LIBRARY
LEABHAR

D1761170

THE PERILOUS ROAD TO THE MARKET

This book is due for return on or before the last date shown below.

25/2 @ 14.02 '11

24/2 @ 18.45.
t P.

11/3 @ 16.00

THE PERILOUS ROAD
TO THE MARKET

THE POLITICAL ECONOMY OF REFORM
IN RUSSIA, INDIA AND CHINA

Prem Shankar Jha

Pluto Press

LONDON • STERLING, VIRGINIA

PATRICK'S
COLLEGE
LIBRARY

First published 2002 by Pluto Press
345 Archway Road, London N6 5AA
and 22883 Quicksilver Drive, Sterling, VA 20166-2012, USA

www.plutobooks.com

Copyright © Prem Shankar Jha 2002

The right of Prem Shankar Jha to be identified as the author of this work
has been asserted by him in accordance with the Copyright, Designs and
Patents Act 1988.

British Library Cataloguing in Publication Data
A catalogue record for this book is available from the British Library

ISBN 0 7453 1852 5 hardback
ISBN 0 7453 1851 7 paperback

Library of Congress Cataloging-in-Publication Data
Jha, Prem Shankar.
The perilous road to the market : the political economy of reform in
Russia, India and China / Prem Shankar Jha.
p. cm.
Includes index.
ISBN 0–7453–1852–5 (hard) — ISBN 0–7453–1851–7 (pbk.)
1. Russia (Federation)—Economic policy—1991– 2. India—Economic
policy—1980– 3. China—Economic policy—2000– I. Title.
HC340.12 .J48 2002
338.9—dc21
2001006647

000171193

ACC.

CLASS 338 . 9 JHA

DATE 0 5 DEC 2002

24 -
HR

Loan

PRICE

UROLM COPY

10 9 8 7 6 5 4 3 2 1

Designed, typeset and produced for Pluto Press by
Chase Publishing Services, Fortescue, Sidmouth EX10 9QG
Printed in India by Replika Press Pvt Ltd, 100% EOU,
Plot No.310 EPIP (HSIDC) Kundli 131 028

Contents

1

Introduction

From Plan to Market:
Forcing the Transition to Capitalism

The Perilous Road to the Market studies the transformation of centrally planned into market economies in three of the largest countries of the world, Russia, China and India. This book seeks to draw some lessons from their experience about what the transformation entails.

Until a little more than a decade ago, all three countries followed autarchic models of development that shunned or mistrusted the market. China began the shift to a market economy experimentally in 1979 and wholeheartedly in 1984–85. India began experimenting with industrial liberalisation in 1980–81, but made its wholehearted commitment to market economics only in June 1991. Russia began experimenting with reform in 1985, but made a sudden and drastic change to 'shock therapy' on 1 January 1992, one week after the Soviet Union was dissolved and Mikhail Gorbachev was forced out of office.

In none of the three countries is the transformation complete. In none has it been easy. Two of the three, China and India, refused to follow orthodox prescriptions for making the transition but were rewarded, at least initially, with rapid economic growth. Neither has been able to sustain its initial burst of growth. China's has proved more enduring, but if the analysis given in this book is correct it is entering into a prolonged crisis during which both its economic and political problems will multiply. By contrast India too reaped the fruits of gradual reform during the first five years after liberalisation, but its growth slowed down after 1997 because of its inability to sustain even the gradual pace of reform that it had adopted in 1991.

In contrast to China and India, Russia followed the orthodox prescriptions for reform developed by the World Bank and IMF out of the structural adjustment programmes of the 1980s known as the Washington Consensus, and devastated the lives of its people. However, by the middle of 2000 there were signs that the worst was over and that its economy was on the road to self-sustaining growth. On the face of it this looks like a somewhat belated success of its shock therapy approach to liberalisation. But even if Russia succeeds in maintaining a brisk 6 per cent rate of growth it will take another eleven years to get back to the GDP it had enjoyed on the eve of shock therapy in 1991. The transformation of a centrally planned into a market economy at the same point on the income curve, via shock therapy, will then have taken 20 years.

THE WASHINGTON CONSENSUS

The sheer unpredictability of the experiences of these countries suggests that something has been left out of the reckoning in the prescriptions that they have followed for making the transition from plan to market. Since the early 1980s an overwhelming proportion of the countries that have made this transition have followed guidelines laid down by the IMF and the World Bank, that have come to be known as the Washington Consensus. In its essentials the Washington Consensus prescribes three broad sets of policy, legal and institutional changes. The first concerns fiscal stabilisation and consists of a combination of deflation – a sharp reduction in the rate of growth of money supply in the economy – and devaluation. This is the time-honoured IMF formula for curing a persistent disequilibrium in the balance of payments. Deflation reduces domestic monetary demand, among other things for imports, and devaluation makes these imports more expensive in money terms, while making exports cheaper and therefore more competitive. The two together exert a powerful corrective pressure on the trade deficit, which is usually the main cause of the chronic balance of payments deficit that signals a structural disequilibrium in the economy.

The second set of reforms are those needed to make a balanced external account sustainable in the long run. These include the removal of quantitative restrictions on imports; the progressive reduction of tariffs and their rationalisation until they perform a revenue-raising and not a protective function; the lowering and rationalising of domestic taxes – preferably through the replacement of other indirect tax regimes with a value added tax, and the adoption of a market determined exchange rate by making the currency freely convertible first on the current account, and eventually on the capital account as well. The rationale for enacting these reforms is to eliminate the underlying distortions of economic policy that inflate the profitability of sales in a protected domestic market, and to make exports at least as much, if not more, profitable.

Quantitative restrictions on imports are a particularly serious hurdle to the efficient integration of the domestic into the world economy, because they offer very high levels of protection to the product in the domestic market. This not only distorts the pattern of domestic investment, but also sucks foreign investment into these very industries. The purpose of foreign direct investment then becomes to exploit the domestic market of the host country and not to promote exports. It can therefore worsen instead of improving the external account.

The purpose of tax reforms is not so much to lower the levels of taxation, as to make the taxes transparent, so that they can be easily rebated in the case of products and inputs that go into international trade. High and widely divergent rates of taxation are in any case undesirable because they distort the signals from the market, and lead to sub-optimal investment. But from the point of view of exports, it is not the level but the simplicity and transparency of the tax system that matter. Needless to say, the simplification of the tax regime needs to go hand in hand with the simplification of bureaucratic procedures for assessing, levying and rebating taxes.

The last set are what might be called structural, or institutional reforms. Their purpose is to enable the state to withdraw from direct involvement in the economic decision-making, and confine itself to setting the ground rules within which the market must function and to create autonomous regulatory institutions to ensure that these are observed. Among the measures that fall into this category are the privatisation of state-owned enterprises, the reform of the banking system to free it from bureaucratic or political interference, the reform of the share and money markets to protect them from abuses such as insider trading, and the elimination of legal and institutional hurdles to the free working of the market for factors of production – land, labour and capital.

The Washington Consensus thus lays out a blueprint for reform, but the blueprint is a static one. It tells reformers what the economy must look like when the reforms are completed. It does not tell them how to get from the existing economy to the desired one. It is here that the role of the state becomes crucial. For, taken together, these reforms are so sweeping, and their impact so unsettling for those who lived and prospered in protected command economies, that the reforms have met with strong opposition almost everywhere. In more than one country this opposition has overturned the government and derailed the reform process. As a result, over years of trying to implement them in various countries, a consensus – albeit a fairly weak one – has evolved that they should be implemented together, in as short a period of time as possible.

Several reasons have been put forward for advocating this type of 'shock therapy'. The purely economic is that coordinated reforms give results in the shortest time, because economic policies are interdependent and mutually reinforcing. For instance, if the goal is to change the pattern of investment within the country in order to promote export oriented industries, lowering tariffs and devaluing the currency will reinforce each other for they will lower the profit on domestic sales and increase those on exports. But lowering tariffs without allowing the currency to get devalued would cause a flood of imports that would severely hurt domestic industry, without boosting exports. By the same token, devaluing the currency without lowering tariffs on imports would neutralise much of the price advantage gained by exports, for it would simultaneously raise the cost of imported raw materials and components, and push up other manufacturing costs by raising the cost of living.

In the same way, reform of the product market alone is of limited use if the factor market remains bound down by regulations and investors are unable to move out of old industries, rendered uncompetitive by liberalisation, into new ones. This creates a situation in which foreign investors and new local entrepreneurs are able to enter an industry unfettered by old machinery, obsolete technology and surplus workers in the most lucrative liberalised areas, while existing domestic industry is denied the freedom to close down plants made uncompetitive by the withdrawal of protection and import restrictions, to shed labour or to sell off marginal lines of their business to concentrate on core areas.

There is also an important political reason for advocating shock therapy. Piecemeal reform may make the wrenching changes involved in the move from plan to market easier to absorb. But they tend to make the reformist urge peter out and leave the reforms incomplete. This happens because the benefits that start flowing from the first reforms, which are usually of the foreign exchange regime and the product market, take the edge off the crisis and reduce the sense of urgency. Spreading the reforms over a period of time also gives those who stand to lose from them, such as the most protected segments of domestic industry and the trade unions, time to organise resistance. The fact that the immediate crisis has been overcome only strengthens their hand.

A FLAWED PREMISE

In recent years, following the East Asian and Russian currency crises of 1997 and 1998, the Washington Consensus has come in for a good deal of criticism. This book suggests that the fault lies not so much with its policy prescriptions as with their underlying assumption that since the problems of all command economies arose out of the extensive intervention of the state in functions that were performed far better by the market, all that the state had to do was to withdraw from these activities and leave them to the market. This premise is misleading. It has been forged by comparing snapshot pictures of *dirigiste* and market economies taken at the same point in time – the present – and concluding that one has only to remove the offending features of the one for the other to be born.

The Washington Consensus therefore underplayed the role of the state as the manager of the transition. The most that the state needed to do was to create, at least for a limited period of time, a political space insulated from the tug-of-war of various pressure groups, in which technocrats could implement the various measures needed to dismantle the command economy and set a market economy in motion. As a result, more than two decades after countries began to dismantle the command economy, the catalytic role of the state in making the transition to the market remains one of the least explored areas of reform. This book argues that eliminating the state from production and consumption decisions does not automatically give birth to a market economy. On the contrary, the market has to be created first and the state is the irreplaceable agent of its creation.

The assumption that the state has only to withdraw for a market economy to take its place is based upon a belief that is so deeply held that it is seldom questioned. This is that markets are 'natural'. They spring from what Adam Smith called 'man's propensity to barter, truck and exchange one thing for another'. From this Smith deduced that exchange is the most natural way in which human beings relate to each other in the realm of the economy. Its scope is restricted only by external constraints such as the amount a family can produce and the distance goods can be transported safely. As the division of labour and improvements in technology increase productivity and improve modes of transport, the area over which goods can be exchanged grows larger. Markets therefore grow naturally until they encompass the world. In this progression local markets come first. These mesh together gradually to form regional and national markets. International trade comes last.[1]

The proponents of this view – that is to say the vast majority of liberal economists – are fully aware that markets do not operate in a vacuum. On the contrary, their smooth functioning requires a large network of regulations and supervisory institutions. But economists have tended to assume that once the state withdraws from direct involvement in the economy these institutions will spring up automatically and in a very short time.[2] The function of advisers and policy makers is simply to smooth the way.

THE TRUE NATURE OF THE TRANSFORMATION

Based upon the experience of the three countries studied here, this book suggests that orthodox economists have seriously underestimated the complexity of the transition from a centrally directed, command economy to a market-guided one and the crucial role of the state in guiding it. The Washington Consensus, which embodies the prevailing orthodoxy, treats it as a matter of mechanics – the replacement of one mechanism for making decisions concerning production and distribution, central planning, with another – the market. It completely overlooks the fact that the rival mechanisms are embedded in, and themselves embody, different principles for the organisation of society. A market is a place where people exchange the goods and services they produce for other goods and services that they need. A market society is therefore one in which economic, and to a considerable extent social, relationships are governed by the process of exchange. Since the purpose of exchange is to maximise satisfaction, and since there are as a rule many buyers and sellers of any given product, the existence of a market implies competition. A market economy is therefore organised around the principle of competition. Socialist and other kinds of centrally planned economies, on the other hand, were born out of a distrust of the market and an attempt to find alternative, less costly (in human terms), ways of organising production and distribution within a society. A centrally planned economy is therefore organised around the *avoidance* of competition, and its replacement by cooperation, albeit cooperation imposed from the top. The real change being attempted is therefore from a society in which economic relationships are not based solely or even mainly upon exchange to one in which they are; that is, from a non-capitalist society to a capitalist one. This requires the creation of an entirely new set of institutions, a new body of law and a new type of state to administer it. All this can only be done by a vigorous and determined state.

Capitalism cannot be brought into being solely by decree. Laws need to be understood and accepted by the vast majority of the people before they become part of a society. Institutions take time to become effective. The reformist state must therefore retain its vigour, and its commitment to making the transformation to capitalism, throughout the period of transition. In Western Europe, the transition from a feudal economy, a large part of which was organised around the principle of redistribution, to an industrial, capitalist economy that is organised around the principle of exchange and competition, took from roughly the mid-fifteenth to the mid-nineteenth century, some 400 years. Japan, a late starter to capitalism, where the state took a direct hand in creating the necessary institutions, was able to compress the changes into a little under a century (roughly from 1868 until 1960). But in Russia, deeply influenced by Western orthodoxy, Mikhail Gorbachev's and later Yeltsin's economic advisers assumed that it could be accomplished in 400 to 700 days!

Smith's concept of Man, elaborated by later economists into the concept of Economic Man – a profit maximising animal – has permeated the humanities so completely that it has taken history out of our attempt to understand the market economy. This can be illustrated by citing a paragraph from a highly regarded work:

> Definitions of Capitalism are legion. Most of them are correct; very few are useful. It is correct for example to say that capitalism is an economic system that uses Capital. It is also correct to define the goal of the system as profit. *But since every economic system in every period of history and in every part of the world has involved the use of capital and the pursuit of profits, these definitions are not useful analytical tools ... Commerce too is as old as written records and so are lending and borrowing money, with or without interest* ...[3] (emphasis added)

Anthropologists have a different story to tell. In early societies, apart from barter, there were three other ways in which people organised the allocation of goods among themselves. These were reciprocity, redistribution, and the household system.[4] Reciprocity created vast and complex rings of interdependence outside the biological family, which in turn helped to identify the society or community to which its members belonged. Redistribution, the most commonly used system other than exchange, involved the surrender of produce to a single authority which decided who would receive what. The household system created the primal division of labour, between husband, wife and children, or the members of an extended family, and was therefore the first system of interdependence within the biological family unit. Redistribution and the household system both reinforced each other in centralising authority and creating societies that were fundamentally patriarchal (but not necessarily despotic) in nature.[5] Exchange, by contrast, transferred the responsibility for making production and distribution decisions from the central authority to the individual. It is hardly surprising therefore that the market system, capitalism and democracy all came into being more or less together and are mutually reinforcing.

Far from developing last, international (to be more precise inter-community) trade was the first form of exchange to develop. This was because it was perceived as an alternative to war. Trade replaced plunder when people realised that they could get what they wanted more easily if they offered something to the vanquished party in exchange. Local markets, based largely on barter but also involving some use of a medium of exchange, developed more or less concurrently with feudalism, but met only a part of a family's needs. In feudal times national markets did not exist. They were created by the emerging modern, sovereign state in order to meet its growing need for a reliable source of revenue.[6]

In Western Europe, the rise of the sovereign state occurred after the Hundred Years' War, roughly between 1453 and 1560. Its distinguish-ing features were the establishment of a system of administration to maintain law and order, resolve disputes and collect taxes; the maintenance of a professional army of mercenaries; and the develop-ment of a system of taxation to meet the expenses of the army and of a paid, professional bureaucracy.[7] The key to success was the ability to raise revenues.[8] Initially kings relied on the revenues of the royal domain. When these proved insufficient, they borrowed money, or taxed their subjects. Taxation was both direct and indirect. The former required consent from the king's subjects and therefore a dilution of his sovereign power. This led to the rise of parliament in England, but also to various Faustian pacts with the landed nobility in Europe in which the king was allowed to tax the peasantry if he spared the nobility. Indirect taxation, consisting mainly of customs duties and sales taxes, were levied on transactions, mainly the transportation and sale of wine, meat, cloth and, over time, a widening range of commodities. These were taxes levied in exchange for the use of a safe and regulated market. The early monarchs relied mainly on borrowed funds and direct taxes. But over time indirect taxes proved to be the most reliable source of revenue and the one that involved the least dilution of sovereign power. The revenues from such taxes thus depended on the volume of transactions, and that in turn depended on the size of the market.[9] It therefore became the goal of every sovereign to expand the size of the market from which he drew his tax revenues. This required him (or her) to destroy other centres of economic autonomy, such as the landed nobility, the church and the independent city states, where these existed. The Thirty Years' War in Europe that ended with the Treaty of Westphalia, the Wars of the Roses and the Reformation in England, Louis XIV's destruction of the independent city states in France, the Customs Union in Germany and the subsequent rise of Prussia under Bismarck, were some of the ways in which the national market was created. More often than not, therefore, the national market was a product of war.

Not only was the state the midwife for capitalism during its birth, it was also nanny throughout its growth to maturity. Throughout the period of commercial capitalism, from the sixteenth to the eighteenth century, states adopted mercantilist policies designed to make them self-sufficient in food (by curbing imports) and to create monopolies in exports (for instance by preventing artisans from emigrating). It was only when the Industrial Revolution made production outgrow the confines of the national market that England began to preach free trade. Today it is the state once again – to be precise the American state – that is playing a key role in removing hurdles to the integration of national markets into a single global market. This is apparent from the lead role it has played in eight rounds of trade talks under the General Agreement on Tariffs and Trade (GATT) and subsequently in the World Trade Organisation (WTO).

Liberal economists' uncritical acceptance of Smith's dictum is not therefore an accident. Every dominant ideology creates its own self-serving myths, and capitalism is no exception. Because in its fully mature form capitalism relies upon the market to take most of the decisions that affect the welfare of the people, its votaries have created the myth that it blossomed because of the minimal role that the state assigned to itself in the economy. Liberal economists concede that among late starters in industrial capitalism – Germany and Japan in the nineteenth century, and South Korea and Taiwan in the twentieth – the state did play a role in accelerating the shift to capitalism. But most committed free-marketeers prefer to regard the autarchic policies of Germany and Japan as an outcome of the wave of hypernationalism that gathered momentum in the last quarter of the nineteenth century, and therefore as a not-to-be-repeated aberration. Somewhat counter-intuitively, when attempting to explain the dazzling performance of the newly industrialised countries of Asia, they extol the South East Asian model of growth as the ideal one and insist that South Korea and Taiwan would have done better had the state confined itself to setting the rules and creating the governing institutions needed by a free and open market economy.[10] But the history of capitalism shows that far from blossoming spontaneously, capitalism would not have come into being anywhere in the world without the active connivance of the state.

ROLE OF THE STATE IN ECONOMIC REFORM

Historically, the transition from pre-capitalist to capitalist economic systems has involved three distinct changes in the way economic activity is organised. The first is the replacement of other forms of distribution with the mechanism of exchange. Since exchange can only take place in a market, the first change entails the *creation of markets*. The second change is from markets to a *market system*. This happens when formerly isolated or specialised markets are merged into a single national or regional market that deals with the exchange of all products. The third is the transformation of the market system into a *market economy*. This involves what Polanyi has called the creation of a 'self-regulating market'.[11] The difference between the markets of a market system and the self-regulating market of a market economy is that in the former exchange exists to serve human needs but human beings and land remain outside the realm of exchange. By contrast, in a self-regulating market, not just the fruits of man's labours but the labour itself becomes part of the process of exchange. Much the same is true of land. Thus literally nothing remains outside the system of exchange. As Polanyi pointed out, while the market system was created during the era of commercial capitalism, the self-regulating market came into being only after the Industrial Revolution.

If the market is capable of regulating everything, then it follows that there is no economic role left for the state to play. This stark formulation formed the core of Manchester Liberalism in England in the first half of the nineteenth century. By the last quarter, however, leading classical economists such as Alfred Marshall and A.C. Pigou had recognised that the market did not always work for the good of all, and that it specifically failed to solve problems of equity in income distribution. This laid the theoretical foundations for the welfare state. Today, however, the wheel has turned full circle and the concept of the minimal state once more reigns supreme in orthodox economic theory. While the roots of this turnaround are to be found in globalisation – the progressive integration of the world into a single market – it is being thrust uncritically upon nations that are still in the throes of the transformation of their *national* economies from pre-market to market economies. The role of the state is therefore complicated by the fact that it has to preside over two wrenching changes at the same time – creating a market economy complete with governing institutions and laws, and integrating it into the global economy.

To sum up, therefore, just as the state played a crucial role in facilitating the birth of capitalism – just as it played a catalytic role in allowing late starters in industrialisation to catch up with the first industrial countries during the era of nationalism – in much the same way it needs to play a facilitating role in the transition from a command to a market economy in the age of globalisation. Ignoring this very important lesson of history, and assuming that the state needs only to dismantle its economic self for a market economy to replace it, is the main cause of the problems that have beset the economic transition in most countries, including the three studied below.

CENTRAL THESIS OF THE BOOK

The central thesis of this book is that economic reforms designed to make a planned transition from a command to a market economy need to respect both the economic and the political logic of the original transition from feudalism to capitalism. Far from needing to withdraw, the state has a crucial role to play during the transition from the command to the market economy. This is to guide and synchronise the transition itself. To do so the state must understand, first, what the transition entails and, second, where the country is in relation to what needs to be done. The precise role that the state needs to play emerges from matching where the country has to go with how far it has already travelled at the point when the decision is taken to hasten the transition to a market economy. Since each country embarks on reforms from a different starting point, the role the state must play will necessarily differ from one to another. What is common to the transition in all countries is the need for the state to maintain a considerable degree of autonomous power through all of its phases.

This is essential because of the sheer complexity of the role it has to play. This involves relinquishing certain powers and abdicating some functions while simultaneously taking on others. Since power is exercised through institutions this means that the state has to dismantle some institutions while it is simultaneously building others. What is more, if it is not to be weakened by the transition and thereby run the risk of losing control of it, the state has to do the former at a pace that matches its success in creating the latter. The elements of this transition are presented in Table 1.1.

All the areas from which the state has to withdraw are listed in column 1. The effect this will have on the economy is listed in column 2. The institutions the state will have to build are listed in column 3.

Table 1.1.
The sequencing of reform:
relationship between policy, markets and institutions

Sequence of economic reforms	Building a market	Building regulatory institutions
1. Free sale of above – plan agricultural produce	Creates marketable produce and permits freer movement of labour	Create free markets for agricultural produce
2. Free sale of above – plan industrial products	Creates marketable products	Allow private trade and shops
3. Legalise private enterprise in the market	Adds to output of goods and services sold	(a) Enact laws governing property and contract, bankruptcy and foreclosure (b) create banking system administered by central bank
4. Permit FDI	Adds to products sold in the market	(a) Create a share market (b) establish securities board
5. Free the exchange rate	Allows currency depreciation in line with inflation	(a) Enact tax laws (b) create tax administration
6. Lift price controls	Creates incentives to produce more	
7. Lift controls on sale and purchase of land and factories	Unfreezes/creates a market for land and enterprise	Enact laws that enable bankruptcy, fore-closure, sale of assets
8. Lift controls on wages and on hiring and firing	Unfreezes/creates a national market for labour. Permits closure of enterprises	Create a nationally administered social security system

9. Privatise state-owned enterprises. Close sick units	Makes them responsive to market signals, reduces government liabilities	Create regulatory boards or authorities for infrastructure industries
10. Lift all remaining production and distribution controls	Completes transition to a market economy	

The complexity of the transition described above requires that the state should have at its command at all times the resources it needs to discharge its functions. One of the disturbing findings of this book is that the reforms embodied in the Washington Consensus tend to reduce the financial autonomy of the state, and thereby its capacity to guide and sustain the process of reform. This is as true of a country like Russia, which adopted shock therapy, as of India where the reform process has been dragged out interminably in the middle of a sea of rising fiscal deficits and growing administrative incapacity.

The three sections of this book examine the experience of each country separately. The model of reform presented in Table 1.1 above helps us to understand both what each country did right and where each went wrong. Russia went in for rapid reform when even that basic requirement of a market economy, a system of production and distribution based upon exchange, did not exist. Not surprisingly it was unable to follow the sequence of reforms outlined in column 1, and failed to synchronise the reforms it did enact with the creation of the regulatory institutions outlined in column 3.

China achieved a much better balance between columns 1 and 3, but in the end, went too fast with the reforms in column 1. The result was a competition between the pre-reform (state-owned) and the post-reform (collective) sectors of industry unregulated by market institutions. This has led to mounting losses in the first sector and mounting over-investment in the second.

In India, by contrast, the creation of capitalist regulatory institutions (which preceded the liberalisation of 1991 by several decades) remained far ahead of the reforms in column 1. India's economy is therefore in balance – with no signs of over-investment, growing indebtedness or inflation. What it has failed to sustain is the momentum of reforms listed in column 1.

Part I
RUSSIA

2

A Society in Torment

In 1997, for the first time in a decade, Russia's gross domestic product (GDP) recorded a small increase. 1997 was also the 700th anniversary of the founding of Moscow and the city had recovered a great deal of its former beauty. But Moscow's beauty was hollow. On its main and longest street, the Tverskaia (formerly Gorky Street), not even one in ten of the elegant shops that lined it was Russian. Nearly all sported famous foreign names, of automobile companies, sports shops, boutiques, fashion houses, electronics multinationals, even bakeries and *chocolateries*. GUM, once the largest department store in the world, has been restored to the elegant eighteenth-century palace that it used to be. Its endless departments with their often empty counters, had long since been replaced by an unending procession of boutiques, Chanel, Bally, Yves Saint Laurent ... In 1997, after almost two years of relative price stability, it was arguably the most expensive shopping mall in the world.

Russia's new entrepreneurs were to be found in humbler premises – in small kiosks that sold foreign cigarettes, photo film, liquor and dresses, or behind even smaller pavement stalls, selling a variety of cheap consumer goods, fruits and vegetables. By local standards these 'entrepreneurs' belonged to the fortunate few whose incomes had kept pace with, or outstripped, the rate of inflation. They were not the only, or even the main beneficiaries of the change. A new class of Russians had come into being in the previous five years. The Russians described them, partly in derision and partly in envy, as the 'New Russians'. These were the new millionaires of the country, a carpetbagger class of capitalists with diverse origins. A few, very few, were truly honest entrepreneurs, like Konstantin Borovoi, who started out as an assistant professor of mathematics at Moscow State University, took advantage of perestroika to start a cooperative and leapt into the then unknown world of business, and in 1994 headed the stock exchange.[1] There was another layer that was more or less honest – the 950,000 small, mostly retail trading, enterprises that had surfaced in the country so far.[2] A third layer originated on the borders between legality and illegality. This consisted of entrepreneurs who had emerged from the underground private retail market that had existed in communist days but became legal with perestroika. Another borderline class consisted of shuttle traders who travel several times a year to and from Finland, China, Turkey, India and other countries. This shuttle trade, which is not quite legal, accounted for $10 billion of imports a year, almost a sixth of the total. But even in these new classes most of the seed money was accumulated through international trade and the sale of imported goods, and through speculation in foreign exchange and commodities. Another class were the new manager capitalists who had diverted funds from the state enterprises they controlled to start their own capital accumulation process. And lastly, there was the ubiquitous Russian Mafiya.

Together these new Russians made up 3 (at most 4) per cent of the population.[3] But they had set new standards for extravagance and ostentation. According to a survey published in *Izvestia*, the new Russians had spent as much as $45 billion on personal consumption by March 1996. About 60 per cent had gone into the purchase of real estate in Western Europe, around the Mediterranean and in the USA. In 1994 Russians spent $6.8 billion on foreign trips.[4] Some idea of the income of the new class of capitalists may be had from the fact that foreign currency exchanges are the most rapidly proliferating business in Russia. These exchanged $10 billion in 1993, and $16 billion in 1994. This may be only a small part of the total annual drain of wealth from Russia. The MVD (the Russian Ministry of the Interior) estimated that no less than $25 billion was transferred to Western banks by organised crime structures alone in 1993.[5] No fewer than 70,000 Russians visited the French Mediterranean coast in 1997 and before the crash of the rouble French hoteliers said they were expecting 100,000 to visit in 1998.[6]

In sharp contrast, the vast bulk of the Russian population was waging a grim struggle for survival. To judge what most Russians were suffering one had only to compare incomes and prices. On the pavements of Moscow, private vendors had set up small tables to sell fresh fruit. In 1997 two apples cost 3,000 (old) roubles (just under 60 cents).[7] Other fruit and vegetables commanded similar prices. These prices were higher than in a Western European supermarket. A check in one of the many 'supermarkets' – mainly medium sized grocery stores – that had opened up in residential districts showed that even milk, eggs, bread and potatoes, the staples of Russian food, were as expensive as in Europe. Rents remained low for those still in the apartments that were originally assigned to them, but they were among the highest in the world for a family trying to move to Moscow from another city, for it had to pay market prices, which were the same for Russians and foreigners. Subway rides were still cheap by European standards –

R1,500 or 30 cents a ride.[8] But they were 30,000 times the 5 kopecks they used to be seven years earlier (in dollar terms the rise was fivefold, from 6 cents to 30. A kopeck is one-hundredth of a rouble). Minibus fares used to be 15 kopecks. They were R5,000 – almost a dollar – in 1997.

Not surprisingly, there was little money to be spent even on essentials. According to a study by a group of academics from the Plekhanov Institute, the average level of consumption for 1990–91 had been about $250 per person per month.[9] But by 1997, more than 80 per cent of the Russian population did not earn anywhere near this amount. In 1996 the average Russian worker earned only R350,000 (old) or $70 per month. This was admittedly not his entire earning. He was still entitled to housing, but rents had begun to rise. He still remained entitled to medical facilities, but the public health system had broken down as, following the wave of privatisation, doctors spent more and more time looking after private patients. A newly appointed lecturer at the prestigious Moscow State University started at $70 a month. The head of department earned $200. Senior professors, including members of the Russian Academy of Sciences, and top scientists in Russia's science cities, earned similar amounts. Student grants had fallen in real terms to only $20 per month. In the hospitals, newly appointed nurses were paid $45 to $50 a month, doctors with their first medical degree started at $60 to $80 a month. The chief of a medical department received $140 to $150 a month.[10] The old age pensioners were the worst hit of all. The minimum pension in mid-1996 in both the armed forces and civil life was between R230,000 to R240,000 – less than $50. In December 1994, the minimum old age pension covered only 53 per cent of the minimum cost of living (food and essentials only) which was then calculated as being R145,000 ($45).[11] There were, officially, around 2.2 million unemployed in the country. But by other, more appropriate definitions the real tally was very close to 10 million. Two years later the official figure was 7 million and the real one about 11 million. There was an unemployment benefit, but it could be as low as $13 per month.

To questions about how ordinary Muscovites managed to make ends meet, there is no single answer. In Moscow and St Petersburg, and to a lesser extent in the other large cities, most people were doing two and even three jobs. Office workers doubled as waiters at night. Aviation engineers worked as gardeners. Many of the fortunate few who had cars, or drove official ones, doubled as taxi drivers. Those who knew English worked as part-time translators or interpreters for hotel guests, for visiting businessmen, embassies and delegations. Professors drove taxis in the evenings, or gave Russian lessons to foreigners. Many wives of academics and civil servants worked as maids in foreign households. A very large number of Muscovites, particularly the *nomenklatura* who had comfortable apartments in central Moscow, had transformed themselves overnight into a new middle class, by renting out their apartments to foreigners for rents as high as $7,000 a month. Some had taken advantage of their position and power to buy up the extensive lands on which their dachas stood, and to turn these into exclusive housing estates for the 'new Russians'. Tens of thousands of others had received handsome compensations from foreign companies and banks for moving out of premises that the latter were buying up to gentrify and turn into corporate offices or hotels. With these nest eggs they had moved out to cheap apartments in the suburbs and put aside enough money to tide them over the nightmare years. In 1995, as the chaos in the financial markets subsided, more and more of them had begun to invest this money with the new investment companies and banks, only to have their savings wiped out yet again in the August 1998 economic crash.

Moscow also had its beggars. Old age pensioners rooted regularly in the city's trash bins. The city authorities helped them to hold on to shreds of their self-respect by providing them with uniforms. Finally, large numbers of Muscovites, drawn mostly from the former KGB, had set up security services and become bodyguards. Some had turned to organised crime and joined the Mafiya.

But those who lived in Moscow or St Petersburg were the lucky ones. Russians never grew tired of telling visitors not to judge the country by Moscow, but to go to the regions (provinces). Seventy-five per cent of the capital raised by the banks and investment companies had been invested in the Moscow region, they said. Another 5 to 10 per cent had gone to St Petersburg. Most of the foreign investment was also taking place in these two regions. But in the other regions, most towns were built around one large plant or factory, and these were either closed or hadn't paid their workers for months. In many the workers reported every day for work but did nothing, for there was no raw material and very little demand for the product. 'Even if the people there hear that there are jobs to be had in the Moscow region, they cannot move because they cannot afford the rent.'[12]

Outside the metropoli, most people were eking out their living by growing food on tiny plots of land. In Academgorodok, one of Russia's science cities 30km from Novosibirsk in Siberia, scientists had not been paid even their meagre salaries for the last six months. Many were growing their own food to survive. Some were making baskets and other artefacts to sell in the local market. A growing number had sublet their apartments to the 'new Russians' who were being drawn to Academgorodok by its pure water, clean air and excellent infrastructure. They had taken to living in tiny apartments in Novosibirsk and commuting daily the 30km to and from work.[13]

But all these expedients had only helped a small minority to hold their own against the devastation of the economy that had followed the sudden introduction of market economics. The most generous estimates put the proportion of the population that had managed to adjust to the new situation at around 20 per cent of the total. Eighty per cent had suffered a catastrophic decline in their consumption standards. Between 1990 and 1994, the purchasing capacity of the average Russian fell by half in real terms, from 58kg of meat and meat products to 32kg per month; from 763kg of milk and dairy products to 329kg; from 1,664 eggs to 1,089; from 114kg of fish to 36kg; from 107kg of vegetable oil to 56kg; and from 426kg of potatoes to 267kg. The sharpest fall took place in the capacity to buy bread, the price of which had previously remained unchanged for 30 years. This fell from 523kg to 162kg.[14] These figures represent the national average. The fall in real incomes of the losers from the change was much sharper.

At the bottom fringe of Russian society, even in the relatively good year of 1996, people were starving. This was apparent from the decline in population that had taken place in 1993 and 1994. Russia's population rose from 148.3 million in 1990 to 148.7 million in 1992. It then fell to 148.4 million in 1993 and 148.3 million in 1994.[15] More ominously, after 1990 there had been a five-year fall in the life expectancy of Russian males, from 63 to 58.[16] In December 1994 there were 30 million Russians who did not earn enough to maintain even the bare minimum subsistence level of consumption. By mid-1999, the number had risen to 66 million – 44 per cent of the population.[17]

3

The Failure of Perestroika

Nearly everyone blames Mikhail Gorbachev for Russia's woes, but for different reasons. Russians blame him for starting a change that he did not understand and could not control. Western analysts and Russia's liberals blame him for not having the courage to push through a complete reform of the political system and enact any one of the several proposals for 'economic reform by shock therapy' presented to him by Soviet and Western economists, when he had the power to do so.[1] The truth, as Yeltsin's 1992 reforms were to show, was that Gorbachev had no option but to proceed slowly, because in 1985 the Soviet Union did not even have the elements of a market system, let alone a market economy. These had to be constructed first, and that virtually mandated that if the reform process was to be reasonably painless, it had to be very gradual. Gorbachev did indeed embark on a course of gradual reform. But he got the sequence all wrong. Largely to blame for this was the stubborn opposition he faced from the hard-line conservatives within the Communist Party.

The weaknesses of the Soviet centrally planned economy had become apparent long before Gorbachev came to power. Industry was monumentally inefficient and agriculture was in a perennial crisis.[2] According to official estimates, the rate of growth of GDP fell from 7.8 per cent per annum between 1965 and 1970, to 5.7, 4.3 and 3.6 per cent in the next three quinquennia. In 1986–87 it fell further to 3.2 per cent. CIA estimates of Soviet growth rates are lower but trace the same curve from 5 per cent in 1966–70 to 3.1, 2.2, 1.8 and 1.9 per cent.[3] The estimates of the growth of net material product by the Russian economist G.I. Khanin are lower still.

The main cause of slowing growth was the failure of the Soviet economic system to harness its technological process to commercial production. The resulting technology gap was reflected in the ever rising capital to output ratio (see Table 3.1), and in the failure of the Soviet Union, after 50 years of rapid industrialisation, to produce manufactured goods, other than armaments, that could be sold in the world market. In 1987, 77 per cent of its exports to the OECD countries still consisted of raw materials, mainly oil and gas, timber, woodpulp, minerals and steel.[4]

By Khanin's estimates, the Soviet economy entered a state of crisis

Table 3.1
Creeping failure of the Soviet command economy

Year	Percentage growth of net material product (Khanin estimates)	Gross investment to GDP ratio	Output to capital ratio
1928–40	3.2	–	–
1951–60	7.2	–	0.72
1961–65	4.4	19.1	0.54
1966–70	4.1	20.1	0.48
1971–75	3.2	22.5	0.41
1976–80	1.0	25.0	0.34
1980–85	0.6	–	–
1985–87	2.0	–	–

Source: Manuel Castells, *End of Millennium*, vol. 3, pp. 12, 17. Original sources: for USSR's GDP, G.I. Khanin, 'Ekonomicheskii rost: al'ternativnaya otsenka', *Kommunist* 17, 1988; for investment and productivity of capital, Padma Desai, *The Soviet Economy: Problems and Prospects* (Oxford: Oxford University Press, 1987).

in the mid-1970s, but the two OPEC-engineered oil price increases of that decade hid this from view by boosting the value of the economy's main export and enabling it to import more consumer goods. The crisis was fully exposed when the price of oil crashed in 1986 to $12 or $13 a barrel, a third of the peak attained in 1981. This was reflected immediately in the USSR budget deficit which soared from 2.9 per cent in 1985 to 11.5 per cent of GNP in 1987.[5] As export earnings fell, consumer goods imports declined and empty shelves became the order of the day.

Since he was starting with a clean slate in 1985, Gorbachev was able to initiate the drastic change of direction that Russia needed. Gorbachev realised that the Soviet Union needed to make its economy competitive; to lower the raw material content of its products, improve their designs, and harness the country's vast technological potential to commercial instead of only defence production.[6] He prepared the ground for the changeover by moving rapidly towards *détente*, reducing defence spending and dismantling Russia's police state (the policy of glasnost). However, the challenge that he faced was to replace centralised planning with the market mechanism as the means of determining production and distribution. This was the challenge that, over six long years, he was unable to meet. Gorbachev's instinct was to make the changeover gradually, but he was constantly buffeted by contrary advice, and by the fact that none of the economists he chose to advise him was able to come up with a blueprint for gradual reform. The result was a paralysis that was reinforced by deep divisions in the Communist Party over the desirability both of specific reforms and of the move from plan to market.

SEVEN AREAS OF REFORM

There were seven main areas in which reforms had to be implemented in a phased manner. These were:

i   Privatising agriculture to increase productivity and generate surpluses.
ii   Granting autonomy to the state enterprises and making them responsible for their own finances, i.e. reducing the scope of the centralised planning system.
iii Legalising private enterprise, especially in the service sector.
iv   Permitting foreign direct investment.
v   Reforming the exchange rate and freeing the foreign trade system from bureaucratic controls.
vi   Lifting controls on prices in a phased manner – on consumer goods first, capital goods next and basic goods, like steel, coal, oil, gas and cement, last.
vii Permitting enterprises to fix their own wages.

It should have been apparent that if a programme of phased reforms were to succeed they had to be closely coordinated and sequenced. Ideally, reforms should have been conceived of in three closely interconnected groups. Agriculture should have been privatised in one form or another first, so that it could generate the additional output that would be needed to cushion the inflationary impact of decontrolling food prices.

Permitting private enterprise, allowing foreign investment and increasing the autonomy of the state enterprises, should have followed close on its heels, and had to be done together. Of these, the last was by far the most difficult task and needed to be planned carefully. In doing this, Russia could have learned a great deal from China.[7] China started by progressively reducing production quotas under the plan, and allowing the enterprises to find buyers and set their own prices for the balance of the output. China followed this by steadily reducing the number of products under the centralised production and distribution system. In this way it forced the state-owned enterprises to sell more and more of their output in the open market. If Gorbachev had been patient and spread these reforms over a decade or more, he would have succeeded in imbuing the industrial sector with a basic capacity to respond to signals from the market. The lifting of price controls, when it finally took place, would then have evoked an increase in production not only from agriculture but also from private producers and foreign enterprises in industry. This would have reinforced the impact of agricultural surpluses in cushioning inflation, made the price rise a self-limiting one.

Lastly, wage, price and exchange rate reforms had to be closely coordinated. The interrelationship between these in a market economy is obvious: an increase in prices without a devaluation can hurt exports; a devaluation without an increase of domestic prices can disrupt domestic supply; and an increase in both without an increase in wages impoverishes all wage and fixed income earning groups, and erodes the legitimacy of the regime. In Russia, since the crisis originated in the external sector with the decline in oil prices in 1985–86, the pressure to devalue came first. Devaluation had therefore to be followed closely by domestic wage and price increases. This would not have led to an endless spiral of administered price inflation. For instance if the import to GDP ratio were 20 per cent, a 50 per cent devaluation would have caused a 10 per cent rise in cost of production and at most a 10 per cent rise in prices. If current consumption accounted for 50 per cent of incomes, the cost of living would have increased by only 5 per cent. The next round of price increases would start with a 5 per cent increase in money wages. One needs only to examine the actual course of reforms during perestroika to see how badly their sequencing went wrong.

REFORMING THE STATE-OWNED ENTERPRISES

Gorbachev began his reforms not in agriculture but in industry. In 1987, he took the first step towards enterprise autonomy by granting enterprises controlled by two· all-Union and three republic ministries greater autonomy in decision making. In effect this meant reducing the production targets set out by Gosplan and allowing businesses to produce more for direct sale in the market. The Law on State Enterprises of January 1988 extended this to all enterprises, and made them responsible for their own finances. By late 1989, all Soviet enterprises had been given this freedom and told that they could no longer rely on budgetary support to make ends meet. In June 1990, the Supreme Soviet passed another law on enterprises emphasising the need to move towards a market economy and further restricting the operations of Gosplan and Gosnab, the state production planning and distribution organisations. Soviet enterprises were admittedly slow to respond to their new-found freedoms, but their failure to do so seems to have been exaggerated by Western writers in the post-Gorbachev era. One index of this is that within a single year after the reforms began, employment in the state enterprises had fallen by 1.7 million.[8] This suggests that there was a serious attempt to trim surplus labour in order to lower the cost of production. Khanin's estimates for 1985–87 reflect the improvement in efficiency. The growth of NMP rose from 0.6 per cent in 1980–85 to 2.0 per cent in 1985–87. This period saw, for the first time since the 1950s, a decline in the materials intensity of production and a sharp rise in the productivity of both labour and capital by 2 per cent per annum.[9]

PRIVATISATION

Gorbachev embarked on privatisation at the extreme edges of the economic system. In May 1987, the state passed a law that permitted students, old age pensioners and cooperatives to indulge in private trade. In July 1988, private companies were allowed to be set up for retail trade and some manufacturing enterprises. Here too, the response was actually far better than the subsequent critics of perestroika are willing to admit. In a single year after the latter reform, the number of workers in the Soviet private sector rose from 0.5 million to 3.1 million. In 1989 the private sector employed 3 per cent of Soviet workers.[10]

FOREIGN INVESTMENT

Gorbachev also tried to liberalise foreign investment in Russia, in a phased manner. A law was passed in January 1987 allowing Russian state enterprises to form joint ventures with foreign companies. In April 1989, the Supreme Soviet passed another law that permitted foreign companies to own up to 99 per cent of the equity in joint ventures. This further liberalisation was forced on the government by the failure of Russian enterprises to take significant advantage of the 1987 reform. One reason for this was that although the 1987 relaxation was sweeping in intent, the capacity to enter into foreign collaborations was limited by the availability of foreign exchange to the enterprises. In all only 200 enterprises had access to foreign exchange and therefore the capacity to enter into such joint ventures.[11]

AGRICULTURE

Agriculture, which should have come first, actually came last. This was surprising because Gorbachev held degrees in agricultural economics and had been the secretary for agriculture in the central committee from 1978 to 1985. He should therefore have known, better than most people, that the problems of agriculture, which had resulted in the ever increasing imports of grain in the 1970s and 1980s, were structural in nature. Indeed Gorbachev had himself repeatedly argued the case for increasing private initiative in agriculture. In retrospect, his failure to push the privatisation of agriculture at the very beginning of the reforms was his greatest error. He got around to elaborating his ideas only in July 1988. He shied away from outright privatisation and proposed instead that much larger chunks of land be leased out to members of the *kolkhoz* (state farms) for private farming. Combined with a reduction of state procurement quotas, which had been enacted in 1988, this would give the necessary flexibility in production by the collective, and free the labour time needed to tend to leased lands. Gorbachev's ideas proved popular among the reform-minded intelligentsia but their enactment and implementation was hampered at every turn by the bureaucracy and the Communist Party ideologues. An enlargement of the land leased to family farms was only finally allowed in January 1990. By then Gorbachev had begun to lose control of the political system and it was too late for agriculture to play the role it had played in China.

WAGE AND PRICE REFORM

The areas in which there was no progress were wage and price flexibility. Wages did not remain totally frozen or controlled by central fiat. The autonomy given to state enterprises also included the right to fix and alter wages and many enterprises took advantage of this to raise wages, in order to attract good workers, even while they laid off other workers. In 1988, wages rose by 7 per cent, while productivity in industry rose by 2.5 per cent.[12] This was not by itself inflationary, because there was a simultaneous decline in the workforce employed in industry of 1.5 million between March 1988 and March 1989. However, what the central leadership of the party baulked at was the kind of wage increase that would become necessary if prices were decontrolled. They feared that complete freedom would push the economy into an endless inflationary spiral. From this it was a short step for the party to resist each and every price change. Nowhere was this more evident than in agriculture.

As part of his agricultural reforms, in 1988 Gorbachev had curtailed subsidies on agricultural inputs and increased state purchase prices by approximately the same amount. However the party leaders were unable to bring themselves to raise the issue prices of foodstuffs, which had not been changed for 30 years. As a result the raising of these prices was postponed to 1989, then 1990, then 1991 and finally 1992. It might not have been implemented even then had the USSR not been overwhelmed by the events of August to December 1991. As a result the deficit in the central budget ballooned from R23 billion in 1985 to an anticipated R120 billion in 1989. Of this, R87.9 billion or 17.8 per cent of total expenditure was accounted for by the subsidy on food.[13] The turmoil within the party over this issue was understandable. The Communist Party consisted of two elites – an industrial elite of enterprise managers and an ideological elite of bureaucrats and the intelligentsia. The former resisted competition because it threatened their monopolies and therefore their rent-seeking ability (salting away part of the proceeds of various sales at home and abroad was a practice that predated perestroika). The latter were afraid of the market because they feared that lifting price controls would unleash inflation and impoverish them. The leaders, including Gorbachev, therefore feared freeing prices because it would split the party. While the industrial elite might benefit from inflation the ideologues and civil servants could only lose.

Despite these hurdles Gorbachev did try to increase prices, even if belatedly. In January 1991, his new prime minister, Valentin Pavlov, raised wholesale prices by 50 per cent. Despite stiff opposition from the parliament, he followed this with a modest increase in retail prices and a 5 per cent presidential turnover tax. But the two measures did not offset the increase in wholesale prices. As a result government subsidies and its budget deficit mounted sharply.

Gorbachev also tried a crude but potentially effective way of taxing the rich. He permitted Pavlov to demonetise the currency. Soviet citizens were allowed to exchange old rouble notes for new, but only up to a ceiling. The ceiling was intended to penalise those with unaccounted wealth, but the scheme was bungled, for it prescribed an unrealistically short time for making the exchange. This ended up in penalising large numbers of honest Soviet citizens – especially the poor in the rural areas, who did not hear of the demonetisation or could not get to the bank in time. Demonetisation made the currency in circulation decline by 30 per cent,[14] but most of this was not black money. Russians therefore rightly saw it as an expropriation of their savings. It was the first of two demonetisations that ended by destroying a large part of the accumulated savings of honest Russians, overnight. It was hardly surprising therefore that in 1995, three-quarters of the national savings in the previous year were converted into dollars.[15]

THE EXCHANGE RATE REGIME

The only area in which transition from an administered to a market regime was substantially achieved was in freeing the rate of exchange and letting it be determined by the demand for and supply of foreign exchange. But this was bungled so badly that it suddenly and catastrophically completed the dismantling of the state procurement and distribution system that had begun with the 1987 Law on Enterprises, and made the shock therapy of 1992 inevitable.

In December 1988 the government announced that on 1 January 1990, the rouble would be devalued by 50 per cent. This was almost certainly too small a devaluation to serve the purpose of making Russia's exports competitive and reflected the hesitancy and internal discord within the Communist Party leadership. But the decision to *announce* the devaluation more than a year in advance was as absurd as changing from driving on the left side of the road to driving on the right, in easy stages. This absurdity reflected the deep divisions within the Communist Party, for the diehards managed to postpone a decision that Gorbachev had wanted to implement immediately. The results were disastrous. Every exporter delayed the repatriation of foreign exchange, and every importer rushed to get goods ordered and paid for before the devaluation came into effect. This plunged Russia into the very foreign exchange crisis that devaluation was meant to avert.

The government had to do something to stop the haemorrhage. As a result the original announcement was overtaken by another half-measure. In November 1989 the tourist rate of exchange was devalued tenfold to 6.23 roubles to the dollar. November 1989 also saw the third half-measure – the first ever auction of roubles by the central bank. At this auction the dollar sold for 15 to 16 roubles.

These two measures effectively devalued the rouble for international transactions. Since the government did not even then raise the domestic prices of exportable commodities the rate of profit on domestic sales fell to a fraction of the rate of profit on exports.

As a result, from November 1989 a strange situation developed in the Soviet Union. Producers and marketing parastatals knew that every unit of output that they managed to export would yield 15 to 16 times as many roubles as a similar amount supplied to the state procurement agencies. Thus they immediately lost interest in supplying the latter and began to explore every possibility of exporting their produce, even at throwaway prices. What is more, since almost no one in the Soviet Union had a clear idea of what international prices ought to be, the underinvoicing of exports became fatally easy for the managers of the exporting enterprises. This was the foundation on which many private fortunes and industrial empires were built. Thus in a matter of months the already weakened state procurement and distribution system created under the command economy broke down completely. In the summer of 1990 Muscovites experienced an acute shortage of bread despite the fact that the USSR had had one of its best ever wheat harvests that year. And Russia still had no alternative with which to replace the command economy!

As the condition of the economy deteriorated, and the gridlock between reformers and diehard communists in the Supreme Soviet and other organs of the party continued, Gorbachev looked increasingly desperately for a solution. Between 1986 and 1991, he commissioned, examined and rejected no fewer than 12 plans for making the transition.[16] In them one can discern a steady progression from gradualist approaches towards shock therapy, a progression that reflected the accelerating deterioration of the Soviet economy as its fiscal imbalances accumulated while the gridlock between the government and the party continued. In this progression one can also discern the growing influence of orthodox Western thinking on structural transformation. For instance, plans 7 and 8, put forward by Grigory Yavlinsky and Stanislav Shatalin respectively, were intended to complete the transition in 400 and 500 days respectively.[17] Subsequent plans tried to merge elements of these two plans with some elements of state ownership and control. But all had one feature in common: they promised a miracle in months and one that would be achieved without too much pain.

Gorbachev ended by rejecting all of them. Although he did not understand much economics, and certainly not enough to chart a course for Russia on his own, as he became conversant with the proposals being made, he became increasingly aware of the flaw that was common to all of them. This was the assumption that a market system would somehow replace the command economy in a very short space of time. His party members shared Gorbachev's fears.[18] Thus there was a growing conflict between the reformers and the Communist Party, which dominated both the Chamber of Deputies and the Supreme Soviet, which came to a head over the issues of price decontrol and the privatisation of agriculture.

MARKET REFORMS WITHOUT A MARKET

Gorbachev baulked at trying to reform the Soviet economy in 400 to 700 days because the Soviet Union was completely unfamiliar with the market system of production and exchange. A market had therefore to be created first for its signals to be heeded by producers and consumers.

In retrospect it is difficult to understand how not one of the Western economists who advocated shock therapy saw this simple truth: the command and the market economies were two alternative ways of achieving the same end – the matching of supply to demand under the 'roundabout' system of production that characterises an industrial economy. The shift from one to the other could only begin, therefore, if there were at least the rudiments of a market already in place. If this precondition was not fulfilled, dismantling the institutions of the planned economy would lead to a complete breakdown of distribution and then production. But by the end of 1991, the Soviet Union had very largely dismantled Gosplan and Gosnab, but still did not have even a rudimentary market economy. As a result, in January 1992, Russia began its journey not to the market but to chaos.

The market did not exist because the Bolshevik regime had done by far the most comprehensive job of destroying it and replacing it with a system of centralised production and distribution than had any of the other socialist countries of Eastern Europe, or for that matter, China. Hungary, which had gone almost as far, had begun to liberalise its economy shortly after the 1956 uprising. By the time that the command economy began to be wound up in 1989, Hungarian enterprises had enjoyed a fair measure of managerial autonomy for more than two decades, and were allowed to trade in the international market on their own and to form joint ventures with foreign companies. There was also a small private sector. As a result Hungary not only had a rudimentary market system, but its enterprise managers had considerable experience of working in market conditions. There was also a private sector that could immediately step in and take advantage of liberalisation by responding to price and investment incentives.

This was also true of Poland. Poland had never succeeded in

collectivising agriculture because 80 per cent of its farmers had successfully resisted it. Poland had also had a small private sector in trade and construction.[19] In China too, the market never ceased to exist. At the height of central planning in China, the state controlled the production and distribution of only 500 products. The corresponding figure in the Soviet Union was over 20,000![20] Even for these 500 products, enterprises had developed an elaborate system of trading their above-plan output among each other. By the time economic reform came to industry in 1985, this had been institutionalised into semi-annual buyers' conferences where bewilderingly complex swap deals were regularly arranged. Chinese state-owned enterprises also enjoyed considerable autonomy over the disposal of their operational surpluses even before 1985. The central and provincial governments allowed this grudgingly, but laid down the proportion that had to be reinvested in the main enterprise or in subsidiaries, known as collectives. Thus when reform came, China had both a substantial body of private and collective entrepreneurs, and a reservoir of experience with the market mechanism.[21]

In 1986, Russia had neither. Even before the Revolution, Russian agriculture had not been truly private. The abolition of serfdom had led to the pre-eminence of the *mir*, the village commune. In the *mir*, communal farming prevailed. Not only was separating one's land from the *mir* frowned upon by local custom, but various exactions by the landowners from the *mir* for the separation of such lands further hindered the establishment of private farms. By 1915, private farming had taken root and 14 per cent of the land was in private farms. But the communal tradition in agriculture remained strong. When Stalin collectivised agriculture, he snuffed out an institution – the private farm – that had never been strong. But Stalin was even more thorough in uprooting capitalism from the industrial and tertiary sectors. Well before the Second World War, he had completely nationalised all industry and the entire service sector. Private enterprise of any kind was, quite simply, a crime. Private trade was dubbed blackmarketing, and was punishable with death. The destruction of capitalist forms of ownership did not take place on its own. It was an offshoot of an even more comprehensive drive, backed fully by economists, to destroy every vestige of the market (that is, of competition and autonomy in price setting), whether of commodities or factors of production. Like the Indian planners of the 1950s and 1960s, Russian economists believed that competition was wasteful. Armed with a fanatical belief in the economies of scale, they provided Stalin and the Communist Party with the intellectual justification they needed for consolidating existing factories, large and small, into huge monopolies, and doing the same with trading establishments. As a result, in 1991, out of 7,664 products manufactured in the machine building, metallurgical, chemical, timber and construction sectors, 5,884, or 77 per cent, were produced by monopolies. Whereas only 26 per cent of all industrial enterprises in the USA employed more than a thousand workers, the proportion in the USSR was 73 per cent.[22] In 1988, large and medium sized enterprises with more than 200 employees accounted for 95 per cent of production and employees.[23]

Thus when he launched perestroika in 1986, Gorbachev had no market, no price mechanism and no entrepreneurs who could respond to price signals even if these were given, and no economists who could give him blueprints for a phased transition that he could 'sell' to his party members. Opposition within the party was both covert and overt.

State enterprise managers were slow to take advantage of the autonomy they had been given. Central and republic ministries were reluctant to part with the power of control that centralised planning gave them.[24] Average Russians also entertained a deep mistrust of the market. The success of the early private entrepreneurs had created a new class of relatively rich Russians who excited the envy of the vast majority. This led to accusations of profiteering, which fell on ears conditioned by 70 years of distrust of trade and private enterprise. Distrust was fanned by the fact that some of the first people to take advantage of the new legalisation were members of the Russian underworld, the Mafiya.[25] The Mafiya also lost no time in battening on to the defenceless individual traders and extorting protection money from them. This effectively reduced the entrance of new entrepreneurs to a trickle, lent a criminal flavour to trade and strengthened popular prejudice against private enterprise. As a result, in January 1989 Gorbachev was forced to pass a law to regulate and reduce monopoly profits. This set back the emergence of a private sector, and completed the job of strangling the growth of an entrepreneurial class that the Mafiya had begun.

THE BREAK-UP OF THE SOVIET UNION

The breakdown of the Soviet economy in 1991 was made immeasurably worse by the fact that it coincided with the loosening of the bonds of the Soviet Union. This gravely weakened Gorbachev's capacity to take more decisive action after 1988. Glasnost, and *détente* with the West, encouraged demands for independence from the Baltic states. Gorbachev was prepared to concede this independence, but drew the line at any further disintegration of the Soviet Union. But the release of the Baltic states from Moscow's iron grip stimulated increased self-assertion and demands for independence in other republics as well. The self-assertion was not confined to politics, but was equally evident in economic demands for greater autonomy. When the rouble was devalued in 1989, these republics were among the first to ignore the central government's procurement orders and encourage their enterprises to hold back their output for export. The Ukraine, for instance, the USSR's breadbasket, began to drag its feet on the supply of wheat. The Central Asian republics did the same.

Yeltsin hammered the last nail in the coffin of perestroika. In 1988 Gorbachev was selected as Chairman of the Praesidium of the Soviet Union, but only five months later, Boris Yeltsin (whom he had removed from candidate membership of the Politburo only a year earlier) won a genuine election to win the Moscow seat in the Congress of Peoples' Deputies. A few weeks later Yeltsin became a member of the Supreme Soviet, when another member vacated his seat for him. From that point on, his main aim became to oust Gorbachev. In May 1990, Yeltsin was elected Chairman of Russia's Supreme Soviet. From then on Gorbachev had to work in tandem with Yeltsin if his programmes were to be more than paper decrees. The bitter rivalry between the two did not take long to come to a head. In August, a panel of economists headed by Stanislav Shatalin produced a 500-day economic reform plan. Under Yeltsin's guidance this was overwhelmingly accepted by the Russian Supreme Soviet in September but rejected by Gorbachev in October. In November, Yeltsin announced that Russia could not implement the Shatalin plan by itself without the cooperation of the Soviet Union. When he received no response from Gorbachev, he began to campaign for his ousting and for the dissolution of the USSR. In February 1991, Yeltsin demanded in a televised address that Gorbachev should resign, as he was a nominated and not an elected president. A nationwide referendum revealed a widespread desire for a directly elected president and the replacement of the USSR with a voluntary union of states. The fact that he was first a nominated president and from 1990 a president elected only by the Supreme Soviet which, by its constitution, had a majority of Communist Party members anyway, was Gorbachev's Achilles' heel, for it put him at a disadvantage to Yeltsin. In the public eye, this worsened when Yeltsin was elected president of the Russian federation in Russia's first free presidential election in June 1990. From 1989 onwards, therefore, Gorbachev was politically permanently on the defensive. He now needed the Communist Party more than the party needed him. This was hardly a position from which he could either disregard the party or bring it around to his views. From 1989, therefore, the political agenda took precedence and economic reform was pushed into the background. The kind of compromise he was forced to strike on price reform in 1991 reflected his weakness.

Gorbachev kept on rejecting plan after plan in 1990 and 1991 not because he had become indecisive or lost his taste for glasnost and perestroika, but when he realised that it threatened his own position as head of state. It was because by then the growth of the budget deficit was almost out of control.[26] The more it grew the greater would be the rise in prices if these were decontrolled. What he needed was a plan that achieved the reforms in gradual stages. What batteries of economists kept offering him were plans that leaned more and more heavily on shock therapy. Politics thus pulled increasingly in one direction while the advice of economists pulled in the other. The result was a paralysis that ensured the steady deterioration of the government's finances until the country was overwhelmed by crisis.

4

Descent into Chaos

One year after the partial freeing of the exchange rate in November 1989, the Russian distribution system was in ruins, production was falling and inflation was rising to what was, in those days, unheard of levels.[1] Black markets were developing in even the basic necessities while the shops for the ordinary people remained empty. Predictably the fissures between the reformers in the Communist Party, who said there was no way to go but forward, and the conservatives who wanted to go back somehow to the not necessarily good, but familiar and therefore safe, old days, widened rapidly. The country had to move in one direction or the other, and the failure of the August 1991 *coup* ensured that it would move towards radical reform. But as subsequent events showed, both the timing and the speed of the reforms, which were dictated by politics, turned out to be wrong.

Within ten days of the dissolution of the Soviet Union, Yeltsin opted for shock therapy on 2 January 1992. The first model, prepared with the help of foreign advisers, including Jeffrey Sachs, A. Aslund and M. Dabrowski, was of a strictly classical type. It aimed at freeing prices altogether, and severely curtailing the growth of money supply to curb the resulting inflation. The new regime moved forcefully to cut government expenditure to eliminate the deficit. Expenditure on the purchase of military equipment was halved and subsidies to farms and factories drastically reduced.[2] Yegor Gaidar, his finance minister, aimed first at reducing the budget deficit to 3 per cent of GNP and, when it became apparent that this was unattainable, tried to hold it at 5 per cent.[3] The intention was to remove the monetary overhang that had built up during the previous years and allow higher prices to spur an increase in production. After an initial period of great stress, the economy was expected to emerge in balance and start growing again. Gaidar was not, however, able to adhere strictly to this model. The removal of price controls led to an immediate 200 to 300 per cent increase in all prices and a 600 per cent increase in three months.[4] The government softened the blow, however, by keeping the prices of 15 basic consumer goods, including bread, milk, gasoline, heating and electricity, under controls.

Gaidar did not have the political strength to enforce the freezing of money supply. An agreement with the powerful coal miners' union to increase wages opened the floodgates for other demands and more concessions. Nor could the government freeze exchange rates after an initial devaluation. From July 1992 the value of the rouble began to fall. In August it fell by 18 per cent; in October by 57 per cent. By the end of the year the inflation rate had reached 60 per cent per month, and money supply had increased by 600 per cent.[5] Overall, during the year, consumer prices rose by 2,323 per cent.[6] Demand far outstripped supply. Thus by March, the regime's policies had already slipped into a pattern that was to continue until the second economic crash in 1998. It would attempt to stabilise prices and the exchange rate exclusively through the control of money supply. But this would cause arrears of pay and social security benefits to mount and a sharp drop in real wages. Eventually the government's fear of social turmoil and pressure from the Duma would overcome its determination to stabilise prices. It would then attempt to pay at least some of the wage arrears, and increase the money wage, pension and social security rates. This would increase money supply once more and the whole cycle would start afresh.[7]

It did not take Yeltsin long to see that shock therapy was not working as it had been expected to. His first attempt to set things right was to give Gaidar more power. In June, therefore, he promoted Gaidar from finance to prime minister. In December, he sacked him. This too became a pattern that was repeated time and again as the Russian government struggled with a problem to which there was no solution.

The problem was the absence of a functioning market system that could convert price signals into output decisions. The winding up of Gosplan and Gosnab (the production planning and wholesale distribution organisations of the Soviet state), which began under perestroika and was completed under shock therapy, left behind a vacuum. To make matters worse, the rudiments of a market system that had come into being after the reforms of 1987–89, had come firmly under the control of the Russian Mafiya. The Mafiya controlled prices and rapidly developed an interest in ensuring that increases in supply that would force prices down did not reach the market. In one instance when a group of peasants tried to bring a larger than anticipated watermelon crop to the market, the Mafiya torched their trucks and beat them up. On another occasion kiosk owners in St Petersburg were beaten up and their kiosks burnt for trying to lower their prices.[8] It also controlled the entry of new small businesses, and thereby choked the growth of entrepreneurship in the country.

As for price decontrol transmitting signals to the producers, the slim chance that Yeltsin and Gaidar had of making a smooth transition was destroyed by the timing of their reforms. Shock therapy was implemented on 2 January 1992, exactly eleven days after the dissolution of the Soviet Union.[9] Had the break-up not taken place it is just possible that over time the budding entrepreneurial class and the soon to be privatised state enterprises might have begun to respond to the stimulus of higher prices sufficiently to dampen the shock waves of price decontrol. But the simultaneous break-up of the Soviet Union put even this slim chance out of reach. In both Russia and the new states, in factory after factory, production ground to a halt. As prices skyrocketed in Russia after price decontrol, sellers in the other CIS states began to flock to it to sell their wares. The ensuing shortage in their domestic markets pushed up prices rapidly. Rising prices in Russia also meant that factories in the other CIS states found that they could not afford the raw materials, components and sub-assemblies they needed from Russian factories. They therefore raised their prices and demanded huge short term loans from their banks to meet their need for working capital. The disruption was proportional to the degree of complementarity in the production of the giant factories that had been sown across the length and breadth of the Soviet Union.

Since the central banks of the new states were linked to the Russian central bank and had the right to increase money supply in roubles, they did so with abandon, knowing that Moscow would have to pay the bill.[10] As a result the Russian government could not prevent the increase in money supply even if it wanted to. Not until late in 1993 was this link finally broken. To complicate matters further, the Russian central bank was not under the president and prime minister (that is, the executive), but under the Supreme Soviet. Under pressure from it Gaidar appointed a hardliner, Victor Geraschenko, who assigned a higher priority to keeping Russia's factories running than to controlling the money supply.[11] Thus, Gaidar's decontrol of prices and production did not move the economy towards a new equilibrium, because he did not have the means to control the supply of money. Instead it caused hyper-inflation and a collapse of the economy: in short, chaos.

The statistics for the next three years tell their own dismal tale. By official estimates Russia's GDP contracted by 18.5 per cent in 1992, 12 per cent in 1993, 15 per cent in 1994 and 5 per cent in 1995. By January 1996, four years after shock therapy, in real terms, Russia's GDP had fallen to 50.4 per cent of what it had been in 1990. In dollar terms the GDP had declined even more steeply, by 72 per cent.[12] This was just over a quarter of the per capita income of South Korea and one-eighth that of Hong Kong.

The combination of plummeting production and a complete lack of control over money supply triggered hyperinflation. The rate of inflation was 1,354 per cent in 1992 (2,323 per cent from December to

December), 896 per cent in 1993 and 320 per cent in 1994. By the end of 1994 prices had risen by 750 times from 1991; by the end of 1995 by 1,500 times. The exchange rate for the rouble had fallen from the auction rate of 15 to 16 to the dollar in 1990 to 4,584 to the dollar in November 1995, and to over 5,000 in May 1996.[13]

Not only did the average per capita income decline, but income differentials widened sharply. The difference between the wealthiest and poorest people had risen to 12.4 times in April 1994. One year later, it had widened further to 13.3 times.[14] Widening income differentials, combined with rapidly falling income, produced poverty and starvation. In April 1995, 43 million persons were living below the poverty line as defined by the government.[15] Ten months later, after a year of almost stable although artificially propped-up exchange rates and rapidly falling inflation, this had improved only marginally to 36.6 million persons.[16]

THE APPARENT SUCCESS OF SHOCK THERAPY

Despite the severe trauma inflicted upon the people, in 1997 it seemed that shock therapy was having the desired effect. The decline of production had stopped and inflation had almost come under control. GDP rose for the first time by 0.8 per cent in 1997.[17]

The inflation rate also declined from 215.1 per cent in 1994 (year-end to year-end) to 11 per cent in 1997.[18] The depreciation of the rouble slowed down from 400 per cent in 1992 to 7.5 per cent in 1997.[19] Both these results stemmed from the government's success in curbing the growth of money supply, which fell from 200 per cent in 1994 to 11 per cent in 1997.[20]

Russia's trade balance with non-CIS states also remained strongly positive all through this period. In 1997, despite a fall in energy prices, and the contraction of the East and South East Asian economies, Russia recorded a trade surplus with the non-CIS countries of $18 billion.[21] There was also a decline in food imports. This was partly made possible by increased domestic production of sugar, alcohol and alcoholic beverages.

The Yeltsin government was also extraordinarily successful in privatising the economy. By June 1996, Russia had privatised around 80 per cent of its economy, measured in terms of contribution to GDP.[22] Banking was entirely in private hands. Management of the large natural resource companies had been privatised even where the state continued to hold the majority or the largest single chunk of shares. There was a rapidly growing share market trading in the shares of the privatised companies.

It is hardly surprising, therefore, that the world began to believe that Russia had at last turned the corner. Foreign direct investment grew by 150 per cent to $6.4 billion, and foreign lenders invested no less than $10.9 billion in short term treasury bills (GKOs) issued by the central bank to tide over (temporary) shortfalls in revenue.[23] On 18 June 1998, Russia entered the Eurobond market for the first time with the sale of $2.5 billion worth of bonds bearing an interest of 12.75 per cent.[24]

The years 1997 and 1998 saw a strange and tragic paradox: so far as economic reform was concerned, Russia proved a model performer; but underneath the false gloss of these bloodless statistics, things had gone deeply wrong.

THE BREAK-UP OF DISTRIBUTION

The steep decline in GDP was a direct consequence of the break-up of the distribution system erected under the socialist system. Perhaps the worst hit was the country's agriculture. The output of foodgrains fell from an average of 104.3 million tonnes between 1986 and 1990, and a peak of 106.9 million tonnes in 1992, to 93 million tonnes in 1993, 81.3 million tonnes in 1994, and 65 million tonnes in 1995.[25] This drastic fall did not affect human consumption but had a disastrous effect on the availability of feed to the farmers' livestock during Russia's seven-month-long winter.[26] Before shock therapy, the Soviet Union made up for shortfalls by importing the grain needed for its livestock. But after shock therapy, the skyrocketing price of imported grain and the withdrawal of subsidies closed this option. Farmers therefore responded to the crisis as their grandfathers had done to famine and dislocation in the first years after the Revolution and again during the first Five Year Plan – by slaughtering their livestock. The number of cattle fell from 57 million in 1991 to 42.7 million at the end of September 1995.[27] Paradoxically, therefore, as Russian grain harvests fell its imports of grain also declined from 25 million tonnes in 1992 to 11 million tonnes in 1993 and to 4.2 million tonnes in 1994.[28]

The sharp decline in agricultural output was caused directly by the disruption of the distribution system. This took the form of a breakdown in the supply of inputs and arrangements for the marketing of the output. On the input side, the supplies of fertilisers and pesticides dried up as the manufacturing units began to hold back their production for exports. As the engineering industries ground to a halt, the availability of spare parts for tractors and harvesters, ordinary and refrigerated trucks, and other farm implements dwindled and their prices also skyrocketed. Farm machinery therefore also stopped functioning for want of repairs. State farm managers responded by cannibalising existing machines. But many of them also took advantage of the rise in prices to sell off machines and spare parts after declaring them unfit for further use. In an election speech in the Altai region, an important wheat-producing area, Boris Yeltsin told his listeners, 'Last year your collective farms ordered 72 new machines, but they scrapped 4,500.'

Increasingly, therefore, farmers found it difficult to sow their crops, and what they sowed, or what dairy produce they obtained from their farms, they were not able to take to the market. In 1996, Russian officials told the author that milk and other dairy products being produced in abundance just 100km from Moscow were being fed to the pigs or poured into the ground because there were no refrigerated trucks to bring it to the city.

The breakdown in supply to the cities created a vacuum that was immediately filled by imports. In 1989 only $10.5 billion of the USSR's imports of $72 billion consisted of food, drink and tobacco. In 1995 and 1996, 54 per cent of the total food being consumed in Russia was imported. In Moscow and St Petersburg, the figure was as high as 70 to 80 per cent. While farmers were still slaughtering their cattle in millions, Russia imported 486,000 tonnes of red meat and 440,000 tonnes of poultry meat in the first eight months of 1995[29] from countries outside the former Soviet Union.

IMPACT ON INDUSTRY

The impact on industry was only marginally less disastrous and followed a pattern of which the full significance has still not been grasped. Between 1991 and 1993, the output of basic and intermediate products fell by 18 to 37 per cent[30] but that of textiles fell by 47 per cent.[31] Between January and September 1994, and the same months of 1995, the output of electricity, coal, oil, gas, steel, cement and automobiles stabilised but the output of textiles fell by another 22 per cent, while that of TV sets fell by 55 per cent, of refrigerators and freezers by 33 per cent, and of meat and meat products by 29 per cent. The pattern remained unchanged in 1996. In January and February, the steel, metallurgy, chemicals and petrochemicals industries stabilised or increased output, mainly because of bounding exports. But the machine-building industry recorded a decline in output of 19 per cent, and light industry of 33 per cent over the same months of 1995.[32]

The pattern is unmistakable: the industries worst hit by the economic 'reforms' have been the consumer goods industries. Production in these has fallen by as much as 60 to 80 per cent since 1991.[33] Why did textiles, arguably the simplest of industries and, in market economies, the first one normally to be set up during the course of industrialisation, suffer the highest decline in production? And why did the basic industries, which are usually affected much later in the course of industrialisation, being more capital intensive and technologically complex, fare much better?

The answer was the lack of a market-based system of distribution to replace the centralised command system that had been dismantled. The larger the number of buyers that had to be reached, the more marked was the impact of the breakdown of distribution. This explains why the decline was most marked not in the high technology sectors but in simple areas of manufacture like textiles and other consumer goods. Even in the cities, where private shops had been opened and a market was being born, Russian consumer goods suffered because they were denied protection from imports.[34] As a result the signals from the nascent market, which were not getting transmitted to the local consumer goods industry, were picked up instead by producers in the world market who rushed in to fill the gap.

By contrast, steel, cement, oil and oil products, non-ferrous metals and chemicals were complex to produce but relatively easy to market. This was because the products were undifferentiated and had only a handful of buyers who were easier to reach. In addition there was a well established export market for these products. Russian producers in these industries were therefore plugged into the international market, which remained immune to the disruption that the winding up of Gosplan and Gosnab caused in the domestic 'market'. Russia thus ended by retracing in its *de-industrialisation* the course traced by the market economies during their *industrialisation*.

TURNING OUTWARDS – THE EMERGENCE
OF DUALISM IN THE RUSSIAN ECONOMY

In view of what has been said above, it should come as no surprise that the one sector of the economy that did not contract was foreign trade. The total value of trade with the non-CIS countries did shrink from $98.3 billion in 1991 to $78.8 billion in 1992, the first year of shock therapy. But it rapidly recovered to $94 billion in 1994, and forged ahead to $108.5 billion in 1995. Most of the increase in trade occurred because of a rise in exports. Between 1991 and 1995, while exports went up from $53 billion to $63 billion, imports shrank from $44.5 billion in 1991 to $37.2 billion and $34.9 billion in 1992 and 1993, and barely recovered to $45.1 billion in 1995.[35] This was because the international market remained the only functioning market for Russian companies. All of them therefore strained every nerve to increase their exports. The most readily saleable products were oil and gas. Thus it is no surprise that their export not only grew most rapidly, but became the mainstay of Russian exports during this period. Between 1994 and 1995, the export of raw materials rose by $5.3 billion.[36] Oil and natural gas accounted for $3.86 billion of this increase. Oil and oil products and gas accounted for 20.7 per cent of total exports in 1994, 27.6 per cent in 1995,[37] and 47.4 per cent in 1997.[38]

Overall, trade grew by 11 per cent in dollars during a period when the real GDP had shrunk by 50.4 per cent. Thus by the most conservative estimate, the trade to GDP ratio had more than doubled in just four years. Converted into dollars, the change was even more striking. From an estimated 8 per cent in 1987, the trade to GDP ratio jumped to 44 per cent in 1995.[39] The sheer speed at which the Russian economy turned outwards therefore far exceeded the speed of change in China. The reason was that while the internal distribution system, which had been based upon *redistribution*, had collapsed, the international distribution system, which is based on *exchange*, had remained hale and hearty, and hungry for the goods that it had been importing from Russia all along. The sharpness of the jump in 'openness' thus reflects the speed of collapse of internal distribution.

Shock therapy therefore turned the Russian economy outward very abruptly, but this turning outward was very different from the outward orientation that is the main goal of economic reform. The purpose of structural adjustment programmes designed to end autarchic development is to integrate the industrial growth of the concerned countries more fully with global production. The model everyone has in mind, albeit implicitly, is that of East and South East Asia, and some countries in Latin America that have become major outsourcing locations for American industry. China is the most recent and most spectacular example of this type of successful reorientation: more than a third of its exports are manufactured by joint ventures and foreign companies that have located their subsidiaries in its special economic zones. But unlike China and South East Asia, Russia has joined the world market as a producer of raw materials, while its immense industrial and technological superstructure continues to decay. This regression was underlined by the decline in its exports to the CIS countries, which included a large component of machinery in the days before the transformation began. In 1995 these fell by 7.7 per cent over the previous year.

Russia's experience thus bears out the validity of the theories of underdevelopment of Marxist economists such as Samir Amin and Andre Gunder Frank. Whatever its failings might have been, the Soviet economy was an integrated one in which the different industries and sectors related to each other in such a way as to leave the entire economic system balanced and self-sufficient. That self-sufficiency was reflected in its low trade to GDP ratio. The sudden shift to capitalism in 1992 has disarticulated the economy and broken up the internal network of interdependence. It has thus created a classic dual economy in which one segment, which is linked to the global economy, is faring reasonably well and expanding its production, while the rest of the economy remains stagnant. The growing income differentials between Russians and 'new Russians', referred to earlier, is a direct conse-quence. The difference is that this is not a true dual economy, of the kind that Frank and Amin analysed, but a parody of one. Russia is not a traditional, pre-industrial economy but a highly industrialised one. So there is no traditional sector to which people thrown out of work can return and get absorbed into; no extended family that accepts the obligation of looking after those who left for the cities and have been forced back; and no subsistence economy consisting of agriculture and artisanal industry that will continue of its own accord, largely unaffected by the turmoil in the modern sector. In Russia the creation of dualism involves the de-industrialisation of the modern economy – what one writer on Russia has called the de-Modernisation of a twentieth-century state.[40]

THE RETURN OF THE BARTER ECONOMY

By 1996 and 1997, although Gaidar was gone, his policy of controlling the money supply to curb inflation seemed to be working.[41] But in the absence of a functioning market system, this had a completely unexpected effect on the Russian economy: demonetised it and regressed it to a system of barter. Intent upon keeping their factories working and their workers employed, plant managers began to exchange IOUs with each other. Over time these became a kind of parallel money. Western observers saw in this only another example of Russian managers' determination to avoid paying taxes, but the structure of industry under communism had made this virtually the only possible response to the control of money supply. At each stage of manufacture the production of the required components and materials had been centralised in one or a few plants. Their dependence on other plants to supply inputs and purchase their outputs was therefore exceptionally high. Thus each plant was able to exert a degree of coercive power over those above and below it in the chain of production. This meant that managers had no option but to accept IOUs in place of cash when their buyer or supplier insisted on them doing so.

Factories were under an equally strong compulsion to continue producing at any cost. Outside Moscow, St Petersburg and a few other cities, most towns were factory towns that had grown up around a single dominant enterprise. If that enterprise closed down the workers would have to find work elsewhere. But there was little work to be had in their home towns, and moving to another was nearly impossible because, there being no market for living accommodation and no money in their pockets to rent whatever little space was available, they could find nowhere to live. Thus if their plants closed down completely, they would starve. Few plant managers and union bosses were prepared to take such a decision. So they continued to produce, and issue IOUs for their inputs.

The breakdown of distribution and the virtual absence of protection for domestically manufactured consumer goods also meant that the factories producing such goods could not sell more than a fraction of their output. So they began to pay their workers in kind – in everything from rubber tyres to cigarettes and stockings. The workers in turn exchanged these products for others that they needed from those who produced them. Thus was born Russia's barter economy.

The growth of parallel money, and of barter, took place in stages and was facilitated by active help from local governments. The separation of the Russian central bank from the central banks of the CIS states in 1992 did not immediately bring money supply under control. The chairman of the Russian central bank, Victor Geraschenko, continued to expand the money supply as he believed that this was a lesser evil than cutting off the state enterprises from all sources of working capital and allowing their workers to starve. Geraschenko eventually lost his post, and his successor tightened control on the supply of money as directed by the Kremlin. The enterprises countered this by beginning to issue promissory notes (IOUs). These IOUs were issued both by very large companies like Gazprom, under their own seal of credibility, and by commercial banks, which were prepared to make loans to the manufacturing enterprises. Eventually these began to be traded, and swapped for each other until they became another kind of monetary instrument.[42] There even developed a discount market for the sale of IOUs. Until the end of 1995, moreover, banks continued to make bridging loans to the federal and regional governments to cover the lag between revenue collection and disbursal of payments by the state. But in 1996, as the control of money supply was inexorably tightened at the behest of the IMF, this practice too was discontinued. As a result the shortage of cash in the economy became even more marked and the use of parallel money increased.

By 1998, barter had developed far beyond the initial exchanges of consumer goods, into a vast parallel economy where money had simply vanished. In August 1998, for instance, the manager of a textile design bureau in the town of Kostroma, 320km north-east of Moscow, paid part of its local taxes with 6,000 pairs of stockings intended for the police but which the town authorities did not have the money to buy. As a bonus, the police stopped asking the director of the enterprise to pay its local tax arrears. To get stockings the Kostroma Design Bureau first exchanged primitive nuts and bolts, washers and spare parts (which was all it was able to produce once the market for its main product had collapsed) for wool that it obtained from a textile mill in Uzbekistan. In the same way it got paid in blankets, table linen and flax for keeping other plants running. In 1998, while the bureau used the socks to pay the police on behalf of the municipality, it gave the blankets to the local electricity utility in payment for its electricity bills. The electricity utility in turn gave the blankets to a camp for handicapped children and thus got a hefty rebate on its taxes. The Kostroma plant rounded off its accounts by paying its own workers in stockings.[43]

Similarly, a textile mill paid its electricity bills in concrete electric poles by shipping its fabric 300km to a garment factory. The garment factory made shirts for the security guards at a nearby automobile factory. In exchange the auto plant shipped a car and a truck to a cement plant, which paid for them by delivering the concrete poles to the textile mill. To survive, the factory was making 50 to 60 barter deals a month.[44] By the time of the second economic collapse in 1998, barter had become the rule rather than the exception throughout Russia. An official survey of 210 of the most important enterprises in Russia showed that barter, debt swaps, and other non-monetary transactions accounted for 73 per cent of their transactions in 1996 and 1997.[45] Gazprom, perhaps Russia's largest company and its principal exporter, conducted 80 per cent of its transactions in barter and other non-monetised deals.[46]

THE DISAPPEARANCE OF THE TAX BASE

The collapse of the Russian economy in 1998 can be traced directly to the rise of barter and the use of unofficial monetary instruments. Whether these transactions generated income or profit became irrelevant, because to measure either one needed a medium of exchange. The abandonment of money abolished the unit of measurement itself. As a result there was nothing left to tax. Russia therefore witnessed the following paradox, for which the IMF and its Western advisers had no answers because they had never experienced it before: as the decline in GDP slowed down, Russia's exports picked up, trade and balance of payments surpluses increased and inflation moderated; but its tax revenues dwindled. These shrank from 20 per cent of GDP in 1992 to 12.4 per cent in 1994, to 11 per cent in 1995 and 8 per cent in 1998.[47] In Russia, federal revenues formed only a part of the total tax burden of the people. By far the larger part consisted of payments into social security funds that finance health, education, housing, pensions and unemployment. Together these exactions accounted for approximately 55 per cent of Russian GDP. As Russia's tax base literally melted away, the sums paid into these funds also fell in proportion to the decline in federal revenues.

Until 1994, members of the government attributed the fall in revenues to the effects of the shock therapy administered in 1992 – painful but likely to be short-lived. Nor was there any specific reason to doubt this. In 1994 revenues from all sources were sufficient to cover 73 per cent of federally budgeted expenditure. In 1995 the government was able to balance its budget for the first time as its revenues amounted to 100.6 per cent of expenditure, but the storm clouds were already visible. The expenditures had been covered by attracting some R27.7 trillion (27.7 billion new roubles, i.e. a little over $6 billion) of private savings into government securities.[48] While Russian budgeting practices do not distinguish between current and capital account expenditures and revenues, this suggests that there was a current account deficit of approximately this amount that was covered by drawing upon capital account inflows. The balance was, moreover, achieved by not paying out 7 trillion (old) roubles ($1.7 billion) of wages; by cutting back sharply on budgeted social welfare and science expenditures; by not paying another R7 trillion into the pension contingency account; and deferring expenditure of another R12 trillion on other accounts. In short, the shortfall of revenues on current account, even in 1995, was of the order of 53 trillion old roubles or $12 billion.[49]

The fiscal crisis became noticeably more acute in the first quarter of 1996, when the actual revenue received amounted to just 33 per cent of projected receipts.[50] The government had no explanation for the sharpness of the shortfall and there ensued a frantic search for explanations that was regularly reported in the Russian press. One that was seized upon immediately was the decision not to provide central bank credit to the federal government to bridge the gap between accrued revenue and expenditure that resulted from the slow accrual of revenues during the early part of the year. The deputy finance minister, Oleg Vyugin, let it be known that the practice of accommodation had been discontinued under pressure from the IMF because the credits were not repaid and were adding rapidly to the federal debt and therefore to the interest burden it had to sustain. This was because of the very high interest rates at which the loans were being taken.[51] Whatever the justification, there can be no doubt that this cut-off increased the arrears of government payments, and therefore the infusion of cash into the economy. It therefore accelerated the shift to barter, and reduced the economy's capacity to generate tax revenues.

Over the ensuing months the fiscal situation worsened. Not long after Yeltsin was re-elected, the government announced that it was going to have to cut down budgeted expenditures by one-third because of the continuing severe shortfall in the collection of revenue. This came as no surprise because all through the first half of 1996 the fiscal imbalance had continued to worsen. 1997 turned out to be even worse than 1996. Tax revenues continued to shrink, and amounted to barely half of what the government had anticipated.[52] There was a spate of explanations and accusations.

The tax regime was blamed for being faulty; for instance there were too many exemptions from import duty given to special interest groups and these were being abused with abandon. The National Sports Fund for example, headed in early 1996 by Alexander Korzhakov, a member of the Federal Security Service (former KGB) and security chief for Boris Yeltsin, had been granted exemption from import duties for sports goods. In May 1995 the import duty forgone on its exports came to $200 million a month.[53] Since the average nominal import duty then was 20 per cent, this meant that the NSF was importing $12 billion of sports goods a year. This amounted to just over a quarter of Russia's total imports in 1995!

Shuttle trade by Russian peddlers crossing over into Finland, China, Turkey and India, which accounted for $11 billion of imports in 1995, was untaxed or at best imperfectly taxed. The Russian Mafiya controlled nearly all of it by 1996.

There was a similar under-taxation of exports. For instance, in 1996 the export duty on oil and gas was being levied on the basis of their domestic prices and not international prices, which were several times higher.[54]

The Duma was blamed for insisting that wages be increased by 54 per cent from November 1995, a decision that was expected to cost an extra 5 trillion (old) roubles, and then advancing the date of indexation to September, a move that would double the unforeseen expenditure.

According to the prosecutor general's office, banks were playing an important role in heightening the financial insolvency of the government, because they were delaying the transfer of revenues collected and payments made on behalf of the government by as much as a full twelve months. The lack of accountability enabled them to speculate with these funds, often in the foreign exchange or commodities markets. Both delays worsened the shortage of cash in the system, and worsened the collection of taxes.[55]

Investment banks and trust funds that had mushroomed to attract the savings of Russians for investment did exactly the same thing with private deposits, except with even greater impunity. Thus it was a regular phenomenon in Russia for banks to default on the payment of interest to their depositors. The government had found that in the Moscow area alone 232 companies had stopped making payments to their depositors, and that overall some 2,100 Russian companies across the country had done the same thing. The sums lost ran into trillions of (old) roubles. In all, according to one estimate, a quarter of the Russian population had lost its savings or had them sequestered by investment funds that were not paying interest.[56] In March 1996 this provoked Yeltsin into enacting a law to protect investors, which included five- to ten-year prison sentences for bankers and fund managers who criminally defrauded their investors in the money and stock markets.

As in the case of import duties on shuttle trade, the Russian Mafiya was held responsible for thwarting the collection of domestic taxes as well. In the businesses it controlled, estimated to be more than 50 per cent of all economic entities in the country,[57] it was known to threaten anyone who dared to investigate their transactions.[58]

Another important culprit was the judicial system. The deputy governor of the Russian central bank, S. Alexashenko, ascribed the unwillingness of banks to give bridging loans to government and private enterprises to a very high rate of default and the absence of an effective legal and judicial system that could enforce contracts.[59]

Lastly, privatisation was held responsible for the withering away of revenues. The bulk of all Russian enterprises had been turned into joint stock (i.e. limited liability companies). This according to many Russians allowed the new owners to amass huge debts by pledging their companies' property alone. Their own, often ill-gotten, wealth remained untouched when the company went bankrupt. Thus a strong disincentive to profligacy and debt default, which was very much present in the US (where 90 per cent of all companies were unlimited liability ventures), was absent in Russia.[60]

But neither singly nor together could these explanations account for the speed at which revenues declined. The real problem was the rapid demonetisation of the economy. Accounts were still kept in roubles. But payments were either not made, made in kind, or in promissory notes and IOUs. As a result the taxable base of the economy kept shrinking. An Urgent Issues Commission, which held its first meeting on 20 March 1996, was informed by first vice-premier Vladimir Kadannikov that as of 1 February 1996 the arrears of payments of local enterprises added up to R281.2 trillion ($68 billion), and was increasing by 9 per cent a month. Of this, R70 trillion was owed to federal and local governments. On 4 March, wage arrears of the production sector (i.e. excluding government and armed forces) had risen to R18.1 trillion ($3.8 billion).[61] In a press interview, first deputy economics minister Yakov Urinson admitted that even the biggest enterprises, in the oil, gas and other sectors, only entered 30 per cent of their receipts into their accounts. The remaining 70 per cent was used to write off debts and redeem promissory notes, and held in trade credits.[62]

As barter and parallel monetary instruments took over the role of money, the government's revenues literally disappeared, swallowed up in a welter of claims and counter-claims. Gazprom refused to pay R12 billion in taxes because it claimed that it was owed R13 billion by its consumers. RAO Unified Electricity Systems said it was unable to pay the government R5–6 billion in back taxes because it was owed twice as much by insolvent customers. The survey of 210 enterprises mentioned above also found that these paid only 8 per cent of the taxes that they owed to the government with 'real' money.[63] Wages continued to remain unpaid. By mid-1998, arrears had climbed in the production sector of the economy to $11 billion.[64] Arrears of payment to civil servants rose in step with the arrears in the rest of the economy. In April 1996, these were about one-fifth of the arrears in the production sectors, that is about R40.8 billion (old).[65] Even if the ratio remained unchanged, they would have risen to $2.2 billion in July to August 1998. But there were indications that government arrears had worsened. In 1996 the arrears in armed forces salaries amounted to six months' pay. By the end of September 1998, some armed forces units in Siberia and the far east had not been paid for 18 months, and were threatening rebellion.[66]

The years 1997 and 1998 saw a strange and tragic paradox: judged by the yardsticks of the Washington Consensus, Russia had proved a model performer; but the greater its success in reforming the economy, the more acute was its breakdown as a functioning state. To cover the gap between earning and spending, the government borrowed more and more heavily at progressively higher rates of interest. This increased the burden of interest payments at an alarming rate, and these payments consumed a progressively larger share of the falling revenues. It should have been obvious to any close observer that the Russian state was becoming steadily less viable and that this was a one-way street. But so compelling was the ideology of the free market that no one, except perhaps some of the ideologues of the Communist Party, could see that Russia was heading for collapse, and that every measure the government took, supposedly to stabilise the economy, only hastened the end.

Throughout this period the government kept up the fiction that it was on course with reform. Tax revenues were only falling because no one wanted to pay their taxes, not because they could not pay. In 1997 the government adopted strong-arm tactics to literally force Russians to pay their taxes. This too had little effect. It then pinned all its faith on a reform of the tax code. The premise behind this reform was that people were not paying their taxes because there were too many, and their cumulative impact was expropriatory. If the number of taxes was reduced and rates brought down to a realistic level, tax compliance would improve and revenues would rise. The logic was impeccable for a market economy, and had been applied with great success to reduce tax evasion in *dirigiste* countries like Turkey in the early 1980s and India in the late 1980s and early 1990s. But Russia was not a market economy. Incredible as it might seem in retrospect, while anxious statements kept appearing in the Russian and the foreign press that highlighted the growth of the barter economy on the one hand and the shrinkage of revenues on the other, only a handful of Russian and almost no foreign commentators made the connection between the two. What is more, almost none of those who did make the connection saw that the link between the two was not causal but contingent. Both were the effect of a third, epic blunder – the attempt to impose market reforms on a country that was not a market economy.

THE ONSET OF THE CRISIS

Western, and most Russian, analysts ascribed the second collapse of the rouble on 17 August 1998 to external shocks – two shocks to the real economy and three to the virtual economy of the financial markets.

In the real economy the price of oil, Russia's principal export, fell to $14 a barrel. This was largely responsible for a 14 per cent decline in government revenues in January to April 1998.[67] Simultaneously Russia suffered an unusually bad harvest. Grain output fell by about 30 per cent and severely reduced the supply of fodder. This increased Russia's dependence on imported foodstuffs to feed its cattle in addition to its human population.

As for the virtual economy, the Russian government and the IMF ascribed much of the blame to three waves of panic among investors between November 1997 and May 1998, all of which were triggered by the spreading currency crisis and depression in East Asia.

The common feature of all these explanations was that they pinned the blame for the growing insolvency of the Russian government not on internal structural weaknesses but on external shocks. Everyone, from President Yeltsin to President Clinton and the managers of the IMF and the World Bank, persuaded themselves of this. Thus it was hardly surprising that at the end of June, when Russia's foreign exchange reserves had fallen to a mere $15 billion, the government turned to the IMF for a bale-out package that would bolster its reserves and restore confidence in the stability of the rouble. With considerable reluctance the IMF agreed to lend Russia $22.6 billion, on condition that it improved its tax collection and cut down federal spending.

But the entire exercise was one of politically and ideologically motivated self-delusion. As has been described above, the financial crisis of the government in 1997 and 1998 could hardly have been prevented by a 14 per cent increase in its revenues; for its fiscal deficit was at least four times as large. The financial turmoil and economic recession in East and South East Asia did heighten the nervousness of foreign investors. But all that did was to advance the date of the collapse.

What followed was a textbook descent into bankruptcy. By summer 1998, Russia's short term borrowing, through treasury bills known as GKOs, had become dangerously high. As a result the burden of interest payments on the budget rose from 25 per cent in 1997 to 32 per cent in January to April 1998.[68] By mid-1998, Russia's position had become untenable. It had issued $40 billion of GKOs, $10.9 billion to foreign banks. Private banks had taken another $15 billion in short term loans, and the first payments on another $160 to $180 billion of longer term foreign loans totalling another $160 billion, on which the first payments were nearly due. All in all Russia had to pay $30 billion by way of interest and debt service in 1998, but had reserves amounting to only $15 billion.[69]

In this situation even the promise of a loan of $22.6 billion and an immediate release of $4.8 billion did nothing to stop the slide into crisis. The Russian central bank lost $1.4 billion in just two weeks ending on 13 August 1998. Reserves continued to run out at the rate of $1 billion a week as the central bank tried desperately to defend the rouble.[70] In just one month after receiving the first tranche of the IMF loan the bank spent $3.5 billion.[71] On 17 August, the government suspended trading in dollars, and announced that it would reschedule its debt. But this did not stop the haemorrhage.

Russia was clearly insolvent. But the insolvency had not been brought on by an imbalance in the external payments account. It had been caused by the shortage of money, the rise of barter and the ubiquitous use of a parallel 'non-money' in the domestic economy. The pity of it was that the barter economy that had sprung up was a market economy, only a very inefficient one. The very extremes to which managers had been pushed to keep their plants working had created much of the know-how needed to operate in a market economy. The next logical step would have been to monetise all the debt, redeem the IOUs and pay off all the arrears. This would have put enough money into circulation to allow transactions to be made in real money once more. But money supply had been choked for so long that the increase needed to remonetise the economy would have triggered hyperinflation and collapse anyway. There was no way out of the dilemma. Thus while the government dithered, the state headed inexorably towards collapse.

THE SECOND ECONOMIC CRISIS, 17 AUGUST 1998

Three events within 48 hours of each other finally brought on the crisis. The first was the failure on 11 August of two of Russia's biggest banks, the Inkombank and the SBS-Agro bank, to meet margin calls on foreign loans of $4.5 billion and $4 billion respectively. Both had pledged Russian government securities and bonds as collateral to the lending banks abroad. When the Russian financial crisis escalated, these securities depreciated heavily. This prompted the lenders to ask for more collateral. The only way either bank could have raised the money was to sell some of their securities and convert the money into dollars. But by then the value had fallen so steeply that this way was to all intents and purposes closed.[72] Both banks were forced to default on their margin calls. On the very next day the rate of interest on the GKOs, which had been rising rapidly, crossed 140 per cent.[73] Finally on 13 August the *Financial Times* published a letter from the Hungarian-born international financier, George Soros, saying that the Russian financial crisis had reached a terminal stage. Soros urged that the rouble be devalued and a currency board established to manage it.[74]

On 17 August the government suspended repayment of its short term treasury bills (GKOs) and federal savings bonds (OFZs) coming due until the end of 1998, and announced that it would redeem the former over a longer period at lower, fixed rates of interest. These were to be redeemed over three, four and five years, at an interest rate of 30 per cent for the first three years and 25 and 20 per cent for the fourth and fifth years. The government also stopped supporting the value of the rouble in the foreign exchange market and announced a 90-day moratorium on the repayment of all foreign loans, no matter who had taken them.

The devaluation, and the restructuring of government debt, did not come as a surprise, but the moratorium on repayment of all foreign loans did, and caused immense harm to the economy. Private banks had taken $15 billion in short term loans, and the first payments on another $160 to $180 billion of longer term foreign loans were nearly due. These amounted to $2 billion in 1998 and $13 billion in 1999. In all, $11 billion invested in GKOs lost about 30 per cent of its value, and the future of about $33 billion of longer term loans and interest payments became extremely uncertain.[75]

The government's default set off a collapse of the banking system somewhat like a house of cards. Its first effect was to rob a large number of banks of liquidity. Since this coincided with a rush of depositors trying to get their roubles out and exchange them for goods or other currencies while these were still to be had, they had no option but to bring down their shutters. On 26 August, therefore, the government formally banned trading in the dollar. The value of the rouble immediately dropped 40 per cent against the Deutschmark. This made its imputed value about 13 to the dollar. But the central bank had no options left because by then it had spent $8.8 billion (or half of Russia's foreign currency reserves, excluding the IMF's loan tranche) in its bid to defend the rouble.

The panic continued unabated, however, as Russians struggled to get their money out of the banks before it became worthless. On 3 September, therefore, the government began to enforce a two-month ban on the withdrawal of savings. Six private banks were ordered not to pay R14 billion they held in savings deposits ($2.3 billion before the crash).[76] The rouble depreciated further to 7 US cents, or 14 to the dollar. Even if the rouble had not dropped further, this meant that in November when the ban came to an end, those members of the Russian public who had made the mistake of holding their money in rouble savings deposits had lost 60 per cent of their savings. This was the third time since 1991 that the government had 'solved' the problem of 'excess' liquidity by simply expropriating the people's savings. But not the savings of all the people. It was mainly the poor who were made to pay for the follies of the government and its Western advisers. As was mentioned in Chapter 2, the majority of the savings in Russia are held as dollars. But the rich and middle income families hold a disproportionate majority of the dollars. A survey carried out in 1995 showed that while 57.5 per cent of the rich and 47 per cent of the medium income families kept their savings in hard currencies, only 15 per cent of the low income families did so.[77] These were the families, who already lived close to the edge of destitution, who suffered the most.

By destroying the creditworthiness of not just the weaker or more rash banks but of all Russian banks the across-the-board moratorium on the repayment and servicing of foreign loans also destroyed the creditworthiness of Russian importers. The immediate reaction of foreign suppliers was to cut off credit to all buyers who could not arrange payments in cash.[78] Imports therefore began to drop. They dropped by 15 per cent in August, and by half in the first half of September. Since about half of the food consumed in Russia was imported, this caused a growing shortage of everything that people needed most to survive. Meat and cooking oil supplies dwindled, and potatoes, where the local crop had been hit by heavy rain, became hard to find. Soaps, diapers/nappies, butter and sugar disappeared from the shelves. Moscow and St Petersburg, which had begun to enjoy a genuine new prosperity, were among the worst hit, because Moscow food processors bought 85 to 90 per cent of their supplies abroad.[79] Initially Moscow retailers were cushioned by the panic buying that took place when the government defaulted on its payments and the rouble began to fall. In August 1998 sales went up by 5.8 per cent (in roubles) compared with the same month of 1997. But in dollar terms the value of these sales was falling rapidly. By the end of the month retail sales in dollars had declined to half the average monthly level of $12 billion.[80]

As the stocks of food ran out, prices skyrocketed. In just two days at the beginning of September, the price of canned peas at a Moscow supermarket rose from 6 to 8.1 roubles per kilo, nectarines from 17 to 33, and cauliflowers from 17 to 20.1 per kilo.[81]

Yeltsin's decision to replace Kiriyenko with Victor Chernomyrdin and the Duma's point-blank refusal to accept him left Russia virtually without a government for four crucial weeks after the crisis erupted. During this period the central bank made ad hoc efforts to shore up other banks' liquidity and finance the fiscal deficit. As a result, between 17 August and 4 September, the central bank was reported to have pumped R27 billion into the economy to bail out banks and finance the budget deficit. This increased the money supply by 17 per cent. It was estimated that this could cause a 60 per cent rise in consumer prices.[82]

The third group that was severely hurt consisted of companies that had financed investment with capital borrowed abroad. These faced both reduced demand at home and a much higher debt servicing obligation abroad. Unfortunately, as Russian economists were quick to point out, the strongest Russian firms were the ones that had borrowed most abroad. Thus these were the ones most seriously hurt. Overall, the crisis left Russian industry severely weakened.[83]

As the effects of the crisis revealed themselves it became clear to Russians that shock therapy and the opening to the West had devastated their country. In September and October Russia plunged headlong towards hyperinflation, renewed destitution and bankruptcy. The state Statistics Committee reported that prices had risen by 43.5 per cent in August and September. The government clung desperately to the hope that the IMF would bale it out, but the IMF was unable to even comprehend what was happening, let alone find a remedy for it. It therefore continued to harp on about the need for austerity and deflation despite the fact that these were precisely the policies that had brought Russia to bankruptcy. Not surprisingly, intense gloom pervaded the Russian government. According to deputy economics minister, Nikolai Shamrayev, annual inflation could hit 230 per cent by the end of the year if the government could not obtain more funds from the IMF and the World Bank. Other estimates, like those of the Russian-European Centre for Economic Policy (RECEP) were much higher. With or without foreign aid, its analysts felt, Russia was doomed to inflation, possibly of as much as 400 per cent in 1998.[84]

Even more disturbing was the nosedive in production, and no doubt employment, that was taking place. In August, even before the crisis had gained full hold of the economy, the annualised GDP had fallen an estimated 8.2 per cent over the same month a year earlier. Industrial production fell even more steeply, by 11.5 per cent.[85] But most alarming of all was the accelerated decline in tax revenues. In September federal tax revenues fell to R9.3 billion ($580 million). This was almost R3 billion less than the revenue received in August, which was around R12 billion. However, the August figure was half the average monthly inflow in the pre-crisis period. Thus in two months after the crisis set in, federal revenues fell by more than 60 per cent.

In the beginning of October 1998, as winter set in and the mercury dropped below zero in many parts of the country for the first time, there was not the faintest single silver lining to the doom-laden cloud that hung over Russia. Not surprisingly a wave of resentment built up, and Yeltsin and the pro-West reformers became its main targets.

5

The Unmaking of Russia

On 23 June 1998, while pleading with the Duma to pass a new tax code, Sergei Kiriyenko, the last reformist prime minister before the crisis, warned that: 'If the State does not learn to collect taxes, it will cease to exist.'[1] Kiriyenko may have thought he was indulging in a bit of hyperbole, but he was, if anything, understating the peril that Russia faced. Shock therapy had turned Russia into a country that engaged in international trade at one extreme, and barter at the other, but left it without a national market. It did this inadvertently by depriving Russia of the one thing without which a market cannot function – a medium of exchange. That had been the effect of the severe curb imposed on the growth of money supply after 1993. Shock therapy had thus succeeded in reproducing in Russia at the end of the twentieth century, a condition not unlike that of Europe in feudal times. But economic systems do not exist in isolation from political and social systems. In Europe the rise of the nation state had gone hand in hand with, and would not have been possible without, the creation of a national market.

The Soviet Union had deliberately eschewed the creation of a market economy, but it had created an alternative, nationwide system of production and distribution based on centralised planning and distribution which served exactly the same political purpose as the national market in *laissez-faire* countries. When this was destroyed and not immediately replaced by a national market, the Russian state too began to journey back in time towards approximately where Western Europe had been in the fourteenth century, before the Hundred Years' War. As nationwide interdependence broke down and people went back to subsistence farming for food and barter for other necessities, the modern nation state became more and more of an anachronism – a leftover from the future in its journey to the past.

When Yeltsin adopted shock therapy in 1992, the Soviet state was already in the process of dissolution. What followed almost put an end to the Russian successor state as well. It did this in two ways: by loosening the economic links between the federal state and the 'regions', and by emasculating the federal state and permitting the rise of competing centres of power within it.

NATION BUILDING IN RUSSIA AND THE SOVIET UNION

Russia was the last of the European states to go through the twin processes of state building and national market creation that was described in the introductory chapter of this book. When the Bolsheviks came to power in 1917, nation building in the sense described above was far from complete. Even in Tsarist Russia, most of its central Asian territories had been annexed only after 1865. After the break-up of the Soviet Union Russia remained, territorially, the largest country in the world. But it contained scores of imperfectly assimilated ethnic groups, large and small.[2]

Tsarist Russia did not have a nationalities policy. Its treatment of ethnic groups was based almost entirely on religion and concepts of 'core' (superior) and 'other' (inferior) peoples. Administratively, Russia had a central area ruled directly by the imperial administration, and a periphery in which Tsarist rule was indirect. The imperial administration followed a somewhat whimsical policy of favouring or discriminating against various ethnic groups according to need and circumstance. The trans-Caucasian region was treated more or less as a colony. Jews were regarded as an inferior group by virtue of their religion, and were lumped together with a variety of 'black' Russians such as the Kalmyks, Kazakhs, Samoeds, Chechens, Tatars, and various peoples of Siberia.

In the eighteenth and pre-Emancipation nineteenth centuries, Russian nation building was mainly administrative in nature. Tsarism imposed a new state order – laws and taxes – on societies that had, until then, had little knowledge of strong state structures. To curb an ethnic backlash the Russian Tsars created an avenue for 'spontaneous' (i.e. voluntary) Russification.[3] The elite of any ethnic group could gain in status by adopting the attributes of the European 'white' Russians.

Economic unification was greatly speeded up in the second half of the nineteenth century by the extension of the railway system first to the Caspian Sea, and then across Siberia to Vladivostok. With this came economic integration and an increase in homogenising pressures on other Russian peoples. As has happened elsewhere, this 'pressure from above' gave birth to an increased awareness of ethnic differences among the ruling groups. But simultaneously, the growth of horizontal economic links among the various national elites also speeded up the process of voluntary and administrative Russification. Economic class formation thus tended to work against the development of distinct ethnic consciousness except among nationalities that had no representatives in the economic elite. The intersection of nationality and class therefore made for weak loyalties to both.

During the Revolution, therefore, the Bolsheviks followed a mixed policy of enlisting both nationalist and class sentiment against the Tsarist regime. The former was employed mainly in the trans-Caucasus region and Central Asia. This decisively shaped the constitution of the Soviet Union, which was the first constitution to be federative and based on ethnic federal units.[4] Being keen to harness ethnic nationalism to the proletarian revolution, Lenin believed that a nation could be fully independent if it chose and could therefore retain the right of secession. The first decade after the Revolution therefore saw a consolidation of nationalist tendencies within the Communist Party and the education systems of the various republics.[5] But this was not a view popular within the Communist Party as a whole. One of its staunchest opponents was Stalin. Thus when he succeeded Lenin, there was a renewed drive towards national integration.

Stalin was not able to reverse the nativisation of the communist parties of the republics. But he pushed national integration in two other ways: by creating elite educational institutions within the Soviet Union, where teaching was done in Russian, and by setting out deliberately to turn the whole of the Soviet Union into a single interdependent economic unit.

Stalin's decision to set up huge production units in far-flung places was not solely, or even primarily, intended to maximise efficiency. An equally, if not more, important purpose was to knit the Soviet Union together in an interdependent mesh of production and distribution that did for a socialist state what the national market did for a capitalist country. Thus Stalin pushed ahead rapidly with a modern variant of the Tsarist policy of administrative Russification. When Gosplan and Gosnab were wound up during the course of the 1980s and early 1990s, the socialist 'national market' system ceased to exist. One important prop of the Russian nation state was severely weakened.

THE WEAKENING OF THE FEDERAL STATE

The damage did not, however, stop there. The inflation touched off by the decontrol of prices had not only destroyed private savings, but reduced the value of the state's resources by an equal amount. This left the state with only two options: either, like the early sovereigns it could borrow money, or like those who followed a little later, it could raise the resources it needed through taxation.

The borrowing option meant getting money from the Western nations and the IMF. Had the West extended Russia even a small part of the help that West Germany gave to East Germany after unification, the Russian state might conceivably have weathered the transition without being severely weakened. But the ideology of the free market, and possibly the remnants of the Russophobia of the Cold War years, stood in the way. Both decreed that while Western governments would certainly not prevent, and would even encourage private investment in Russia, they were loath to extend official assistance to the Russian state. The only economists who recognised that Western aid had a political in addition to an economic role to play and had therefore to go to the state were Graham Allison and Jeffrey Sachs of Harvard University and Grigory Yavlinsky, whom Gorbachev had made his deputy prime minister in the summer of 1990. Had their pleas for massive aid to Russia in return for rapid economic reform been heeded the subsequent crises, both economic and political, might have been avoided. But the West turned a cold shoulder to their proposals, and left Gorbachev with no option but to reject their plans for reform. As a result, in contrast to the $80–$120 billion that the 18 million people of East Germany have received *every year* since 1990, in June 1998 all that the Russian state, with its 147 million people, had been able to borrow was $21.55 billion.[6]

The state was therefore left with no option but to tax, but its tax base had been destroyed by two catastrophic decisions, both of which were foisted upon it by the economic orthodoxy of the Washington Consensus. The first, which has been dealt with extensively in the previous chapter, was the effort to stabilise the economy by limiting the growth of money supply. This led to the rise of a 'parallel' economy using barter and promissory notes, that was, almost by definition, outside the tax net. The second was privatisation. Privatisation deprived the state of the natural resource companies which were its sole remaining income earning assets, and created the conditions for the rise of a new and often lawless oligarchy that came close to hijacking the Russian state.

PHASE ONE: VOUCHER PRIVATISATION

At the beginning of 1991 Russia had 23,766 medium sized and large industrial enterprises. Five years later more than 77 per cent of these had been privatised. These enterprises accounted for 88 per cent of Russian industrial output. Eighty-two per cent of shops and stores had also been privatised and the number of new, private ventures had gone up to 900,000.[7] The story of this failed privatisation has been told elsewhere.[8] It is sufficient here to sum up its main features.

Many explanations have been put forward for the speed at which the Russian government undertook privatisation. These range from an uncomplicated belief in the superior efficiency of private enterprise, to the need to restore initiative to managers who had never had to take entrepreneurial decisions.[9] But the main reason was that a kind of covert (also described as spontaneous) privatisation had already begun before 1992, and had urgently to be brought under control. This process had been triggered, inadvertently, by Gorbachev's 1991 decision to abolish the control of the big Soviet cabinet ministries over the general directors of the state enterprises.[10]

It soon became apparent that a few thousand state managers would be able to strip the entire federation of its industrial assets. The solution adopted was not to reassert the control of the state, but to push ahead with privatisation as fast as possible. If the state's assets could be equitably divided among the people, Yeltsin's advisers reasoned, the stripping would stop.

The first scheme for privatisation, the voucher scheme, was born out of this expectation. It was modelled on a scheme that had been implemented in the Czech Republic.[11] The broad principles followed were as follows: a part of the shares – 25 per cent in the most popular of the schemes – was distributed free to the workers. They were able to buy another 10 per cent and 5 per cent was sold to the managers. But workers accounted for only 17 million of the country's 149 million citizens. Thus to give the others a share of the assets the government evolved the voucher system. Each citizen was given one voucher, valued at R10,000 or $84 in June 1992.[12] He or she could use it to buy a share in any enterprise, or give it to a licensed voucher investment fund that was expected to work like a mutual fund, and invest the vouchers on their owners' behalf. The vouchers could be used to buy some of the remaining shares of the enterprises, which were to be auctioned. In the auctions, 29 per cent of the shares were reserved for sale against vouchers.

On the face of it, the scheme was highly successful. In 97 per cent of the privatised large and medium sized firms workers were able to acquire 40 to 41 per cent of the shares. On average the managers and workers paid one-fortieth of the real value of the shares to acquire them.[13] But the shares-for-workers scheme turned out in practice to be far less egalitarian than the promoters had hoped. In 1996, only 30 per cent of the privatised enterprises, mainly those producing and exporting natural resources, could be considered profitable. As a result the shares in the remaining 70 per cent had become virtually worthless. In these the employees lost both their livelihood and their capital.

As for the vouchers, 3 per cent of Russians never received theirs; 5 per cent received but didn't use them; 20 per cent sold off their vouchers usually at nominal prices; 15 per cent invested through investment funds most of which did not declare dividends;[14] 10 per cent used them directly to bid for shares; and 47 per cent invested them in shares of their own enterprises. Those who invested in oil, gas, metallurgical industries, timber, paper and non-ferrous metals came out the winners.[15]

Thus on a rough estimate, at most a third of the workers and somewhere between 25 and 40 per cent of the voucher recipients fared well initially. But many of these recipients were later expropriated by other indirect means. As a number of surveys later showed, despite every effort to explain the voucher privatisation scheme to the people, it remained poorly understood. As a result few Russians – outside the managers in investment funds, banks and government departments, and of course the managers of the enterprises themselves – realised that the assets of the companies were grossly undervalued, and that the shares of companies that produced mainly for export were already worth many times their nominal value. With their real wages were in a tailspin, and even these not paid for months on end, relatively few of the worker-shareholders were able to resist the temptation to sell their shares to the first person who came along.

Managers in several of the most profitable enterprises added to the workers' distress by deliberately withholding their wages, partly to speculate with the money and partly to force the workers to sell their shares in order to survive.[16] They also withheld dividends for the same reason. That was one of the reasons why, by June 1996, nearly half of the voucher holders who had invested in their own enterprises had sold off their shares.[17]

The end product of the voucher-cum-employee privatisation was not therefore a broad-based ownership of companies, with the accompanying shareholders' control of the enterprise. Instead, the manager-capitalists' drive to concentrate industrial wealth and exercise unfettered control over the former state-owned enterprises, was barely dented. Most important of all – despite a variety of rules that were promulgated along with the scheme, which barred the managers from opening subsidiary companies, transferring assets to them and giving them lucrative contracts, the essential element needed to give these restrictions teeth – an active body of shareholders and a board of directors accountable to them never came into being. On the contrary, the general directors of the companies, aided willingly by the employee shareholders, left no ruse unused to prevent outside shareholders from getting on to the boards of directors, or receiving a part of the profits where these were being earned. They opposed the open trading of stock in their companies, arguing that this would enable the Mafiya to buy its way in; kept control of the shareholders' registers; often refused to register sales of shares, or to allow shareholders to look at the registers; and dispossessed outside investors by passing resolutions that created new blocks of shares which were sold only to insiders at nominal prices.[18] The shares-to-workers and voucher privatisation schemes therefore ended by reinforcing the power of the manager-capitalists and the financial-industrial conglomerates that had sprung up after the reforms began.

PHASE TWO: 'PINPOINT PRIVATISATION'

In contrast to voucher privatisation, the aims of which had been honourable even if they were not realised, the next phase of privatisation, which some Russian officials described as 'pinpoint privatisation', was corrupt from the outset. It was shaped by the growing impoverishment of the state, the resulting erosion of its authority, and the emergence of new centres of financial and economic power that took advantage of the state's impoverishment to make a bid for political power.

By the time the auctions against vouchers ended in June 1994 the state was left with between 29 and 40 per cent of the shares of the erstwhile state-owned enterprises.[19] In 1995, as fiscal pressures mounted, the Russian government began to sell these shares. In contrast to voucher privatisation, these sales were confined to a handful of buyers who were asked to bid for the block of shares that had been put up for sale. In theory these were not sales at all, but loans to the government against a transfer of shares to the bidder. The state retained the right to redeem the shares at a later date, but everyone knew that this was a convenient fiction.

Pinpoint, or as it is better known, 'crony' privatisation, ruled out participation in the auction by any but the large banks or the emerging financial-industrial combines. The management of the auctions was handed over to lead banks – Western style. But Russian banks were not Western in any sense of the term. They used a variety of often inventive pretexts to ensure that bids were not won by the wrong people. Thus it did not really come as a surprise when the managing banks won all the auctions. For instance in 1996, when the auction of a large block of shares in Norilsky Nikel, one of the largest non-oil natural resource companies in the world, was won by the managing bank Oneximbank for a paltry $160 million, it was widely reported in the press that a bid for almost twice the sum was declared invalid on the grounds that it had been received minutes after the auction closed. Similar charges were hurled against the winners in almost all the deals.

PRIVATISATION AND THE NATION STATE

The above description of privatisation makes it possible to assess its impact upon the Russian state. In the pre-reform period the whole of Russia (and the Soviet Union) was a kind of royal domain. The state simply determined how much the nation would consume and appropriated the rest of the product – the gross saving – for itself. Privatisation whittled down and eventually destroyed that royal domain, and left the state facing the task that the early sovereign states had faced in the fourteenth century, of finding other, reliable sources of revenue. It did this at a time when taxation, the only alternative way to raise resources, was being ruled out by the division of the economy into an international trade sector that would not pay taxes, and a domestic sector that worked on barter, and therefore could not. Privatisation thus took place at the worst possible time. Far from stopping the hijacking of the state that was going on under spontaneous privatisation, it only accelerated it.

As barter took hold of the Russian economy, the only substantial tax base left was the portion of the economy that was hitched to the world market. Even before the 1992 reforms, raw materials, metals and chemicals had made up almost 90 per cent of the Soviet Union's exports to the non-Warsaw Pact countries. They had therefore been the main sources of both saving and foreign exchange for the Soviet state. But these were precisely the industries in which the spontaneous privatisation and voucher privatisation had reinforced each other most strongly to dispossess the state and create a rival power elite that was able to ignore all demands of the state because it, in large measure, controlled it. Pinpoint privatisation was an early sign of the growing weakness of the state; for the shares-for-loans deal that it involved was a hybrid between borrowing and selling off further pieces of the 'royal domain'. This had become possible because by 1995 Russia too had spawned its own breed of bankers who behaved in ways that were not much different from the moneylenders-turned-bankers of Europe.

If privatisation's first effect was to weaken the state, then its second was to facilitate the rise of competing centres of power, a process that weakened it still further. Three separate economic power centres emerged in the years after 1992. The first was a new class of manager-capitalists who accumulated power with a rush during the 'spontaneous' privatisation that followed Gorbachev's 1991 decision to wind up the controlling ministries. In effect this phase saw the birth of several hundred powerful entrepreneurial families and business groups which rapidly accumulated capital at the expense of the state. Because it vested the power to determine the mode of privatisation in the hands of the managers and workers in each enterprise, the voucher privatisation scheme only ended by reinforcing and legitimising their power. It did this by providing the manager-capitalists with an opportunity to convert the capital they had accumulated during the spontaneous privatisation into large blocks of shares in their own enterprises (if these were profitable) or others (if their own were not).[20]

The privatisation of the banking system created a parallel financial elite which amassed capital by using enterprise and government deposits as well as savings deposited by individuals to finance the lucrative import trade, and speculate in currency and commodity markets.

A third potent focus of power was the Mafiya. By 1995 there were more than a million small businesses in Russia, nearly all of which paid protection money to the Mafiya. The rake-offs ranged from $50 a month from pavement kiosks and $100 from shops, to cuts in the profits from the shuttle trade, and tax evasion. As the Mafiya accumulated capital it began to invest in business and finance.

By late 1995, business and finance had begun to integrate in new conglomerates. In January 1996, a newly formed Association of Financial-Industrial Groups (FPGs) held its founding conference. The first FPG had been formed in September 1995. By January there were no fewer than 28 of them embracing more than 450 enterprises, and some of the largest private banks in the country. These included giant enterprises such as GAZ, Norilsky Nikel, and very large private banks such as Oneximbank, Promstroibank, Avtobank and Rossiisky Kredit.[21]

In 1997, a study commissioned by the central bank and carried out by the Russian Academy of Sciences revealed that a small number of Russians had amassed an estimated $140 billion.[22] It concluded that the oligarchs opposed both investing this money into industry and developing a 'market acting according to law' because this would threaten their financial-political dominance.

The creators of these new empires soon began to be referred to as the 'oligarchs'; a term that reflected the peoples' awareness not only of the political power they wielded, but the ruthless struggle for power that they engaged in among themselves. They first showed their power in the 1996 presidential elections when all but one or two supported and heavily financed Yeltsin's presidential campaign. President Yeltsin's election campaign was headed by Anatoly Chubais, who took the help of oligarchs such as Boris Berezovsky who owned, among other things, one of the main television networks in Russia, and Vladimir Potanin, the owner of Oneximbank. This election was one of the few occasions in which the emerging financial-industrial oligarchy closed ranks and acted together. The did so because they were united by their fear of the Communist Party, which had heavily defeated all the liberal parties in the 1995 parliamentary election, and which spoke of going back to the 'transitional stage' of a mixed economy. What followed in the Kremlin was little short of Byzantine. Chubais' first *coup* was to get rid of the powerful chief of Yeltsin's personal security service, Alexander Korzhakov. Korzhakov, who came from the old KGB and therefore a different and older branch of the Russian elite, knew perfectly well the crucial importance of money in the new Russia. He had therefore made a determined bid to gain control of the National Sports Fund, a so-called non-profit organisation intended to safeguard the future of Russian sport (by becoming financially independent), which had been granted duty free import privileges that were costing the Russian customs service $200 million a month.[23] During the election campaign Korzhakov's men arrested two top campaign aides for allegedly trying to sneak $500,000 out of the Russian White House. Chubais insisted that Korzhakov had had the money planted on the campaign aides in order to discredit them, and got Yeltsin to fire Korzhakov.

The two years that followed saw the virtual takeover of the Russian state by the oligarchs. After the elections, Yeltsin rewarded his supporters with choice posts in the government. In August 1996, Potanin became first deputy prime minister for the economy, and in October, Berezovsky became deputy secretary of the Security Council, the ultimate seat of power in Russia. Shortly after his appointment, he gave an interview to the *Financial Times* that was a surprisingly candid manifesto of the Russian financial oligarchy. 'We', said Berezovsky in the name of the Moscow group of seven bankers, 'hired Chubais and invested huge sums of money to ensure [President Boris] Yeltsin's election. Now we have the right to occupy government posts and enjoy the fruits of our victory.' This was not an isolated piece of bravado. A year earlier, in a no less cynical interview he gave to *Nezavisimaya Gazeta*, Mikhail Khodorkovsky, head of Rosprom (the industrial holding of Bank Menatep), had remarked, 'Politics is the most lucrative field of business in Russia. And it will be that way forever. We draw lots in order to pick out a person from our milieu for work in power.'

'For these gentlemen', wrote Andrei Piontkovsky, director of the Centre for Strategic Studies in Moscow, 'the fruits of victory meant abusing public office for personal gain ... as long as Berezovsky opens the door to Chubais' office with his foot, Russia won't have reform. There will be continued rule of oligarchs who entered the government in order to channel state budget financial flows into their private companies.'[24]

Neither Yeltsin nor Chubais reacted immediately to Berezovsky's brazen assertion. Yeltsin may have been constrained because Berezovsky had forged durable and extremely lucrative links with his son-in-law, Valery Okulov, the head of the Russian airline Aeroflot, with whom he allegedly connived to funnel out some of the airline's foreign exchange earnings into Swiss bank accounts. He also lavished opulent gifts on Yeltsin's daughters.[25] Chubais was unable to react immediately because he was himself a creature of the oligarchy. But Berezovsky's blatant boast gave him the opportunity to work for his ouster in the name of clean government and an end to crony capitalism in the Kremlin. Berezovsky had been able to pick up the shares of Sibneft, a Russian oil company in Siberia, for a song. But that was his last easy acquisition. In the summer of 1997 Potanin of Oneximbank won the two major share auctions, namely of Norilsky Nikel and the Russian telecommunications giant Svyazinvest. In both Berezovsky was aligned with another banking, industry and newspaper tycoon, Vladimir Gusinsky. After the Norilsky deal in August, Berezovsky flew to France to meet Chubais who was vacationing there, to sort out matters, but evidently failed. When Svyazinvest also went to Potanin, the knives came out. Both Berezovsky and Gusinsky accused Chubais of using state power to ensure that Potanin would be able to outbid them. Coincidentally, a short while earlier, Chubais had given Oneximbank the responsibility of 'servicing' $1 billion of money collected by the State Customs Committee. Berezovsky and Gusinsky alleged, probably with good reason, that Oneximbank had been able to outbid them by using this money.[26] On 4 November 1997, Chubais struck back and dismissed Berezovsky. Berezovsky and Gusinsky retaliated by turning the full blast of their newspapers and television stations on them. The first head to roll was that of Alfred Kokh, the head of the privatisation committee, who, it was found, had accepted a $100,000 advance from a Swiss publisher connected to Oneximbank. Then a jounalist on a Gusinsky newspaper, Alexander Minkin, dug out a $450,000 book deal signed by Chubais and four of his colleagues with Segodnya Press, another company financed in part by Oneximbank. As mentioned earlier, Chubais had set up a foundation, a popular method among Russian leaders for building a cushion against adversity. When it was also revealed that this foundation (set up to help Yeltsin win the 1996 elections) had accepted a $3 million interest free loan from another bank that had benefited from crony privatisation, his days too became numbered. Within two weeks of Berezovsky's dismissal, three of Chubais' top aides had been forced to resign, and he had been deprived of the finance portfolio. Eventually, he was replaced by Sergei Kiriyenko.

The following remark by Andrei Piontkovsky gives some idea of the stakes in the game described above:

> I recalled a conversation I had with a very prominent Russian politician several months ago. We both spoke at a seminar about corruption in Russia and the power of the financial oligarchy. After my talk, he told me: 'Allow me to give you one piece of advice. You mentioned Boris Berezovsky's name five times today. And I didn't do so once. Do you know why? I have known for too long and too well that man. Be careful. He is very dangerous.'[27]

The Byzantine intrigue outlined above shows that by the time the crisis occurred in 1998, the state was no longer in command, but had itself become a spoil of war. The economic crisis of August 1998 destroyed the remaining shreds of Yeltsin's legitimacy. This was first reflected in his decision to nominate Victor Chernomyrdin to replace Kiriyenko, and then in parliament's total rejection of the man and its choice of the conservative Yevgeni Primakov. The oligarchs – notably Berezovsky, whose links with the first family had remained unaffected – had chosen Chernomyrdin. The communists and their allies in the Duma had chosen Primakov.

As state power collapsed at the centre, the regions began to pull away. First Chechnya became independent in all but name. After the August crisis, the governors of the regional provinces and even municipal mayors began to go their own ways. As federal subsidies petered out, the regions ignored Moscow's *diktats* and introduced administrative and price controls to cushion the social impact of the meltdown. Many regions banned shipments of food to others. Some stopped paying federal taxes. And the collapse of Russia's biggest banks has forced some regions to set up closed banking systems of their own. The governor of Sakhalin described these developments as the 'beginning of Russia's dissolution'.[28]

6

An Uncertain Future

On 6 October 1998, almost a month after being appointed prime minister, Yevgeni Primakov unveiled some of the policies he intended to adopt to get Russia out of its economic crisis in a televised address to the nation. Winter was closing in on the country even as he spoke. The maximum temperature in Moscow had already sunk to 7 °C. Food prices had tripled at a time when a third or more of the people were already below the poverty line. And even those who had savings were unable to get them out of the banks. Primakov's first task was to make sure that the people of the further reaches of Russia, especially the cold Siberian north, did not starve or freeze to death in the onrushing winter. To avert this his government pumped small sums of money into sending essential foodstuffs and fuel to the depressed regions and promised to send more. It also halved freight rates on the transport of fruit, vegetables and potatoes to them. The government prepared a list of food products and medicines that Russia needed most urgently and released foreign exchange on a priority basis to buy these abroad. It also requested Ukraine and Byelorussia to repay loans in the form of food.

His second priority was to make sure that ordinary Russians had some money with which to buy the bare essentials. To this end the government decided to pay two months' arrears of pay to the armed forces and transferred R3.782 billion before 2 October. In addition Primakov promised that while others would not receive their wage arrears, no one would be denied their current pay any longer.

Turning to structural issues, Primakov correctly assessed that the government's priority had to be to save and restructure the banking system. The onset of the financial crisis had been hastened by the banks wilfully or inadvertently holding up about R40 billion of payments – to each other, to the government and to the corporations. He therefore prevailed upon the central bank to unfreeze R30 billion of these payments. Primakov warned the bankers, however, not to expect the government to nationalise their banks. For many of them, this would simply amount to nationalising their liabilities while they walked away with the profits. Instead, he said, the government was drawing up a list of banks that it would save and another of those it would allow to go under.

His next task in order of priorities was to reconcile inter-corporate accounts in order to untangle the web of non-payments that was suffocating the economy. Primakov made it clear that he believed that the greater part of corporate liabilities could be cancelled out against receivables in their balance sheets. This would minimise the increase in money supply needed to remonetise the economy. Significantly he said that in order to prevent abuses, this rationalisation of debt would be carried out through state channels and would completely bypass the banking system.

Primakov further promised to lower tax rates and toughen the tax administration in order to bring transactions out of the shadow economy. He also asked the Customs Committee to release $1 billion of mainly producer goods that had been impounded because the tax had not been paid. This had brought production to a halt in parts of several enterprises.

Lastly, Primakov announced measures to regulate the production and sale of alcohol and alcoholic beverages, that fell just short of nationalisation. The aim was to ensure that the sizeable revenues from the sale of vodka and other alcoholic beverages would not be avoided and would come directly to the state.

Taken together these measures amounted to little more than a fire-fighting effort. They left a number of crucial questions unanswered. The first was the IMF's fear that however restricted the increase in money supply might be, it would further raise prices. How would the government prevent the development of hyperinflation? How would it find the foreign exchange it needed to finance imports of food and medicine when foreign suppliers were no longer offering credit? There were more serious lacunae too: nowhere in the speech was there a reference to the fundamental cause of the crisis – the disappearance of the state's revenue base following the destruction, through privatisation, of its 'Eminent Domain'. Since the Russian government had not succeeded in replacing the direct extraction of surpluses from state property with tax revenues, a partial return to direct appropriation, at least in the short to medium term, was necessary to tide over the fiscal crisis. Yet nowhere did Primakov mention the logical alternative to taxation – a system of revenue (as opposed to profit) sharing, especially with the natural resource companies.

In spite of these lacunae, the speech gave ample indication of the direction in which Primakov intended to take the country. He wanted the state to reassert itself vigorously and take on the role of a regulator of the economy. He wanted it to assure itself of a minimum supply of revenue from the sale of alcohol to carry out its functions. And he would remonetise the economy to make it start functioning once more. If Primakov had his way there would be no more cosy back-room deals in which the state literally liquidated itself in favour of a handful of emerging tycoons.

His intentions were even more apparent in his appointments. He brought back Victor Geraschenko as the head of the Russian central bank – a clear sign that he would not shrink from increasing the supply of money if needed; and as his first deputy premier for the economy he appointed Yuri Maslyukov, former head of Gosplan, the Soviet planning agency. Maslyukov had been a close adviser to the Communist Party leader Gennady Zyuganov in the 1996 presidential campaign and was identified with Zyuganov's proposal to regain control of the natural resource companies. He was therefore reviled by the Western and the Moscow English-language press as author of a plan that had 'called for the eventual mass nationalisation of the economy'.[1] To balance Maslyukov, he appointed a liberal, Mikhail Zadornov, as his finance minister. Zadornov was not in favour of nationalisation and was intent upon increasing tax revenues of the state as this was the only sure way to bring the state out of crisis.

The weeks after Primakov's address saw a profusion of explanations and suggestions that reflected the confusion that prevailed over policy. Conspiracy theories abounded. The prosecutor general's office claimed that the entire financial crisis might be a criminal plot. 'Not everything is clean there', said prosecutor general Yury Skuratov in September, as he announced an investigation of the functioning of the central bank during the Kiriyenko era. A milder indictment came from a well known economist, Andrei Ilarionov, who put the blame squarely on the central bank for not insisting on buying up all the foreign exchange that came into the government debt market. Had it done so the country's reserves, he claimed, would have been richer by $21 billion at the time of the crisis. When asked whether this was not because the central bank would have had to print roubles to buy the foreign exchange and was reluctant to do so, he correctly pointed out that the bank had in any case had to print roubles to buy government securities to fund the budget deficit. It preferred to do this because the return on these bills was very high whereas simply buying up foreign exchange did not yield much revenue to the bank. More significantly he accused the central bank of choosing this alternative because it helped it to finance its own swollen expenditures on itself. He accused it of feeling no compunction in spending R15 trillion (old) on its own staff and administrative expenses. This was one and a half times as much as the entire personnel cost of the Russian administration and parliament.[2] In short, Ilarionov concluded that even the Russian central bank had succumbed to the lure of profit and in effect been 'spontaneously' privatised.

There was also no dearth of suggestions on what to do. At one extreme the governor of Sverdlovsk emerged from an interview with Yeltsin to announce that the president had responded favourably to his suggestion that the dollar should be outlawed, a suggestion that caused blind panic until it was speedily denied. At the other Anatoly Chubais resorted to the scare tactics that had won Yeltsin the 1996 elections and predicted a communist takeover. However, somewhat inconsistently he also asserted that the privatisation of the Russian economy was irreversible.[3] In between fell a spate of suggestions which shared one common feature: they all wanted the state to reassume the regulation of the economy. One set of suggestions, made by economists of the Russian Academy of Sciences had considerable effect on the government's policies. In an open letter to the president written in the first half of September, they urged the government to fully index not only wages but also the savings of individual Russians, held with not just the state-owned Sberbank, but also all commercial banks. They asked the government to make it mandatory for exporters and other recipients to sell 100 per cent of the foreign exchange they earned to the Russian central bank, and to severely restrict the purchase of foreign exchange to those with genuine import contracts. The academicians also urged the government to regulate the banks and tighten the procedure for monitoring their activities, and create an 'interbank pool', similar to the US Federal Reserve Board.[4]

None of these measures suited the oligarchs who saw in them the end of their freewheeling days of 'bandit capitalism'.[5] These worthies wanted the state to pump money into their banks to prevent them from going under. They did not want the state to exercise discretion in deciding which banks to support and preferred blanket measures. Even less did they want the market to decide which banks would survive and which would fail. Thus they began a rearguard action to minimise the damage. Their first effort, spearheaded by Boris Berezovsky, who retained his influence with the first family, was to get Victor Chernomyrdin back as prime minister. When this failed and Yeltsin appointed Primakov, they used their control of the media to spread disinformation. After Primakov's appointment, hardly a week went by without *Kommersant Daily* or *Interfax* shrilly reporting that Maslyukov was contemplating one or another coercive measure – to monopolise trade in the US dollar, to monopolise the banking system, to monopolise the alcohol industry. When the new finance minister, Mikhail Zadornov, proposed that the taxes levied on oil and gas be adjusted to take into account the windfall earnings bestowed on them by the devaluation of the rouble, the oil barons, driven by another oligarch, Mikhail

Khodarkovsky, declared open season on him. Khodarkovsky sent a letter to the government saying, 'It is time to stop following the instructions of the IMF. Russian producers must be supported, and controlled inflation can prop up the budget.'[6]

In the midst of this maelstrom of confusion, fear and self-interested pressure, Primakov and his team rebuilt brick by brick the edifice of state regulation. The first step was to regain control of Russia's foreign exchange earnings. To do this the government made it compulsory for all exporters to deposit half their foreign exchange earnings with the central bank. It also limited the release of foreign exchange to commercial banks to the extent needed to finance genuine imports. The money released would have to be used within seven days for the stated purpose or returned to the central bank.[7]

The government also did not shrink from printing money to meet the urgent commitments of the banking system and its own expenses. By the end of October the central bank had released R55 billion into the economic system.[8]

On 3 November, the cabinet approved a plan to bring the crisis under control. The plan's main elements were: the indexation of wages and pensions to protect ordinary people from further deprivation; an increase in the ratio of foreign exchange earnings to be sold to the central bank from 50 to 75 per cent; and the lowering of tax rates from 20 to 15 per cent in VAT and from 35 to 30 per cent in corporation tax to ensure better compliance. Faced with a yawning expenditure gap of R70 billion, the government announced that it would try to hold down deficit financing to R12 billion in the last quarter of 1998. However, as economists were quick to note this would only be possible if the IMF were to come through with the second tranche of its $22.6 billion loan. The IMF, however, continued to frown on Russia's return to controls. After a special mission in August, it had recommended sweeping cuts in federal expenditure and had opposed the return to a regime of controls. The first was completely unrealistic at a time when the collapse of the rouble could only push government expenditures upwards. Primakov therefore ignored the IMF's recommendations as impractical, and pursued the logic of the suggestions made by the economists of the Russian Academy of Sciences. He announced that the government would sell another 5 per cent of Gazprom's shares to tide over its difficulties, and would soon unveil plans to force the privatised companies to declare dividends. On 31 October he remarked at a press conference that the state owned a major chunk of the shares in 5,000 companies but had received a paltry R900 million as dividends in 1997.[9]

RUSSIA'S TURNAROUND –
THE EMERGENCE OF A MARKET ECONOMY

Primakov thus set about methodically restoring the primacy of the state within the framework of the reforms that Yeltsin had initiated. Despite the severe stress that Russia was being subjected to, he did not show any desire to nationalise assets or to go back to a system of administered prices.[10] Instead he contented himself with reimposing those elements of state control that he deemed absolutely necessary to guide Russia through its crisis. In the year that followed, against all expectations, the Russian economy stopped shrinking and began, for the first time since the 1980s, to grow. Early in 1999 the IMF had predicted that the Russian economy would shrink by a further 9 per cent in 1999. Instead its GDP rose by an estimated 3.2 per cent, and industrial output rose by 8.1 per cent.[11] By October 1999, tax revenues had increased by more than 60 per cent – R30 billion more than the target the government had set – and were being paid in real money. During the year as a whole they rose from 9 per cent of GDP in 1998 to 13.4 per cent in 1999.[12] As a result, pensions were paid in full for the first time in years.

This remarkable turnaround was an unexpected byproduct of the crash of the rouble in August 1998. The decline in its value from 6.3 in July 1998 to 24.62 to the dollar by the end of 1999, and the curbs the central bank put on the convertibility of the rouble led to a strong revival of Russia's food processing industry and a less marked but nonetheless significant improvement in its consumer goods industries, notably textiles. The fall in the value of the rouble made Russian foodstuffs suddenly far cheaper than the food that was being imported from Western Europe. Shop owners reacted to skyrocketing import prices, the decline in the real income of their consumers and the sudden shortage of cash when accounts were frozen, by replacing imports with local produce. This was greatly facilitated by Primakov's October 1998 decision to halve the freight rates for a wide variety of agricultural produce. The combined effect of the devaluation and the reduction of freight rates was to restore the link between agriculture and industry – between town and country – that had been disrupted when central planning and distribution was discontinued. The non-availability of dollars also spurred this shift. Much the same thing happened in the food processing, garments and textiles sectors. In effect, therefore, the devaluation did what economists close to the Communist Party had been proposing all along – protect the domestic market in order to give Russian industry space in which to grow.

However, industry would not have been able to fill this space so promptly if producers had not learned to respond to the signals that they began to receive from the market after the crash of the rouble. The fact that they did so, and with celerity, revealed the extent to which the trauma of the previous seven years had forced them to develop the rudiments of a market economy. This was where the barter economy that they had been forced to develop during the years when the centrally planned economy was disintegrating around them, came to their aid. Barter is the most primitive form of exchange, and a market economy is its most sophisticated form. Thus in developing their barter economy Russian producers had taken their first and most difficult step away from the chaos created by the abandonment of the centrally planned economy towards the creation of a market economy. The sudden surge of demand from the retailers and wholesalers enabled them to take the next steps in a hurry.

For the first time ever, the Russian farmers, manufacturers and traders responded to a crisis in exactly the same way as their counterparts in market economies do. A 14-city survey by the Russian division of the *Gesellschaft für Konsumforschung*, a European market research organisation, whose results were released to the press in December 1999, showed both the extent to which the crisis had immiserised Russians further and the manner in which it was leading to a revival of domestic industry.[13] The survey showed that between March 1998 and November 1999, the Russian market for foodstuffs shrank by a fifth, and for non-food items by a third. The contraction was sharpest in the Moscow region, where a third of Russian personal income is concentrated. Here personal consumption expenditure fell by 60 per cent.

But this decline impinged far more sharply on imported foodstuffs and consumer goods than Russian. The sale of foreign brands fell by half. The gap was filled by domestically produced goods. The overall consumption of yogurt and chocolates had fallen by around half, but the consumption of imported yogurt had fallen by 88 per cent, that of Russian brands by only 17 per cent. In the case of chocolates, all the decline was concentrated in the imported brands. Russian sales had increased by 2 to 5 per cent for several categories. The sale of Russian brands of tea had similarly risen by 11 per cent while overall consumption had declined by 6 per cent.

In the case of non-food items the substitution effect was even more marked. For instance the overall sale of toothpaste fell by 16 per cent, but that of imported brands declined by 46 per cent while the sale of local brands rose by 130 per cent. For shampoos the corresponding figures were an overall decline of 25 per cent, decline in imports of 43 per cent and a rise in domestic sales of 86 per cent. The market for detergents contracted by 18 per cent, but while imports fell by half, domestic sales rose by 200 per cent. These responses show, as nothing else could have, the long way Russia had travelled during the years of chaos, from the vertically linked 'statist' economy of the Soviet Union to the horizontally linked market economy it had set out to build.

Primakov inadvertently kick-started a recovery in much the same way as the governments of Thailand and Malaysia had done in the second half of 1998 – by ignoring or renegotiating the increases in money supply permitted by the IMF in its standby agreements. But this was only the beginning. The increase in the trade surplus began exerting an anti-inflationary pressure on the economy by remonetising it, when this was most needed. Since the compulsory deposit of export earnings had to be converted into roubles, it increased the liquidity in the economy and accelerated its remonetisation. Under Putin the government also adopted a sliding scale of export duties in March 2000 that rose with the export price of oil. This enabled it to convert a large part of the continued oil bonanza in 2000 into tax revenues. Not surprisingly the tax to GDP ratio rose to 19.8 per cent of GDP in April 2000[14] and as GDP growth picked up further, steadied at 16 to 17 per cent in the second quarter.[15] In fact so great was the rise in revenues that in January to March 2000, the federal government registered a surplus on both the primary budget (before deducting debt servicing) and a smaller one on its overall budget. This eliminated the need to resort to deficit financing or borrowing from the Russian central bank, and rapidly brought inflation under control.

Against most predictions, the Russian economy continued to strengthen in 2000. Inflation, which had soared to 84.4 per cent by the end of 1998,[16] fell to 36.5 per cent at the end of 1999 and to 17 per cent in the first six months of 2000. Industrial production grew by 10.3 per cent during the first half of 2000, and GDP grew by 7.3 per cent. The real disposable income of Russians rose during the same period by 9.3 per cent.

The pattern of growth confirmed the birth of a market economy in Russia, for the very same industries that had experienced the maximum decline in production between 1992 and 1996 were the ones that experienced the highest rates of growth after 1998. Thus in the year June 1999 to June 2000 light industry, which included textiles, toiletries, cosmetics and most household goods, recorded growth of 22.3 per cent; machinery recorded an increase of 17.2 per cent. These dwarfed the increase in output of metals and chemicals, the demand for which came mainly from the world market. Output of ferrous and non-ferrous metals grew by 15 per cent, of chemicals and petro-chemicals by 14 per cent and of timber and woodpulp by 11.8 per cent. This was almost entirely because of the buoyancy imparted to the world market by the American boom.[17]

By the end of summer 2000, to more and more Russians the years 1992 to 1999 had begun to feel like a nightmare from which they had at last woken up. Most wage arrears had been paid off. Real incomes, though still far from adequate were rising and so, less rapidly, were pensions. According to one survey, the index of consumer confidence had risen from a nadir of 40 in October 1998 to 85 in April 2000.[18] There had been a similar improvement in the investment outlook, with two-fifths of all companies reporting plans to expand investment in the coming year. More than 81 per cent of the decline in real disposable incomes caused by the 1998 crisis had been made up.[19] Most Russians had ceased to brood over their economic and political decline and were beginning to look, and plan, ahead.

PEERING INTO THE FUTURE

Any economic recovery is most vulnerable in its early stages. The Russian recovery is no exception. Whether Russia will be able to sustain its burst of growth or not will therefore depend on the extent to which its government understands the underlying causes and tailors its policies to ensure the upswing's continuation. Unfortunately there is no generally accepted explanation of the turnaround. The uncertainty is mirrored by a near-universal lack of belief that it can be sustained. As late as May, despite a 6.8 per cent growth in the first quarter, the most optimistic prediction for the year was GDP growth of 5.2 per cent.[20]

The return of good times has revived the conflict between liberals and conservatives that had bedevilled the six years before the 1998 crisis. These camps differ both on the causes of the recovery and the policies that Russia should follow. The liberals, who overwhelmingly dominate the newspapers and television, and are to be found in disproportionate numbers in Moscow, believe that the recovery was purely a windfall brought about by the collapse of the rouble, which blocked imports, high oil prices and the American boom, which pushed up output in other export industries and gave Russia a 130 per cent increase in export earnings in the first half of 2000, and a tidy budget surplus. This windfall would eventually peter out. In fact several commentators claimed that despite the strengthening of growth in the second quarter, it was already petering out in August. 'Without far reaching change, which requires a major attack on vested interests, the economy was just another big accident waiting to happen.'[21]

Not one of the liberal economists was prepared to admit that the recovery might have had something to do with Primakov's reassertion of state power and imposition of a limited number of controls on the foreign exchange market; or that his decision to increase 'subsidies' by indexing wage rates and pensions, and paying off arrears, might have remonetised the economy, converted potential into effective demand for Russian consumer goods, and greatly widened the tax base.[22]

To many people's surprise, despite the spectacular failure of their policies in 1998, the liberal reformers are neither down nor out. On the contrary, Putin has picked some of his closest advisers, like his economic adviser Andrei Ilarionov, deputy prime minister for finance Alexei Kudrin and minister for economics German Gref, from among the ranks of what are known as the St Petersburg liberals.

The focal point of debate is a ten-year economic reconstruction plan prepared by the Centre for Strategic Research, which was headed, until he became a minister, by German Gref. The Gref Plan calls for balanced budgets; a reduction, through privatisation, of health, educational and social expenditures by 30 per cent in the next ten years; the privatisation of Russia's remaining 24,000 state-owned enterprises; the break-up and privatisation of public utilities such as the railways and RAO-UES, the energy supply monopoly; a comprehensive restructuring of the banking system to make it capable of giving medium term loans for investment – something that virtually no private bank does today; allowing bankrupt or poorly managed banks to fail or be bought up by their competitors; the making of sweeping reforms to the taxation system and enacting and refining laws to facilitate bankruptcy, foreclosure, and retrenchment of surplus labour.

Not surprisingly the Gref Plan has become the focus of bitter controversy in Russia, between the vast silent majority that has suffered grievously in the past ten years and now wants above all else a respite from uncertainty and fear, and a vocal minority that wants to use the present respite from stress to complete the transition to a market economy even if this means some more reduction in socialist life support systems, and increased labour redundancy in the short run. In the Duma the Gref Plan came under severe attack from communist members and their allies, who pointed out that if the plan was implemented Russia's industrial potential would contract by 25 to 30 per cent over the next ten years, the share of the population below the poverty line would stagnate at 23 to 27 per cent (against the May 2000 figure of 35 per cent) and GDP growth would sink to 0.9 per cent until 2006 and rise to no more than 1.5 per cent in the next three years.[23]

Putin – who summed up his philosophy in a phrase that has become famous throughout Russia: 'he who does not regret the passing of socialism has no heart, but he who wants to bring it back has no head' – accepted the Gref Plan in principle and signalled his support for continuing reform by bringing the author into his cabinet, but then went about diluting its rigours. Based on the plan, and called the 'Main Guidelines for a Long-Term Perspective' the government brought out its own plan called the 'Plan for Top Priority Measures for 2000–2001'. The latter accepted the goal of a balanced budget, and outlined a zero deficit budget for 2001, but maintained the state's role in providing, and even enhancing, social security in the short and medium term. It also diluted the proposals for banking reform, and instead of forcing changes in it that would immediately make it capable of meeting the economy's need for investment capital, placed this responsibility on two state investment banks set up after the 1998 crash, the Russian Development Bank and the *Rosselkolkoz* bank (a bank to finance investment in agriculture). In this, therefore, Putin followed a mixed economy model not much different from what was proposed by economists close to the Communist Party.

On three other issues, however, Putin sided with the liberals: on the need to reform the taxation system, to restructure the massive state monopolies in the public utilities, and to complete the privatisation process. In July 2000 he got the Duma to pass a new tax code with only four chapters held up for further discussion. The reforms already enacted included a 13 per cent flat rate of income tax, and the reduction of a number of other nominal rates of tax (which were very high but seldom enforced) with a simultaneous closure of loopholes. In 2000 the government took some preliminary steps to break up some of the state monopolies, but here, as in privatisation, Putin showed that he was not in a hurry. Overall, the government made it clear that it regarded the Gref Plan as a statement of eventual goals but recognised the need to hasten slowly.

The influence of the liberals is felt most in the day-to-day making of economic decisions and is most evident in three interlinked areas of policy: the management of the exchange rate; the use of government surpluses; and the consolidation of the industrial revival. The most pressing issue for the government is how to cope with the adverse side effects of the oil revenue bonanza. Thanks to soaring oil prices and sharp increases in the export of other raw materials[24] the trade surplus rose by 130 per cent in the first half of 2000. The central bank has continued to buy 75 per cent of all export dollars to bolster reserves, but the roubles it is releasing into the market as it buys dollars are pushing up prices. The monthly inflation rate rose from less than 1 per cent in March to 2.5 per cent in June.[25] Few economists now expect inflation to be limited to the 18 to 20 per cent target set by the government.

But a higher rate of inflation with a steady nominal exchange rate will mean a real appreciation of the rouble against other currencies. Everyone believes that this does not pose any threat to Russian exports, but prescriptions on how to 'neutralise' the excess roubles differ sharply. One school of liberals argued that the bank should let Russians hold up to 50 per cent of their export earnings in dollars instead of the present 25 per cent.[26] This would reduce the inflow of dollars into the Russian central bank. A second – which included deputy premier Kudrin – advocated sterilising some of the additional money supply by issuing bonds and raising the interest rate (a measure that would have limited success because of Russians' allergy to holding savings instruments denominated in roubles), and using the massive increase in tax revenues to pay back some of the debt to the Russian central bank that the government incurred during the period of growing insolvency before and immediately after the 1998 crisis.[27] This was the direction in which the government seemed to be leaning in July to August 2000.

What no one was examining was the impact of rouble appreciation not on exports but on imports. If the rouble gets sufficiently strong for imports to start displacing domestic products, the revival of Russian industry will be endangered. In reply to a newspaper correspondent the chairman of the Russian central bank, Victor Geraschenko, said that the rouble could appreciate to 20 to the dollar without hurting exports.[28] This did not answer the crucial question: what rate of exchange would start hurting domestic industry once more? The rouble remained severely undervalued only in relation to its value in July 1998, just before the crisis. But that rate had been artificial – a product of the Yeltsin regime's desperate effort to stabilise prices by cutting back the growth of money supply. This had resulted in a real appreciation of 50 per cent over the value in 1995.[29] In April 2000 the real value of the rouble was 52 per cent of its July 1998 level, but 92 per cent of its 1995 level.[30] Since then it has risen further at almost 2 per cent per month. If 1995 is used as a benchmark, the rouble will soon become overvalued once again. A further appreciation will therefore almost certainly lead to a rise in imports and a slowdown of industrial growth.

What is more, it will affect not just consumer goods but the revival of the capital goods industries too. Today an estimated 60 per cent of the capital stock inherited from the Soviet Union is worn out. New investment has been running at barely half of the replacement level. A huge market is thus developing for capital goods. The future of the Soviet economy will in all probability depend upon whether this demand is met by indigenous industry or by imports. In the first case, the demand for domestically manufactured capital goods will rise, and the manufacturers will have the incentive to go abroad and shop for new technology. In the second, Russia's once vibrant capital goods industries will continue their slide towards death, and become rusting relics of a bygone age. A strong rouble will encourage the latter development.

Surprisingly, no one is suggesting, at least in print, that the scope for remonetising the economy and thus increasing demand without causing inflation is not exhausted and therefore that the government should use its windfall tax revenues to pay off the remaining wage arrears and raise salaries and pensions above the subsistence level. Instead the public utterances of government officials reflect a near-unanimous belief that the Russian economy cannot 'absorb' any more purchasing power and so the surplus revenues should be used to pay off the government's domestic debt to the Russian central bank or the foreign debt inherited from the Soviet era.

But this belief is almost certainly too pessimistic. Between the end of December 1999 and the end of June 2000, while the money supply grew by 26 per cent the consumer price index rose by only 9.6 per cent, a sure sign that most of the increase in the former was still being absorbed by the remonetisation of the economy.[31] The need to improve living standards remains urgent. Real wages are still 18 per cent below the level of 1998, and a 30 per cent real cut in health and education expenditures after the crisis has not been made up.[32]

There is still far too much surplus capacity in most consumer goods industries, whose output is still not much more than half of what it was before 1992. Thus, in all likelihood, increasing government expenditure to fuel consumption by the Russian poor would lead to faster growth. It would also not generate any additional inflationary pressure because increased domestic consumption would also push up imports. This would lower the trade surplus and consequently the inflow of dollars that is pushing up the exchange value of the rouble. Russia is therefore in that singularly fortunate situation where a slight alteration of policies away from the liberal paradigm could give it continued industrial recovery, GDP growth and an improved standard of living, with a stable real exchange rate, and only moderate inflation. It remains to be seen whether it will be able to break the grip of economic liberalism on Russian policy sufficiently to take this path.

REBUILDING THE RUSSIAN STATE

In October 1998, when Yevgeny Primakov put Russia back on the long road to recovery, it was not only the economy but the state itself that was on the verge of disintegration. This was a direct consequence of the power structure that Boris Yeltsin had built to stabilise his regime during the political and economic turmoil after the collapse of the Soviet Union. This power structure was quintessentially feudal. Yeltsin delegated more and more political power to the governors of Russia's 89 regions on the one hand and, on the other, economic power to the oligarchs, a new class of robber-baron capitalists spawned by the economic reforms and the privatisation of state-owned industry. The system was based upon individual agreements that Yeltsin made with members of each group, and it worked in Yeltsin's time because they were respected.[33]

The system had come into being during the run-up to the 1996 presidential election when a highly unpopular Yeltsin seemed on the verge of being ousted by the Communists, who had won a resounding victory in the December 1995 elections to the Duma, Russia's parliament. And it worked. The combined support of powerful regional governors and the oligarchs, who among other things owned just about the entire privately owned media groups in the country, ensured that Yeltsin took a small lead over his communist rival Gennady Zyuganov in the first round of voting. A short-lived alliance with the third runner, former general Alexander Lebed, ensured his victory in the second round.

Both the regional leaders and the oligarchs reaped a handsome reward. The former got *carte blanche* to run their regions as they wished; the latter were able to buy up controlling blocks of shares in multi-billion dollar Russian state-owned giants, such as Norilsky Nikel, for a few million dollars borrowed from their own banks. Thus former car salesmen and failed stage directors became industrial tycoons overnight.

The sole aim of this power structure was its own self-perpetuation. The governors did as they wanted in their regions. This included passing laws and even promulgating constitutions that went against federal law and the Russian constitution. By early 2000 the Russian ministry of justice estimated that between 25 and 35 per cent of all laws in force in the regions either violated the constitution or were not in consonance with federal laws. In all, 4,000 laws were found to be in this category while another 4,000 remained to be investigated. In an interview to the

Financial Times, Yegeny Yasin, a former economics minister, described the power of the governors as follows: 'Every governor and every leader of a Republic is a small oligarch. There is no difference between a Boris Berezhovsky [the Kremlin power broker] and a Yury Luzhkov [the mayor of Moscow]. They both use administrative resources to control federal property and seize control of financial flows.'[34]

What Yeltsin's system could not deliver was coordinated decision making for the entire country. By the same token the parasitic economic power structure he helped to create with the oligarchs could not deliver either economic development or equity. While a class of 'new Russians' grew rich the majority of the people, including the entire intelligentsia, the bureaucracy, the working class and the soldiers sank into poverty.

When the economic crash occurred on 17 August 1998, the greatly enfeebled and now bankrupt federal government began to lose control of the country. Every region tried to take as much 'sovereignty' as it could. They began to restrict exports of foodstuffs, impose export duties, and levy customs duties on imports. With each new development the anxiety of the Russian people deepened. The invasion of neighbouring Daghestan by a radical Islamist faction, following a power struggle in Chechnya, became the catalyst for the expression of Russian fears about disintegration. When he decided to crush the Chechnyan insurrection Putin gained instant popularity. Opinion polls in Russia showed that 60 per cent of the people approved of the bombing of Grozny and other insurgent strongholds.

The presidential election of May 2000 crystallised the Russian revolt against Yeltsin's system. In the words of Marina Shahina, a political analyst, Russians saw that

all the deified institutions of a free society – the Press, private business, federalism ... have been distorted and are a far cry from the high standards of democracy. The Press is often immoral and serves the political interests of private persons. Russian business evades taxes ... is immoral, thievish and selfish. Federalism means the denial of rights to the citizens and omnipotence of regional 'sovereigns'. Human rights has turned into the right of terrorists to take hostages, kill and rob people and attack neighbouring republics.[35]

And according to a poll conducted by the All-Russian Public Opinion Centre in July, 60 to 70 per cent of Russians believed that the oligarchs had committed 'quite' to 'very considerable' violations of the law, and 75 per cent wanted criminal proceedings to be brought against them.[36]

This was the 'silent majority' that Yeltsin and his 'family' had ignored during his second term in office. Putin's promise to 'restore the dictatorship of Law' was music to their ears. As a result Putin won in the first round itself with more than 52 per cent of the vote.

Putin lost no time in turning his promises into policies. He first turned his attention to restoring Moscow's power over the regions. In May 2000 he introduced three bills in the Duma that would in his terms restore the 'power vertical' (that is, the writ of federal law over the individual members of society), and abolish intermediate tiers of 'sovereignty'. The first grouped the 89 regions into seven 'federal districts' and created seven plenipotentiary representatives (referred to as federal plenipotentiaries) to oversee the functioning of the regions in each district. While the main purpose of these plenipotentiaries is to oversee the functioning of the regional governments to ensure that they do not pass laws or take action that violates federal law and the constitution, they have also been given executive power to oversee the working of federal institutions in each district. Thus the regional branches of the Russian central bank, the Tax Inspectorate and the Federal Security Service (the former KGB) have been brought under the federal plenipotentiaries. This will reduce the influence of the governors upon them. Lastly the plenipotentiaries are also being given the task of overseeing the use of central grants to the regional governments.

The second bill lowered the regions' share of state revenues. One of the main weaknesses of the Yeltsin constitution had been that while the regions had the right to spend money the task of raising revenues fell mainly upon the federal government. Putin could not tackle this asymmetry while he was struggling to reform the tax code and to put the institutions in place that would enforce it. But his bill was intended to reduce marginally the share of the regions in the total state revenue and bring the disbursement of a larger portion of it under the direct control of the federal plenipotentiaries. The change has provoked an outcry from the governors of the regions, who complain that it will reduce their share of total revenues from 48 per cent to 30 per cent. The federal government has refuted this charge however, by pointing out that once federal project-specific allocations are taken into account, the share of the regions falls only to 43.6 per cent.

The third bill stripped the governors of their membership of the Federation Council, the upper house of the Russian parliament, and required them to observe the constitution in spirit as well as letter by sending two representatives to the Council, one of whom must be an elected member of the regional assembly. Most governors have resented this bill even more than the other two not only because it threatens to reduce their capacity to veto federal legislation in the Upper House, but also because it will lower their position in relation to the federal plenipotentiaries.

Despite their opposition, Putin was able between May and July to get all the three bills passed by both houses of parliament. The governors were reluctant to oppose him because 30 of them were coming up for re-election that year and, with his popularity rating at an astounding 73 per cent (until mid-August) none felt that they could afford to alienate him.

Putin then turned his attention to the oligarchs. Over the months of June and July these began to be hauled in on charges of having evaded taxes and committing other breaches of the law. The Russian law enforcement agencies relished their task. Gusinsky's arrest and imprisonment was therefore the most visible tip of a much larger iceberg. Eventually in July the oligarchs asked for a meeting with Putin. At the meeting, which took place on 28 July, Putin made it clear that he had no intention of expropriating them but that they had to choose between being businessmen and becoming politicians. As businessmen they could not remain above the law as they had been to all intents and purposes in Yeltsin's days. The meeting ended with a promise by the oligarchs to stay clear of politics while Putin promised to ensure that the law enforcement agencies were more considerate in their dealings with them. Despite this Gusinsky left the country and in mid-August was living in Spain.

Putin's intentions are sound but such sweeping changes of policy often have unexpected results. In Russia, his steps to clip the wings of the regional governors and presidents of autonomous republics could very easily take the country back to the inefficient bureaucratic state that Russia was in Soviet days. Over-centralisation is likely to be accentuated by two other factors. The seven federal districts coincide with the existing military districts of the country. Thus the administration that will develop in them will also work closely with and have the support of Russia's military. Secondly, in Moscow real power is vested not in the cabinet but in the Council for State Security whose members include not only the heads of the armed forces and the intelligence service but also the seven plenipotentiaries. The simultaneous removal of the governors from the Federal Council and elevation of the federal plenipotentiaries to the highest and most secret level of decision making, when the former are elected representatives of the people while the latter are bureaucrats, will create a tension in the administration and the regions that could have unpredictable consequences in the 23 ethnic regions and autonomous republics of the country.

Part II
CHINA

7

How Fast is China Growing?

China's economic performance after 1978 has been described only in superlatives like 'outstanding', 'miraculous' and 'record'. According to statistics compiled by the China Statistical Bureau, and published without caveats by the World Bank, the average growth rate was a staggering 9.4 per cent between 1978 and 1995.[1] Since the population had grown at 1.4 per cent per annum, per capita income grew during this period at 8.0 per cent per annum. Between 1978 and 1991, the growth rate was an impressive 9.0 per cent.[2] Then it really took off and reached 14.2 per cent in 1992, 13.5 per cent in 1993, 12.6 per cent in 1994 and 10.5 per cent in 1995.

Until the early 1990s these estimates were accepted more or less uncritically. But the further acceleration of an already phenomenally high growth rate in the 1990s began to raise doubts about the accuracy of the official estimates. In a recent report on China, *China 2020*, the World Bank conceded that 'Measuring China's growth rate is tricky.' The problem, it went on to say, was 'official consumption and investment deflators used to convert nominal into real GDP have increased much more slowly than alternative measures, such as the consumer index or the price index for capital goods'.[3] Using 'reasonable' alternate measures of price increases – the consumer price index for consumption, and the price index for building materials for investment – the Bank estimated that the average per capita growth between 1978 and 1995 was 6.8 per cent.

There are other estimates, notably one by Summers and Heston using purchasing power parity GDP estimates, that are a good deal lower. Their estimate was obtained, however, by 'arbitrarily' reducing the growth of consumption by 30 per cent and of investment by 40 per cent.[4] Angus Maddison, one the most respected of growth statisticians, accepts the Summers and Heston figure for the period after 1978,[5] but the Bank rejects both and leaves it to the reader to choose between its alternative growth rates of 8 and 6.8 per cent per capita. Either, it points out, makes China the fastest growing economy the world has ever known.[6]

The World Bank's alternative estimate is only better than the official estimate if the price indices for consumer goods and building materials are reliable. Following a spate of articles by scholars questioning their

Table 7.1
Unexplained share of growth (%)

Country/Period	Constant returns	Increasing returns
China 1978–95	44	30
Japan 1963–90	30	9
South Korea 1960–93	21	–2

Source: World Bank staff estimates, in *China 2020*, annex 1, p. 107.

reliability, the World Bank recognised that there was a problem with China's statistics: after allowing for the increase in product that arose from an increase in the inputs of labour and capital, assuming constant rates of return to all factors of production, a large portion of the growth of GDP remained unexplained. This is not peculiar to China. Some residual is to be found in all countries, and is usually ascribed to 'technology' or technology-cum-management. This residue is usually much larger in fast growing developing countries than in mature industrialised ones. But as Table 7.1 shows, it is far, far larger in China than in even the fastest growing countries of South East Asia.

The table shows that while 21 per cent of Korea's and 30 per cent of Japan's growth could not be explained by the addition of labour and capital, in the case of China it was as high as 44 per cent. Even the assumption that China enjoyed the same increasing returns to scale as the fastest growing countries of Southeast Asia, fails to explain almost one-third of China's growth rate (i.e. 2.8 per cent per annum).

The World Bank has therefore suggested another explanation for the extra growth. This is the structural transformation of the country. Every shift of labour from a sector where its productivity is low to one in which it is higher, adds to output and therefore to the GDP growth rate, without any change in the total amount of labour being used. In principle the same is also true of capital. The World Bank's calculations show that the reallocation of labour from the state sector of industry to the non-state sector has added 0.5 per cent to the annual growth rate between 1985 and 1994, while the reallocation of labour from agriculture to industry has added 1 per cent. Thus if one assumes that these trends also held true for 1978–84 and for 1995, then fully 1.5 per cent of the 2.8 per cent of residual growth is explained in this way.

Table 7.2
Components of China's growth*

TFP** at constant returns	5.1
Plus increasing returns	1.5
Plus factor reallocation	1.5
Plus inflation	1.2
Unaccounted	0.1
Official GDP growth	9.4

* All figures are percentages   ** Total factor productivity

Allowing 1.2 per cent for the understatement of inflation, this leaves only 0.1 per cent of China's 9.4 per cent official growth rate unexplained.

There are, however, two weaknesses in the factor reallocation theory. The first is that its impact is suspiciously large. By the Bank's own calculations, factor reallocation contributed only 0.26 per cent to Japan's and 0.34 per cent to South Korea's growth rate between 1960 and 1993, and nothing to that of the US during the period 1950–92. While the US may be dismissed as a mature economy, how could factor reallocation have contributed almost *five times* as much to China's growth as to South Korea's? South Korea, after all, went through exactly the same structural transformation as China and actually grew at 6.9 per cent per capita, which was 0.1 per cent faster than the World Bank's revised estimate for China.

The second problem is that of distinguishing the effect of factor reallocation from that of changes in technology and management. To find a quotient for the increasing returns to scale caused by changes in technology and management practices, the authors of *China 2020* used a 1995 study by Kim Jong-il and Laurence Lau which showed that, in a sample of other Asian countries, a 1 per cent increase in all factors of production led to a 1.3 per cent increase in output.[7] But Kim and Lau had related the *total* increase in output to the increase in labour and capital. The 'factor reallocation effect' was therefore part of the quotient of 1.3. In adding a separate factor reallocation effect to the 30 per cent increasing return to scale, they were guilty of double counting. If one therefore excludes the 'factor reallocation' effect China's growth rate (of total GDP) amounts to 6.6 per cent.

CALCULATING GROWTH VIA ENERGY CONSUMPTION

There is another way of calculating the rate of growth of GDP; a way that is both reliable and free from the element of arbitrariness found in Summers and Heston's assumptions. This is to see it as the sum of the rate of growth of energy consumption and the increase (or decrease) in energy efficiency. In the case of China this method immediately reveals a major anomaly. During the period 1978–95, China's energy consumption grew by only 4.8 per cent per annum.[8] Thus even if we take the World Bank's lower estimate of growth of 8.2 per cent, China achieved one of the highest growth rates in the world with one of the lowest rates of growth of energy consumption. Between 1997 and 2000 the anomaly has become a great deal more marked. During this period GDP, according to official statistics, grew by 24.7 per cent. But energy consumption actually fell by 12.8 per cent. As Thomas Rawski of the University of Pittsburgh points out the two figures are almost impossible to reconcile.[9]

This disparity raises two questions: first, when the growth of energy consumption has consistently outstripped the growth of GNP in other developing countries, why is China an exception? Second, while GNP growth may in exceptional circumstances outstrip energy consumption for a few years, is it possible for it to do so continuously for 20 years?

The answer to the first question is that the very special circumstances in which China began it reforms did make it possible for economic growth to take place with a less than proportionate increase in the use of energy, and yield a sustained improvement in energy efficiency. The answer to the second is that the actual magnitude of the annual increase in energy efficiency that China claims is simply not credible. Thus either the growth of energy consumption is grossly underestimated, or the growth of GDP in constant prices is grossly overestimated. For reasons given below, the former is far more likely than the latter.

The China Statistical Bureau compiles data for energy production and consumption (including exports and imports) and for the energy used per billion yuan of GDP. During the pre-reform period the relationship between the growth of GDP and of energy consumption reflected all the built-in inefficiencies one has come to expect of a non-market, and therefore non-competitive, economy in which input prices are fixed arbitrarily by government and heavily underpriced. Thus between 1965 and 1978 it took a 1.5 per cent increase in energy consumption to yield a 1 per cent growth of output.[10] When economic reforms came, first in agriculture and then in industry and the service sectors, it was expected that the energy intensity of growth would fall. But the reforms transformed this relationship to an extent that scarcely seems credible. According to the *China Statistical Yearbook 1996*, and its two predecessors, the energy consumed per billion yuan of GDP at 1990 prices fell from 1 million tonnes of coal equivalent (mtce) in 1978 to 0.4 million tonnes in 1995.[11] The drop in average energy consumption is staggering enough. But that in marginal consumption defies belief. In 1990 prices China's GDP grew from Y680.9 billion (yuan) in 1978 to Y2,582.8 billion in 1993. During this period energy consumption grew from 571 mtce to 1,074 mtce.[12] Thus it took only 0.26 mtce to produce an additional billion yuan of GDP. The almost instantaneous drop from 1.5 mtce to 0.26 mtce in marginal energy consumption per unit of additional GDP is simply not credible.

Some idea of the extent to which the improvement has been overestimated can be had from projections of the energy needed to sustain various rates and types of growth from 1980 to 2000 made by a World Bank study team in 1984–85.[13] The study team made projections of what China's energy consumption would be in 2000 at various rates of growth based on three scenarios about the future change in the structure of the economy (measured by the share of output originating in agriculture, industry and the services), the capital intensity in each sector (dubbed Quadruple, Balanced and Moderate estimates) and three assumptions regarding the improvement in energy efficiency per unit of output in each sector (dubbed High, Base and Low). It thus offered nine different projections of energy consumption in 2000, associated with two rates of growth of per capita GDP.[14]

The Bank estimated that, if China were able to change the structure of growth so that by 2000 the share of the service sector went up while that of industry plus agriculture came down (the Balanced scenario) and attain a 6.6 per cent GDP growth rate, then, using the base rate of improvement in energy consumption of 2.1 per cent per annum, China would have to increase its energy consumption from 605 mtce in 1980 to 1,420 mtce in 2000. In 1995, China's actual energy consumption reached 1,290 mtce. If the rate of growth attained from 1990 to 1995 was maintained until 2000 this was likely to go up further to around 1,680 mtce; i.e.,18 per cent more than the projections made by the study team. This could mean either that China's growth rate had exceeded 6.6 per cent (by about 0.8 per cent) or that the share of the service sector had not risen as the 'Balanced' scenario had assumed.

A closer study shows that while the share of the service sector did go up from 25.8 per cent in 1980 to 28.3 per cent in 1995,[15] the study's more important assumption, that the share of industry plus infrastructure in the GDP should rise only marginally from 48 per cent in 1980 to 50 per cent in 2000, was not met. On the contrary, the share of industry and mining alone has risen from 40.5 per cent in 1980 to 54.4 per cent in 1995, an increase of almost 14 per cent.[16] This is almost twice the 8 per cent increase that the Bank had forecast for its 'worst case' Quadruple scenario.

One can therefore get a somewhat more accurate estimate of GDP growth by turning to the World Bank's Quadruple scenario, which has been framed for an increase in the share of industry and infrastructure from 48 per cent in 1980 to 58 per cent in 2000 and by taking its lower estimate of the rate of improvement of energy consumption of 1 per cent per unit of GDP. According to that projection, to achieve a 6.6 per cent rate of growth of total GDP China's energy consumption would have to rise to 1,765 mtce in 2000. This is 85 mtce (or 4.8 per cent) more than the projection of China's energy consumption in 2000 given above. That would imply that the actual growth rate is about 0.2 per cent below 6.6 per cent – 6.4 per cent. The per capita income has therefore most probably grown at around 5.0 per cent per annum. Perhaps not coincidentally this is very close to the growth rate that the World Bank estimates in *China 2020* after deducting the effect of insufficient accounting for inflation and the so-called factor reallocation effect.

WHY IS GROWTH OVERESTIMATED?

There are at least three reasons why China's GDP growth rate is being overestimated. The economic reason is the weakness of China's statistics.[17] These weaknesses are: that estimates of agricultural output given by the ministry of agriculture tend to be on the high side; that the estimates of the real growth of output of the township and village enterprises (TVEs) and of the rapidly growing service sector are at least partly in current prices and therefore inflated; and that the price indices used to deflate current into constant price estimates 'have some problems'. Prof. Dong Fureng thus confirmed the validity of Summers and Heston's decision to reduce the growth rates of the industrial and service sectors, although not the magnitude of the correction.[18]

The bureaucratic reason for overestimation is that data on performance are collected by the same agencies as are entrusted with the attainment of output and other targets. This leads to a systematic overestimation of achievements and underestimation of failures. This had reached epidemic proportions during the Great Leap Forward, and later during the Cultural Revolution, but it has never completely disappeared despite strenuous government efforts to weed it out.

Almost six years after the above interview with professor Dong Fureng, Xiao Zhuoji, another professor at Beijing University, also bemoaned China's misleading statistics. 'When drafting economic growth Plans', he told *China Daily* in an interview, 'local governments should take actual conditions into account, rather than vying to present statistical bubbles likely to burst under closer examination'. Xiao Zhuoji attributed the inflation of Chinese figures not so much to difficulties in collection and deflation, as to the desire of 'some local governments' to report 'artificially high' economic growth rates in order to 'show off or at least save face'. He also ascribed some of the inaccuracies to the haste with which the data were collected and presented. (China, for instance has quick estimates of GDP growth within the days of the end of the calendar year, and these are seldom if ever revised.)[19]

This charge is made frequently by others in China. *Liaowang Weekly* (no. 18), reprinted in *Wenzhai Zhoubao* (Chengdu) carried the following article on 20 April 1998:

'The village deceives the township, the township deceives the county – in deception upon deception as a report moves up the hierarchy' and 'Officials create statistics and statistics create careers for officials'. These sayings have become very popular among the people during the past few years to describe the bad working style in which some local governments and cadres in some departments falsify statistics.

During the latter half of 1997, the State Statistical Bureau, the Department of Supervision, and the State Council Rule of Law Bureau carried out a large nation-wide survey to check the compliance of statistics with the applicable rules and regulations. The survey discovered 60,000 instances of illegal actions in producing statistics. False reports, exaggerated reports, falsified reports, and illegal alteration of statistical data comprised 56.7 per cent of the total. Refusing to report statistics, consistently delayed statistical data comprised 18.4 per cent. Interfering with legal statistical data collection and other illegal actions accounted for 24.9 per cent of the total. These activities are not among the most serious offenses, so they are called 'illegal actions related to statistical work'. In addition to these less serious offenses, another 15,000 serious violations of laws related to statistical work were also discovered.

THE MYSTIQUE OF GROWTH

The third reason why the growth rate is being overestimated is political. During the Cultural Revolution, Mao Zedong turned the masses against the Communist Party, and destroyed the party. When Deng Xiaoping took over as leader of China in 1978, he rehabilitated the party cadres, but his programme of economic reform demoralised the party by disavowing the ideology of communism. When 'to get rich is glorious' replaced 'serve the people' as the national watchword, any remaining illusion the party cadres cherished, that they were helping to create a new society, was shattered. Deng's belief that 'practice was the sole criterion of truth' completed the demolition of the communist ideology. But economic liberalisation brought a new set of issues to the fore. Within the leadership it touched off a conflict between the old conservatives and the reformers. This conflict resulted in a seesaw between reform and reaction, in three clearly identifiable phases, the last of them ending with the student demonstrations in Tiananmen Square. Not surprisingly, the split tended to run along the lines of age, with the bulk of the veteran leaders opposed to the new ways. Only the towering pre-eminence of Deng Xiaoping made it possible to paper over the rifts and keep the country on a course of piecemeal reform.

The period from 1985 to 1989 saw an increase in prices and a precipitous fall in real incomes for the bulk of society, such as China had not known since the Second World War. But not everyone suffered. Inflation and the multiplying opportunities to make money suddenly created income differentials in an egalitarian society, and the sheer pace of China's growth after 1985 made these widen rapidly. A new schism between the rich and the poor therefore appeared, which coincided to a disturbing extent with the schism between the honest and the dishonest. The advent of capitalism therefore brought with it envy, and anxiety. And none were as seriously affected as the young, who previously used to be assigned their jobs, and now faced an increasingly uncertain future. Large numbers therefore reacted in the only way possible – by trying to gain a greater measure of control over their lives. This was the origin of the movement for democracy.[20]

China's leaders had no answer to these problems. Throughout the 1980s, as prices rose and a new moneyed elite began to emerge, the veterans of the party felt more and more threatened. Inflation reduced their real incomes, making it more and more difficult to make ends meet, even as the rise of a new economic class of relatively well-to-do farmers and small traders and independent entrepreneurs in towns began to erode their influence in society. Not surprisingly, as inflation sharpened in the second half of the 1980s the middle ground between the reformers and the conservatives began to disappear and Deng's task of keeping China on a middle path became more and more difficult. In the end it was the threat posed to the Communist Party's monopoly of power that tilted the scales drastically against any political liberalisation. Not only could the party leaders not countenance such a drastic change, but even less could they live with the loss of control over China's evolution that it implied. Their conviction that China needed strong political control exerted from the Centre was founded not only on communist ideology and a reluctance to part with power, but two millennia of warlordism, and internecine warfare. The result was the brutal suppression of the Tiananmen demonstrations in June 1989.

The aftermath saw the largest conservative backlash China had witnessed since the beginning of reforms. Since Deng was closely associated with the reforms that were held responsible for endangering the Chinese state and the Communist Party, this backlash posed the biggest threat to him in all the years that he held power. He rode it by urging, tirelessly, that ideological battles be downplayed as they only further debilitated the party and country, and by allowing a distinction to be drawn between 'economic development' and 'bourgeois liberalisation'. This distinction had been made earlier to cope with conservative criticisms of the reform process. Deng put it to good use. On 9 June, addressing the leaders of the martial law troops, he declared that the line of 'one Centre, two basic points' which had been adopted by the Thirteenth Party Congress in 1987 had to be pursued even more vigorously. The 'Centre' was economic development, the 'basic points' were, first, economic reform and opening up to the outside world and, second, opposition to bourgeois liberalisation.[21] Deng also distanced himself from the fray by plucking Jiang Zemin out of the secretaryship of the Chinese Communist Party in Shanghai and making him general secretary of the party in Beijing. It was left to Jiang to draw the distinction between reform and bourgeois liberalisation.

After a torrid two years during which he had to give ground repeatedly, several factors helped him to restore his primacy and get reforms moving ahead once more. The collapse of communist regimes in Eastern Europe, beginning with East Germany and Romania in 1989, and the rapid weakening of the Soviet Union the following year, all palpably brought about by their economic failure, did not fail to reinforce the case for 'one Centre, two basic points'. However, what completed the rout of the conservatives was the eagerness with which provincial authorities in the dynamic coastal provinces seized on Deng's ideas, to raise their own banners of revolt against Beijing. Deng provided them with this opportunity in 1991, perhaps inadvertently, by writing a series of articles in the main Shanghai daily *Jiefang Ribao* (he had retired to Shanghai in late 1990 in frustration at his inability to stem the conservative backlash). In these he debunked the special ideological position of the planned economy, asserted that the market mechanism and state planning were not 'capitalist' and 'socialist' respectively, but only instruments (methods), and that their merits had to be judged by the results they gave. The touchstone was economic growth. The leaders of Guangdong, Tianjin, Hebei and elsewhere, who were chafing at the brakes that the resurgence of conservatism, with its reinforcement of planning and price and distribution controls was putting on their continued rapid growth, took up Deng's criterion. This internal support proved crucial, and helps to explain why Deng launched his drive to make economic growth the centrepiece of policy with a tour of the southern provinces in 1992.

However, the motives of the provinces in supporting reform had little to do with ideological battles and were entirely pragmatic. This, combined with Deng's own readiness to distance himself from bourgeois liberalisation, ensured that economic freedom had no sustaining ideology, and had to justify itself solely by its success. Deng himself enshrined this in his call to create a 'socialist market economic system' which was endorsed by the Fourteenth Party Congress in October 1992. Thereafter, simply to minimise internal divisions, and to keep the restive younger generation reasonably happy, China simply had to succeed, and succeed spectacularly. Growth itself became the new ideology. It would have been surprising if its computation had not become at least somewhat politicised.

DID THE GROWTH RATE SPURT IN THE 1990s?

While China's overall growth rate has been impressive there are a number of indications that it has been slowing down in the 1990s; that the slowdown may have started as far back as 1992 or 1993; and that the 14.2, 13.5 and 12.6 per cent growth rates of 1993, 1994 and 1995 reflect China's inability and perhaps unwillingness to sift out the effect of the very high inflation rates of those years from its calculations of the GDP. This was a full seven years before Premier Zhu Rongji admitted to the Tenth Peoples' Congress that the country faced a grim situation, at home and abroad.[22] This suspicion is reinforced when one examines the actual growth of various sectors of the economy after 1990. Table 7.3

Table 7.3
China's GDP at factor cost by sector of origin in constant 1990 prices

Sector	Weight	1990 (billion yuan)	1995 (billion yuan)	Growth rate (%)
Agriculture	29	501.7	615.0	4.1
Industry	45	771.7	1725.7	15.7
state	24	421.3	586.0	6.6
non-state	21	350.4	1139.7	26.8
Services	26	581.4	925.8	9.6

Source: World Bank, *China 2020*, tables 2 and 26 (from *China Statistical Yearbook 1996*).

gives the output of various sectors of the economy in 1990 prices.

Between 1990 and 1995, the average growth of output of the energy, steel, cement, timber and fertiliser industries, the main areas in which the big state-owned enterprises (SOEs) are concentrated[23] was far from impressive. It was approximately 3 per cent per annum for coal, gas and oil; 10 per cent for electricity (8.7 per cent for hydroelectricity); and about 8 per cent for the main intermediate goods, steel, cement, timber and fertilisers.[24] Light industry, which accounts for at most 30 per cent of the state sector's industrial output, almost certainly fared worse. Its main component, the state-owned textiles factories, consisting of 4,031 firms that employ 4 million workers, has been making mounting losses since 1993. In 1997, 40 per cent of the mills were on the brink of collapse. This could hardly have happened if the output of the sector had been showing a high rate of growth.[25] Overall, therefore, the state sector's industrial output grew by approximately 6.6 per cent per annum during this period. By the official statistics, agriculture grew at 4.1 per cent per annum. Thus non-state industry and the service sectors had to grow at 26.8 and 9.4 per cent for China to attain an overall growth rate of 12 per cent per annum.

This is where one encounters a serious anomaly. By official statistics in the non-state sector, the output of the urban and rural collectives grew by 18 per cent per annum.[26] But employment growth in the collectives plummeted from 17 million in 1993 to a mere 1.4 million in 1994 and 1995.[27] Employment in the urban collectives actually declined by 4.8

million, from 35.6 million to 31.8 million, between 1991 and 1995. It is difficult therefore to believe that such a sharp slowdown in growth of employment was not accompanied by a substantial slowdown in the growth of output.[28] Overall, urban employment of all kinds, collective, individual and joint venture, grew by 18 million during these five years (i.e. at 6.8 per cent per annum). Figures for the rural collectives are not easily obtained but the growth rate is unlikely to have been much higher. One is thus invited to believe that at most a 7 per cent growth of employment in the non-state sector yielded a 26.8 per cent rate of growth of output. That too stretches credibility very thin.

DECLINING GROWTH OF ENERGY CONSUMPTION

In the period 1992–95 the mismatch between energy consumption and growth becomes even greater than in the 1980s. Whereas from 1982 to 1988 a 6.9 per cent rate of growth of energy consumption yielded an 11.7 per cent rate of growth, between 1990 and 1995 by the official figures a 5.5 per cent rate of growth of energy consumption yielded a 12.5 per cent annual growth of GDP. If the high growth of energy efficiency in the 1980s was hard to believe, the jump in energy efficiency in the 1990s, from 4.8 to 7 per cent per annum, is even more incredible.[29]

THE SOFT LANDING THAT NEVER WAS

The above interpretation of the available data helps to clear up one of the greater mysteries of China's recent economic performance. When the only way in which the Peoples' Bank of China was able to bring the inflation of 1988–89 under control was by cutting off the expansion of credit, and permitting economic growth to fall close to zero, how has it been able to impose ceilings on credit again, and bring inflation down from 24.1 per cent in 1994 (urban consumer prices) to 8.3 per cent in 1996, and still keep the growth rate up at 9.8 per cent in 1996? The claim has surprised not only some foreign economists, but Chinese economists also. Thus on 14 November 1996, shortly after Dai Xianglong, the head of the People's Bank of China, had announced the 'soft landing', a Shanghai economist told the *New York Times* that the latest growth and inflation figures 'don't seem to fit'.[30]

The solution to the mystery is that there was no soft landing because the spurt in growth was a statistical myth: China's growth·rate had in all probability already responded to the curbs imposed on credit after July 1993 by the central bank. That is also the most likely explanation for the sharp drop in employment growth in the collectives and the absolute decline in the number of persons employed by the urban collectives. Even in a market economy when credit growth is reined in, for instance by raising the rate of interest, the least economically creditworthy enterprises suffer disproportionately while the stronger ones get away with only marginal reductions. In China, where the laws of the market do not apply to loans to the SOEs, the denial of credit to the collectives must have been far sharper because the SOEs simply had to be financed first.[31] What is more, between 1992 and 1996, the proportion of SOEs showing operating losses rose dramatically from 26 to 50 per cent.[32] As a result, keeping them afloat pre-empted more and more of the available credit. Since the growth of bank credit was also being cut back, the credit available to the collectives was squeezed from two directions at the same time.

8
From Plan to Market

The estimates of China's growth given in the previous chapter are not intended to denigrate its achievements. A growth rate of 6.4 to 6.6 per cent, sustained for 20 years, may look disappointing to those who have grown used to hyperbolic praise of China's 'double-digit growth'. But to anyone else it is sensational. China achieved such sustained, long term growth by introducing competition into an economy where it was virtually absent, incrementally, and pragmatically.[1] China introduced them sector by sector, and changed one policy parameter at a time in each sector. Beijing further hedged its bets by allowing some of the advanced provinces to experiment with new ideas and systems first. If these were successful other provinces copied them, and Beijing eventually endorsed them on a national level.

Partly by chance, therefore, and partly by design, and in glaring contrast to Russia, China kept the centrally planned system intact, and created an outward looking market-guided economic system beside it virtually from scratch. That system has gone through the stages of evolution of a market economy in a remarkably short time. Through the various cycles of reform and reaction the market economy has expanded steadily and the planned economy has shrunk. In the 1980s, and again after a brief pause in the 1990s, the goal of the central leaders was to merge the centrally planned system with the free market system in such a way that China would manage to retain many of the beneficial features of socialism while ensuring that production, distribution, pricing and investment decisions were guided more and more by signals from the market. This was the endeavour to which Deng Xiaoping gave a formal shape when he unveiled the goal of creating a 'socialist market economic system', in 1992.

BUILDING THE MARKET SYSTEM

No master planner could have constructed a blueprint for the kind of reform described above. China's strategy emerged out of the policy makers' attempts to grapple with its mounting domestic problems. The most important one, by far, was unemployment. In contrast to India, whose planners and policy makers have tended to turn a blind eye to the problem of unemployment, in China, where the state took upon itself the responsibility for finding everyone a job, Beijing did not have this option and had to face the problem squarely. As in India, agriculture was saddled with huge underemployment.[2] But underemployment had become a normal feature of industry also. State workers were assigned to enterprises, and there were far too many of them. Their productivity was therefore so low that the World Bank estimated it to be half that of industrial workers in India in the early 1980s.[3]

In the communes and the industrial enterprises, a quiet desperation had begun to seize the workers and directors. Not only were there too many workers, but their children were coming on to the job market, and had also to be provided with work. The only way out was to *grow*. But both in agriculture and in industry, the closed, centrally planned system seemed to have reached its natural limit. Chinese agriculture was in particularly bad shape. Only 23 per cent of China's 9.6 million sq. km is arable, against 79 per cent of India's 3.7 million sq. km. Thus the land available per person in China is only about three-fifths of the arable land per person in India. Unlike India, yields per hectare were already very high in China. Total grain output therefore stagnated during the 1970s and a number of droughts and floods, which strained the country's exceedingly weak distribution system, made matters worse. China became a regular importer of foodgrains.

THE REFORM OF AGRICULTURE

Reform therefore came to agriculture first. The only way out was either to create work opportunities outside agriculture, or to improve the productivity of agriculture itself. The Chinese did both. The reforms began in 1978. Some industrial activity had been allowed earlier in the communes, by 'production brigades'. In that year the communes were formally given permission to set up small industrial ventures to absorb labour, and prices were increased sharply for grains and other produce, while being reduced simultaneously for key inputs such as fertilisers. The sharp shift of terms of trade back in favour of agriculture and against the cosseted industrial sector, gave the communes their first jump in savings. This was invested rapidly in village enterprises and became the nucleus of the rural collectives sector of industry – the township and village enterprises (TVEs).

In 1983 the government took the second crucial step in reforming agriculture: it introduced the contract leasing system by which peasants tilled a piece of land on contract, gave a fixed amount of produce to the state and kept the rest for themselves. Previously they had had small plots for personal cultivation but these were intended only to provide them with a food supplement. The peasants used these plots to grow vegetables and to rear pigs and chickens for their own consumption. Once peasants had only to give a fixed amount of grain to the government, they were free to grow whatever they wanted on the rest of the land. There followed a dramatic diversification from cereal into cash crops, fruit and vegetables. The resulting increase in output and income caused a further rise in savings in the rural areas and gave another fillip to the growth of the TVEs.

In one crucial respect, therefore, agricultural reform played the same role in China as the enclosure movement and the agrarian revolution played in Britain 300 years earlier: it generated surpluses that could be invested in industry, and more importantly, since the peasants had to sell their surpluses of grain, fruit, vegetables, meat and dairy products in the towns, it created a nascent free market in agricultural products, something that had not existed until then and without which a more rapid and more efficient industrialisation was out of the question.

THE ORIGINS OF A LABOUR MARKET

The gradual emergence of a market for agricultural products made possible the next important step in the creation of a market economy: the emergence of a province and then a nationwide market for labour. Well before the industrial reforms of 1984 and 1985, in fact from the 1960s onwards, Chinese state enterprises had been employing not only workers assigned to them – known locally as 'state workers' – but also workers on contract. These were workers who had taken courage in both hands, decided to leave the provinces, cities and communes to which they were assigned, or where they had been born, and looked for employment in factories often located far from their homes. By doing so they not only forfeited the welfare, pension, medical, housing and children's education rights they enjoyed in their places of residence, and assigned locations, but also their food coupons, which were only valid in these places.

In the absence of a free market for food, such a move was fraught with danger and only the most courageous, foolhardy or desperate, made it. But, for the same reason, those who found work as contract workers invariably proved to be far more efficient than the state workers. As a result, despite the immense difficulties that plant directors (general managers) had in arranging even food rations for their contract workers,[4] they continued to hire them, to provide them with dormitories and give them health benefits while they worked in their enterprises. The emergence of a free market in foodstuffs in the early 1980s made the lives of the contract workers much easier, and their numbers multiplied rapidly. By 1993, in Guangzhou province alone, 400,000 peasants had left their farms every year since 1983 to become industrial workers.[5] The growing free market in food enabled workers to migrate in huge numbers from the backward provinces to the special economic zones – more than a million came to Shenzen alone – and large numbers moved from the backward provinces to become farm labourers in the rich plains and deltas of the eastern and south-eastern provinces. A national market for labour thus began to take shape.

CREATING A MARKET FOR INDUSTRIAL PRODUCTS

Reforms in industry were similarly driven by internal necessity. These ran on two parallel tracks: the creation of a market for manufactures, and the enlargement of the autonomy enjoyed by the state enterprises. Looked at schematically, the state created a market for manufactures in three stages. The first was to set up a 'unified (as distinct from centralised) buying and selling system' which legitimised the informal market. The second was to sell or buy only a predetermined share of outputs and inputs from the state. Beyond the amount contracted for by the state authorities the enterprises were told to look to the market for sales and supplies. The third stage was the gradual decontrol of prices.

China's centralised planning was never as comprehensive as that of the Soviet Union. Against 65,000 producers' goods subjected to mandatory centralised production and allocation in the Soviet Union, there were only 837 such products in 1980 in China.[6] In both countries the centralised planning and distribution system covered broadly similar areas of industrial output. Centralised allocation covered the basic industries, and all but the most highly specialised machinery – machines that could only be made against special orders. Where Russia and China diverged significantly was in their planning for consumer goods. In Russia the Gosplan and Gosnab determined the allocation of both inputs and outputs to the last detail. In China the state attempted to do this only for the inputs. In practice this meant that it planned both production and distribution for the producer goods industries, because here one factory's output was another factory's input. In the case of consumer goods, the factories received their inputs from the state and their orders from state commercial organisations. This meant that, unlike Russia, if there was an excess of production over demand the manufacturing SOEs were left free to arrange the sale of the surplus output themselves. Over time they learned to respond by making hidden price cuts, improving quality and styling, and offering warranties.[7] An informal buyers' market also emerged to dispose of the 'surpluses'.

Even in inputs, the relative lack of sophistication of the Chinese allocation process, which was reflected in the much broader classification of products, meant that mismatches between the type of product supplied and required (e.g. steel) were common. From the beginning, therefore, enterprises were forced to make supplemental purchases 'directly'. There was therefore always a grey market in which products not under the plan, and above plan output, were traded. They did this through more and more complicated systems of barter. Until 1979, barter was expressly forbidden. Instead the planning and supply agencies of central, provincial, municipal and autonomous region governments tried to organise exchanges of surplus output between the enterprises and their supply agencies.

Just how cumbersome this could be is revealed by the following example. In 1977, the Materials Bureau of Wuxi county exchanged AC electric motors produced above the fixed quota for 2,160 tonnes of silicon steel in the following way: it first exchanged the motors for pig iron and steel billets from eight separate provinces. It then exchanged 1,000 tonnes of the pig iron for 500 tonnes of small silicon steel sheets from the Shanghai Handicrafts Administrative Bureau. That left 1,660 tonnes to procure. It then sent the steel billets to a steel works under the Shanghai Metallurgical Industry Bureau to be rolled into 2,800 tonnes of steel sheets of which one-eighth (350 tonnes) would be silicon steel. It then exchanged the bulk of the rolled steel with no fewer than eight other materials supply bureaus and power companies to obtain another 1,110 tonnes of silicon steel. Finally, it exchanged 250 tonnes of rolled steel for 500 tonnes of silicon iron, and then got this converted into 200 tonnes of silicon steel sheets.[8]

Where centralised allocation broke down was in the production of machinery. All over the world, except for the simplest of machines and tools, plant and equipment has to be made to special order, usually in small batches. Russia responded to this problem by making its planning system more and more complex until it was nearly a hundred times more detailed than the Chinese system.[9] The Chinese planners threw up their hands and left the enterprises to fend for themselves. As a result by 1979, when the government legalised the barter economy, producers and buyers had made direct links in as many as 357 categories of producers goods – most of them in the machine-building industries.[10] Following the legalisation, in a single year the proportion of direct sales rose from 13 per cent to 46 per cent. By 1982, 48 per cent of all sales of non-agricultural consumer goods by manufacturing to commercial enterprises were voluntary transactions.[11]

The limitations on the central government's capacity for detailed planning also made it devolve progressively more of the task of allocation upon the provincial and local authorities. This led to a multiplicity of prices for the same product. In general the smaller the authority the greater the freedom it had. When the government acknowledged the existence of two markets in 1979, it also legalised a 'plan' price and a 'market' price. By 1988, however, there were not two but three prices: a plan price at which the government contracted to buy its purchases; a free market price at which goods were sold on the open market; and a 'plan-adjusted' price at which enterprises supplied goods to other enterprises with a sudden shortening of delivery times. This situation was tailor-made for corruption and influence peddling. In 1988, according to an estimate published in a World Bank report, one-third of the output of the SOEs was being sold at the plan price, and another third at the market or plan-adjusted price. The remaining third simply disappeared.[12]

After 1989 the pace of decontrol of prices accelerated. By the end of 1991 price controls had been lifted, in terms of sales value, on 70 per cent of all consumer goods, all but 111 intermediate products and 17 agricultural products. 1992 saw further sweeping decontrol. The most important measures were the removal of price controls on steel and aluminium in 1992, on petroleum products at the end of that year, and on grain and edible oil in March 1993. The main items still under price control were coal (which is the main fuel of the poor in China), medicines, energy, transport and housing, the last of which remains heavily subsidised.

In 1993, the government still pre-empted about 15 per cent of the total output of the state sector under the plan at lower prices. As in India, the government sold foodgrains through ration shops to the people in the cities at the same price that it procured it from the farmers. The whole of the storage, transport and distribution cost was met from the exchequer.

ENTERPRISE AUTONOMY – THE CORE OF REFORM

By 1993, on the eve of the 'great inflation', Beijing and the governments of the coastal provinces had done a creditable job of changing the macroeconomic framework of the Chinese economy. But

China's leaders were becoming uncomfortably aware that the success of economic reforms would hinge on their ability to transform the state-owned enterprises from production units, which simply carry out orders given from above, in to enterprise units that are able to function in a competitive market economy. In the West, the dazzling speed of China's growth and structural transformation had given rise to the belief, among journalists in particular, that the Chinese policy makers' strategy was to promote the TVEs and urban collectives on one hand, and the foreign and joint ventures on the other, and let the state-owned enterprises die a natural death. But Chinese leaders never harboured this intention, nor the illusion that this was possible. For the SOEs were the core of the communist system; their workers the aristocracy of the proletarian state. In 1995, there were 305,000 state-owned enterprises in China, of which 118,000 were industrial ventures. The latter accounted for one-third of industrial output, while the 305,000 enterprises taken together accounted for two-thirds of urban employment, half of the country's capital assets[13] and employed 112 million workers (i.e. 18 per cent of the work force).[14]

The ultimate goal of enterprise reform was never in any doubt – to make the SOEs function as their counterparts in capitalist countries do, seeking profit and responsible only to their shareholders. The challenge the reformers therefore faced was how to motivate the workers in the SOEs to seek reform. The experience of structural adjustment in countries that had faced far less wrenching changes had shown that the cooperation of the management and workers of the state enterprises could not be taken for granted. As Russia's experience of perestroika in the 1990s, and India's of 'Liberalisation' in the 1990s, was to show, trade unionists and ideologues can be extraordinarily ingenious in concocting reasons why economic reforms should be indefinitely postponed, even when they have no alternative solutions to offer for the country's economic problems. China's solution was to create a 'Socialist Market Economy with Chinese characteristics' – a 'collective capitalism' in which enterprises and not individuals competed with each other in the market. Within themselves each enterprise preserved the tradition of 'eating from the same pot' which had typified Chinese socialism. China therefore tried to create a market, but fought shy of letting it turn into a self-regulating market in which labour also became commodity. The methods it used to do this deserve close study.

It is too often assumed that the personal eminence of Deng Xiaoping, the habit of obedience to the Communist Party and trade union leaders, and the country's Confucian traditions were the main reasons why the Chinese people accepted the reforms so readily. These may well have made the transition easier, but a more important reason was the Chinese leaders' success in harnessing the self-interest of the workers and managers with those of the firm. They did this by applying an astute mixture of economic threat and enticement. As with agriculture, this too was not born out of a master plan but emerged almost by accident from an attempt to deal with problems as they arose.

The threat to the state-owned enterprises was created first. In 1978 four special economic zones for foreign investment were set up, of which Shenzen is the best known. Not only were power, water and other infrastructures specially created, but schools, hospitals and hotels, roads, housing and office buildings were designed to standards more appropriate to Singapore than Shanghai. The thrust from the very start was to make these zones – to borrow a phrase from India's first prime minister, Jawaharlal Nehru – 'temples of modern technology'. The special economic zones enjoyed a number of advantages over the state-owned enterprises. Almost none of the social obligations that the latter had to shoulder, such as paying pensions to retired workers and providing them with housing and schools for their children, were loaded on the foreign and joint venture enterprises. Instead they simply paid the workers a great deal more than the SOEs did. To attract foreign investment, taxation was deliberately kept low at 7.5 per cent for the first three years and 15 per cent after that, as against an average of 30 per cent of profits in the case of the SOEs.[15] Had the joint and wholly foreign-owned ventures been allowed only to export their products and not sell them in the domestic market, they would not have posed any threat to the SOEs. But in fact a sizeable part of their output was intended from the start for the home market. Overall, until 1998, these ventures were exporting around 47 per cent of their output and sold the remainder in China.[16] The modern technology of the foreign and joint venture companies gave them a natural competitive edge over the state-owned enterprises. This was further reinforced by their lack of social overheads and lower taxation.[17] Thus measures that were taken by the central government to attract foreign investment had the unintended effect of shaking up the SOEs and making them look for ways to meet the new competition.

The SOEs have also come under pressure 'from below', from the township and village enterprises. While the defects in the statistics make it difficult to make a firm estimate of their contribution to industrial output, if the estimates of the government, that they now account for about 30 per cent of the total industrial output, are anywhere near correct, then competition from them presents an even bigger threat to the SOEs than the foreign and joint ventures. The main reasons are their lower wages, and the much lighter burden of social overheads on them.

In 1993, against an average wage and bonus package of Y350 (yuan) in Guangzhou City, and Y600 to Y700 in a profitable SOE, workers (all female) in a TVE garment factory at the 'Evergreen' county (a former commune and now a showcase rural community not far from Beijing), were earning only Y200 a month. Social overheads like housing, health and childrens' education were also paid for by the state and were not reflected fully in the costing of their products. The TVEs also paid much lower taxes: an average of 27 per cent of profits taking direct and indirect taxes together, against direct tax alone of 30 per cent on the SOEs.[18]

The threat from the two directions developed over a decade, but because the state ordering and procurement system on which the SOEs depended was reduced gradually, it gave them time to chalk out a survival strategy. The only way ahead was to bring in new technology and management systems, new incentives to work harder, and new designs and products. Thus the state-owned enterprises gradually reconciled themselves to become adherents of change.

Pressure for deregulation was also generated, again not entirely intentionally, by the decentralisation of economic decision-making power to the provinces and city administrations. The provincial administrations turned out to be more pragmatic and more willing to innovate than Beijing. They went out of their way to attract foreign investors and cash-rich Chinese state enterprises to invest in their newly set up development zones. They speedily sold off shops, and service facilities like barber shops and restaurants, that had been run by the state, and gave licences to set up thousands more. Thousands of taxi and minibus operators were given licences. All but a handful of the new ventures were collectives and subsidiary ventures set up by state-owned enterprises. The new investors were overseas Chinese, state-owned enterprises that wanted to set up side businesses (urban collectives) for their surplus workers and for the children of their workers, and individuals.

The explosive growth of the tertiary sector, light industries, and foreign-owned and joint ventures, also created a serious and growing gap between the incomes in the state-owned enterprises and these sectors. The high earnings in the joint venture and service sectors stoked the desire for reform in the state-owned enterprises. The workers realised that so long as their products were under price controls while those produced by the joint ventures were not, or so long as the state purchased a large part of their output at a low administered price, they could not increase their incomes beyond a point. Therefore they also chafed at price and distribution controls, and pushed for their speedy withdrawal.

The formal transfer of decision-making power from the central planning authority to the state-owned enterprises began in 1978. That year saw the beginning of two major initiatives: to devolve decision making on price, output and investment to the enterprise managers; and to create the institutions essential for the success of a market economy.

Before 1978, all decision making on prices, outputs, inputs and marketing was controlled by the central planning authority in the 800-plus products that accounted for the bulk of production in China.[19] The currency played a limited role, solely as a medium of exchange. Credit was of minor importance: there was no commercial banking. The Chinese central bank met the enterprises' need for working capital while a 'Construction Bank' met their need for long term finance to set up new projects. The motto of the government was 'Big finance but small bank'.

All of the surplus generated by an enterprise belonged to the government, and enterprises had to get permission to use even their depreciation funds. The only decisions left to the enterprises were those that related to the 'simple replacement' of capital – of worn-out machines and parts. In practice they were allowed to retain a share of the surplus to meet social overheads for the workers. But all earnings went into a common pool and the investment needs and losses of all were met from this.

Pressure to increase managerial autonomy first developed within the enterprises. Their workers had children who needed to find jobs. The enterprises asked for and obtained permission to open subsidiaries in which more jobs could be created. What is more, efficient plants that exceeded their targets and sold the excess to other enterprises or to consumers, wanted to keep a part of the additional earnings, either to open more collectives or to increase the pay package of their workers in recognition of their efforts.

In 1978, the government changed its rules and allowed the enterprises to retain 30 per cent of the surplus, not only to meet social overheads but also to open such collectives and pay out bonuses to the workers. In the ensuing years the pressure from the enterprises to increase the share of retained profit grew stronger and stronger. Enterprises found ingenious ways to disguise personal expenditure as social expenses.[20]

When the 'unified buying and selling system' was introduced, enterprises strained every nerve to buy and sell more in the newly legitimised market system in order to increase their profits, and thence their retained surpluses. The government also increased the share of profit that the enterprises could retain from 30 to 70 per cent. This was part of a phased transition from profit sharing to a corporation tax, which has still not been completed.

An important corollary of the change was that the enterprises also had to meet a progressively larger part of the cost of new investment from their retained earnings. Budgetary support for the investment by the state-owned enterprises fell from 40 per cent in 1978 to only 13 per cent in 1989. There was a corresponding increase in reliance on bank finance.

To cope with this the banking system was expanded and diversified. Four huge, state-owned commercial banks were opened: the Industrial and Commercial Bank, the Agricultural Bank, the Chinese Peoples' Construction Bank, and the Communications Bank. The government also set up the Bank of China, which deals in foreign currencies and finances imports and exports. The Peoples' Bank of China was created as the central bank to control and harmonise the credit operations of all the others. In theory, as their names implied, these were specialised banks that lent money to the sectors they were intended to serve. But in practice, the banks increasingly crossed these lines and lent money to whoever had a viable project, or the necessary pull to obtain a loan. This was the genesis of commercial banking in China. The large commercial banks were supplemented by 14 smaller commercial banks in the 1990s, and by a network of rural and urban credit societies and more than 300 trust and investment companies. This rapid growth of banking institutions is the main reason for China's very high mobilisation of domestic savings, now touching 45 per cent of GDP.[21]

This transformation too is far from complete. The commercial banks therefore remain far too susceptible to the dictates of local and provincial party bosses to lend to specific persons and enterprises. When it comes to financing the losses of the state-owned enterprises, their autonomy more or less vanishes. The control of the Peoples' Bank of China over the 'specialised' banks is also rather haphazard. The former is able to exercise only limited control over credit creation through normal monetary instruments, such as liquidity ratios or rediscount rates. Control has to be exercised through executive fiats, which are often countermanded by the provincial governments, which insist that credit continue to be given to favoured clients and local state enterprises.

Some idea of the degree of autonomy won by, or granted to, the SOEs from the following indicators by 1989 was obtained from a sample survey quoted by the World Bank.[22] It showed that the portion of profits that could be retained by an enterprise from its plan output had risen from 7 per cent in 1980 to 39 per cent in 1989, and the share of profits from above-plan output from 11 per cent to 27 per cent. Some 67 per cent of the sample SOEs enjoyed autonomy in making production decisions in 1989 against only 7 per cent in 1980, and 35 per cent could fix wages against 1 per cent in 1980. By 1989, 88 per cent were operating under the management responsibility system, against none in 1980, and 94 per cent had exercised the freedom to hire new managers, against only 9 per cent in 1980.

THE RESPONSE OF THE STATE ENTERPRISES

Paradoxically, however, liberalisation increased the vulnerability of the SOEs to competition from the foreign and joint ventures and the TVEs. Price decontrol, for instance, increased the gap between the prices set by the SOEs and those of their competitors. The proportion of the state enterprises that recorded losses therefore rose from 10.7 per cent in 1985 to 31.5 per cent in 1990, and the ratio of their pre-tax profit to revenue fell from 23.8 per cent to 10.4 per cent.

Everyone, from the controlling ministries to the meanest plant worker, knew that further improvements in their incomes and survival in the long run depended on improving productivity and introducing products that could compete with those produced in the special economic zones. This fact was dinned into them tirelessly by chairman Deng Xiaoping, by the Thirteenth and Fourteenth Peoples' Congresses and, at the plant level, by the trade union representatives and the Communist Party secretaries. China had to be competitive or perish; independence came from being in a strong trading position in the world economy; success in trade depended on being able to compete with the other trading nations of the world. China could not grow in isolation any more.[23]

At the heart of this drive lay the upgrading of technology. To encourage this the government insisted that a large part of the profits that the enterprises retained had to go into a 'technology renewal fund'. But new technology invariably meant fewer jobs on the factory floor. The SOEs dealt with the problem of labour redundancy by finding new jobs for the surplus workers. One stratagem was to divert surplus workers into services and other subsidiary enterprises, and into new managerial functions, such as design and marketing, which were simply not needed when enterprises produced to a fixed central plan. The other was to expand the core enterprise itself so that the decline in workers in each workshop or production line was offset by a rise in the number of workshops or production lines.

The first proved far easier than the second. Centralised planning had ensured a severe underdevelopment of the service industries. In 1965, the share of services was 17 per cent of GDP in China against 34 per cent in India and 59 per cent in Mexico. Even in 1990, this had only risen to 20 per cent in China against 41 per cent in India. The deregulation of the services sector by the provincial governments had opened the way for the enterprises to open shops and other service establishments to absorb their own surplus workers. Trading and taxi companies were other favourite ventures. But the most attractive business turned out to be real estate. In the late 1980s and early 1990s, when the market for land was in its infancy and foreign investors were flocking in, this looked like a gold mine in the back garden. Only in the late 1990s, when growth slackened, was the full size of the real estate bubble revealed.

The transition from a centrally planned to market economy also created new types of jobs in the factories. These were in marketing, aftersales service and product design. None of these functions was needed during the heyday of centralised planning. But the transition to a market economy and relentless competition from the foreign and joint venture enterprises made the more progressive SOEs reorganise them-selves in order to compete. In engineering enterprises in particular, while the older workers gravitated towards marketing and aftersales service, the younger and better educated gravitated towards product design.

The response of the SOEs to the pressure of competition has been very uneven. It has understandably been slowest in basic industries where the scope for technological innovation is limited, interference by ministerial bureaucrats is continuous, the workforce is old and social overheads are high. But medium and light industries, which are driven wholly by the market, have fared much better.

TWO CASE STUDIES

Two medium and light engineering enterprises visited by the author in 1993 gave a glimpse of the changes that the SOEs were undergoing. In the 1950s and 1960s, the Guangdong Light Industrial Machinery Works (GLIMW) in Guangzhou used to produce mainly sugar refining equipment and a variety of fermentation tanks and other process plant equipment. The demand for sugar refining plants dried up gradually, and in the 1970s the enterprise switched to making bottling plant machinery. In the days before reform GLIMW was a premier plant, which had been designated a state first-class enterprise for six years running, and was meeting 65 per cent of the demand for bottling plant equipment in the country. But with economic reforms and the emergence of joint ventures and TVEs to give them competition, its stars declined. In May 1993, the plant was working only one shift and producing only at 40 per cent of its estimated capacity. In the previous three years, however, the management had taken a number of steps to reduce its redundant workforce, to diversify production and to make the enterprise more cost conscious. A sizeable part of the workforce had been diverted to shops that the enterprise had opened in Guangzhou, many of which catered to its own needs. It had also opened sales rooms, and three subsidiary enterprises, one of which was a computerised design centre in which it was an equal partner with a firm from Hong Kong.

Internally, the enterprise was in the throes of a complete transformation. In 1985 it had gone in for a systematic diversification of its product. Its mainstay became a 20,000 bottles per hour filling line, for which it imported the technology from Germany. This supplemented a wide range of other smaller capacity machines that it had on offer. In 1993 it was offering a wide range of bottling plants from 4,000 to 48,000 bottles per hour filling capacity, and had set up a separate section for manufacturing 7,500 bottles of plastic (PET) or glass containers per hour. It had replaced 75 per cent of its machine tools with numerical and microprocessor controlled machine tools and machining centres. For the future the company was placing its faith in further product diversification. 'We plan to introduce five or six new products [in the general area of bottling plant machinery and fermentation equipment] every year', the plant director said. The computerised design centre it had created was intended to make this possible. To eliminate overstaffing, the company was placing its faith in expansion: in the next two years (1993–95), when the renovation of the workshops was complete, it hoped to increase its output by 250 per cent.

The Tianjin Hwanhua factory, which the author visited, had taken a slightly different route to modernisation and to solving its problem of surplus labour. Set up originally in 1938, and nationalised in 1956, the plant specialised in making tinplate containers for different kinds of products and aerosol cans. Until 1985, it operated under the centrally planned economy and its growth was slow. In 1985, its total asset value was Y7.5 million (then about $2.6 million). During the era of reform, when the enterprise gained control of its investment plans and was able to retain its surplus for modernisation, it went in for a dramatic widening of its product mix, introducing plastic container production lines and widening the range of tinplate containers. Its total assets increased in current prices to Y260 million ($45 million) and its productive capacity increased elevenfold.

To increase productivity this factory adopted a somewhat different approach to GLIMW in Guangzhou. It first equipped one of its twelve workshops with the latest German machinery for making tinplate containers and took to heart the admonitions of the German engineers who had come to set it up, that machines alone would not give them the productivity that was achieved in Germany. The Germans were fond of saying that one German worker produced as much as three Japanese and one Japanese as much as four Chinese. The managers and workers at the Tianjin factory took this as a challenge. They divided the factory into two parts, even erecting a partition in the administration building to separate the old from the new. Within the new workshop and administrative offices, it deliberately introduced Western concepts of industrial engineering and productivity. In short, they decided to break the age-old Chinese principle of 'eating from the same pot'. Bonuses were no longer pegged to the overall performance of the entire factory, but to the performance of each worker in each shift. Productivity norms were set up wherever possible for each worker and, where this was not possible, for each production line in each shift.

The improvement was dramatic. Within a year, the factory managers claimed, the new part of the factory was touching German productivity norms. This claim, like most of those made during my interviews, was somewhat exaggerated, but not greatly so. The productivity norms were set up in such a way that theoretically it was possible for a worker to earn eight times the basic salary of between Y160 and Y250 a month. But the average earnings of the workers in the new part of the plant had risen, by early 1993, to between Y750 and Y800 a month ($135 to $145). The highest that an individual worker had earned was about Y1,000 per month, or four to five times the basic salary. Assuming that the theoretical maximum had itself been set with some reference to German productivity levels, this suggests that the actual productivity levels attained may not have been much more than half of the German levels. Even this is praiseworthy.

There were other innovations: instead of the personnel department assigning workers to each production team, the workers were allowed to choose where they wanted to work. The work team was also allowed to choose its workers. This too was a radical departure from the past. Initially the workers were sceptical about the reform. However, under pressure from the trade union representatives, and the party committee in the plant, they agreed to give it a try. The success of the experiment and the huge gap that had suddenly opened between the salaries of the workers in the new plant and those in the old, persuaded them to change their production methods also. When the author visited the plant it had nearly completed the modernisation of all of its twelve workshops with equipment from Hong Kong, Singapore, Germany, Switzerland and Taiwan. The enterprise intends to increase its output by five times when the changeover is completed.

The Tianjin plant had gone a long way further in diversification than GLIMW in Guangzhou, and had begun to privatise itself. It had opened in all nine subsidiary companies in real estate, trade, interior decoration, a taxi company, and a financial consultancy venture. It had invested in three joint ventures with groups from Hong Kong and Singapore, in making containers, packaging materials and covers for containers. Forty per cent of the output was intended for export.

In April 1992, the company went public. It created 67.5 million shares of half a yuan each. Some 35 million were retained by the government while the balance was sold to the workers (6 million shares) and to others outside the enterprise, for 3 yuan each. However, these shares are still not traded on the stock market.

GLIMW in Guangzhou and the Tianjin Hwanhua factory exemplify two contrasting ways of coping with the unemployment that is generated when modernising medium sized state-owned enterprises, in order to make them more competitive. While the management at GLIMW concentrated on diversifying and expanding the range of its products and building new managerial capabilities in order to absorb surplus workers, the form of modernisation adopted by the Tianjin factory, which concentrated on downsizing and streamlining the production process, could not fail to create unemployment. The management had therefore decided to give the surplus workers their basic salaries and let them stay on in their flats rather than have them on the factory floor. Such workers were being given their full basic salaries for three months, and 70 per cent of their basic salaries for another three months. After that they were allowed to stay on in their flats but were not given any pay. There was, however, an unemployment insurance paid out of a fund collected by the workers, of Y100 a month. When asked how the laid-off workers had taken this, the managers replied, 'We expect them to look around for work in other factories, and eventually leave. No one likes to stay on in such circumstances for a long time.' The process of unemployment creation was humane, compared to capitalist economies. But the end result was the same. In subsequent years most enterprises adopted the Tianjin model. In 1996, there were more than 15 million unemployed or more or less unemployed urban workers who had joined the ranks of those in absolute poverty.

9

Is China's Transformation Sustainable?

China's policy of incremental reform – what Deng Xiaoping called 'fording the river by feeling the stones' – has given it one of the most impressive and sustained growth rates the world has known. This growth has lifted at least 300 million people out of poverty;[1] created more than 100 million productive new jobs in the township and village enterprises,[2] and another 17 million in the foreign and joint ventures that have come up in development zones and the special economic zones created along the coast.[3] Can China sustain this growth rate, and can the reform process remain as smooth as it has seemingly been so far?

Prior to the Asian economic meltdown, few scholars entertained any serious doubt that it could. Belief in China's future was reinforced by its success in curbing the four year long inflation of 1993 to 1996, and achieving a 'soft landing' – merging the control of inflation with a resumption of growth – in 1997. In 1996 the World Bank expressed an unqualified confidence in China's future. It admitted that China faced 'a number of challenges' in the coming years but concluded that its resilience should not be underestimated. This resilience sprang from its political stability, its high rate of saving (45 per cent of GDP), its strong record of pragmatic reforms, its disciplined and literate labour force, and the strongly supportive Chinese diaspora. The Bank pointed out that while the Ninth Five Year Plan had set a target of 8 per cent GDP growth, China had achieved 9.5 per cent in 1996, its very first year. China therefore needed to grow at no more than 7.6 per cent per annum during the rest of the plan to achieve its target. 'By the standards of recent years, such growth does not seem unduly ambitious', the Bank concluded.[4]

Even after the Asian economic crisis had put brakes on the growth of exports and foreign direct investment, faith in China remained strong among the majority of China-watchers. Writing in *Foreign Affairs*, Nicholas Lardy, a senior fellow at the Brookings Institution, made the following assessment:

> The Asian financial contagion has so far left China untouched. Unlike the plummeting currencies elsewhere in the region, the Renminbi has appreciated against the dollar since the onset of the crisis. In real terms the Chinese economy has also fared well. In 1997, the growth of GDP, while slower than the blistering pace of

the immediately preceding years, was almost nine percent. Inflation was at a five-year low. Exports grew over 20 per cent in 1997, contributing to an unprecedented $40.3 billion trade surplus. Foreign direct investment rose for the seventh consecutive year, reaching $45.3 billion, and China raised an additional $16 billion through debt and equity offerings on international markets. Foreign exchange reserves rose sharply, reaching $139.9 billion by the end of the year, second only to Japan's.[5]

Others, however, were not so confident. *The Economist* pointed out in its 1997 survey of China that spontaneous reforms had run their course. Those that now had to be made – such as the integration of the national market, improved financial accounting in the state industries, and trade liberalisation – had shown up the state's inner contradictions 'in a harsher light'. 'These contradictions', *The Economist* pointed out, 'are immense and so far show no sign of being resolved'. *The Economist* concluded that China's economic transformation and its high growth could not be maintained if gradual reform was not given up in favour of a Chinese variant of shock therapy.[6]

Believers and sceptics shared the view that sustaining the reform process in the new century would become more difficult but differed on their assessment of China's capacity to stay on course and even accelerate the reforms. The World Bank believed China could do it, but *The Economist* preferred to remain non-committal. In 1996 and 1997, however, neither the World Bank nor *The Economist* fully appreciated the real difficulty that lay ahead. This was that China had reached a watershed in its economic transition. Political and economic compulsions had reinforced each other in the reforms carried out until then. But political and economic imperatives were in direct conflict with each other in the reforms that lay ahead.

The convergence of political and economic motives was disrupted only once during Deng Xiaoping's lifetime. This was during the run up to the Tiananmen demonstrations in 1989. After they were suppressed, the provincial leaders picked up the torch of economic reform. Provincial and city governments set up 'special economic zones' (SEZs) and development zones by the score to attract foreign investment. They set up holding companies and International Trading and Industrial Corporations (ITICs) that borrowed heavily in the Hong Kong money market, and incorporated dozens of companies in Hong Kong – the so-called 'red chip' companies – to raise foreign exchange through the sale of shares. This money was funnelled into thousands of investments in their provinces. State-owned enterprises followed suit and set up subsidiary companies in Hong Kong. These also raised money and came back into China as foreign companies to invest in the SEZs and reap the tax benefits and freedom from social overheads that they offered. Not to be outdone, township and county administrations set up hundreds of thousands of urban and rural collectives – the so-called township and village enterprises – to mass produce simple consumer goods. Thus a joyful free-for-all took place in which everyone raced everyone else to set up what were essentially new variants of collective capitalist enterprises bent upon exploiting the seemingly inexhaustible domestic and foreign market. By the mid-1990s there were no fewer than 240 ITICs set up by the provincial governments,[7] and no fewer than 1.9 million township and village enterprises (TVEs).[8] Between them the ITICs and the TVEs accounted for the lion's share of the industrial growth of China during the period of reform.

At the enterprise level, the removal of price controls and progressive reduction of the share of product pre-empted by the state for distribution under the Plan had the full support of the workers because although it raised the cost of living, it also increased the sales revenue of the affected enterprises, and therefore the direct and indirect earnings of its employees. Since the basic needs of the workers were still being met by the enterprise, nearly the whole of the increase in their income represented an increase in disposable income. The new-found freedom this gave to them – to buy and sell, to travel in search of work, to visit one's fiancé(e) or parents in a different city more frequently (and not only when the state decreed and provided travel vouchers for), or even to take a holiday at a tourist resort – were all important new economic freedoms that kept the demand for political freedom at bay, and helped to maintain public order through a period of wrenching economic change. Thus China was able to put through reforms like the removal of price controls and the ending or reduction of subsidies, that have toppled governments in other countries, with hardly a political tremor.

In sharp contrast, the reforms that lie ahead will seriously pit the economic compulsions of the state against its political imperatives. What is worse, this conflict is emerging at a time when the political authority of the Communist Party is waning and when, thanks to slowing economic growth, the Chinese people have begun to get an inkling of what the dark face of capitalism looks like. This makes the challenges that future reforms pose qualitatively different from those of the past.

THE INCOMPLETENESS OF REFORMS

Capital markets

A decade and a half after Prof. Dong Fureng, then the director of the Institute for Economics of the Chinese Academy of Social Sciences, proposed at a nationally telecast press conference in 1985[9] that China needed a capital market in which shares of enterprises could be freely traded, the equity and bond markets in China remain rudimentary by any standard. At just over 100 per cent of GDP, China's stock of financial savings is the lowest of any Asian country, with the possible exception of Vietnam. But equity shares and bonds make up barely a tenth of even this figure.[10] The balance of the stock of savings is held as bank deposits. The reason is that the government determines exactly how much new capital will be raised every year via equity and bonds, and how much of it will be raised in each province. The amounts it is prepared to raise have been very small because of a morbid fear that this will divert savings away from the banks and make it difficult for them to finance the state-owned enterprises.[11] The smallness of the share market has combined with the rapid growth of incomes and profits to create one of the unhealthiest stock markets in the world, in which too much money chases too few shares. While the ratio of trading to market capitalisation in most newly industrialised countries ranges from 25 per cent to 75 per cent, in Shenzen and Shanghai it is a frenzied 250 per cent.[12]

The banking system

The banking system is also far from commercial in its operation. The Peoples' Bank of China (PBC), the apex bank established in 1984, still has only limited control over credit creation, and has to rely excessively on direct instructions and detailed administration of credit ceilings. Despite several formal changes in the structure of the banking system and the introduction of indirect methods of money management in a wide-ranging set of reforms in 1993,[13] the PBC has continued to rely mainly on direct controls to curb the expansion of credit. In spite of this, its control of the money supply has almost certainly become weaker in the 1990s. In 1988 a ceiling set on credit expansion by the PBC was largely observed and succeeded in stopping inflation in its tracks, albeit at a very high cost in terms of growth foregone. By contrast, in the beginning of June 1993, when the PBC called its managers from all over the country to decide on a strategy to contain inflation, the consensus that emerged and was incorporated in the stabilisation programme announced on 11 July was that a hard credit ceiling would probably not be feasible and that the bank should try for a 'soft landing' instead. The soft landing policy was a mix of interest rate increases, credit ceilings, and detailed supervision of loans designed to bring down the growth of investment. A year later it seemed to be having some (albeit limited) effect, but inflation flared once more in the second half of 1994, and continued until 1996. In retrospect therefore the 'soft landing' policy seems to have been, at least partly, a euphemism to hide the PBC's awareness of its loss of control. The reasons for this were twofold: the PBC's inability to prevent the diversion of bank funds into speculation, and the millstone of having to finance the credit needs of the state-owned enterprises. A large part of the money borrowed by the SOEs went into covering their continuing losses and therefore fed inflation. What is more, the SOEs were no less inclined to speculate than individuals and collectives.[14]

Both in 1988, when the economy had also overheated, and during the inflation of 1993–96, the Peoples' Bank of China was unable to use interest rates as a way of preventing the flight of deposits from financial to real assets such as land and gold. One reason was the sharpness of the periodic surges of inflation. In 1988–89, prices were supposed to have risen at an annual rate of 15.3 per cent, but in August 1988, the annualised rate of inflation rose, briefly, to 80 per cent.[15] The second was the poor quality of Chinese statistics on prices. In 1992, when the economy again began to overheat, there was a similar ambivalence about the actual rate of inflation. Understandably, therefore, the PBC places little faith in interest rates and relies instead on taking physical measures to reduce the creation of credit in the economy.[16]

But the inability to rely on the interest rate yielded negative real rates of interest. This led to huge flights of savings from the banks into land and gold. In 1993, the entire amount allocated for capital construction was used up in the first quarter. Much of this went into speculation in land, in which everyone joined. One favourite expedient was to open new 'development zones'. In 1992, local authorities set up no less than 2,800 development zones. Beijing was forced to insist that most of them be shut down. 1993 also saw a heavy buying of gold, so much so that Chinese demand pushed up world gold prices in the first half of 1993.[17]

Ailing state enterprises

Despite the initiative and enterprise shown by some of the medium sized and smaller SOEs, 12 years after the relaxation of control on the state-owned industrial enterprises, not only have the majority still not made the transition from central planning and direction to a market economy successfully, but the number of enterprises failing to do so is mounting.[18] These include nearly all of the 1,000 large enterprises that account for two-thirds of the capital invested by the state in industry. To keep these enterprises afloat, money has to be pumped into them every year and it is coming from the banks. Some 80 to 90 per cent of the loans made by the state-owned commercial banks go to the state-owned enterprises.[19] Of the total advances to enterprises and individuals of Y5.889 trillion in December 1996, about Y5 trillion had been loaned to the SOEs. This was 83 per cent of China's GDP at current market prices. The relentless rise in debt had pushed up the debt to equity ratio of all state-owned firms more than 50 times in a single decade, from 1:10 at the outset of economic reforms (1984–85) to more than 5:1 at the end of 1995.[20] At this level of debt many companies are not making enough by way of sales revenue to cover their interest payments (unless interest rates are subsidised also). Of the 305,000 SOEs, half are making operating losses.[21] At the end of 1998, the non-performing loans of the four largest commercial banks, the China Construction Bank, the Agriculture Bank, the Industrial and Commercial Bank and the Bank of China, added up to more than Y2 trillion ($241 billion) – a quarter of their total outstanding loans at the end of 1998.[22] Since these banks accounted for 64 per cent of total credit in 1998, it is likely that the total volume of non-performing loans had exceeded Y3 trillion, or almost 40 per cent of the GDP, by the end of the year.[23]

More disturbing than the actual level of non-performing loans is the fact that the amount they are having to be loaned every year keeps rising as their losses mount. Chinese estimates suggest that bad debts are mounting at the rate of Y50 to Y60 billion a year.[24] Since the Chinese criteria for non-performing loans are a good deal less stringent than the international norm, which is to miss payments of interest or principal for 90 to 180 days, the actual level of non-performing loans may be a good deal higher.

The failure of the majority of SOEs to become competitive is also the reason why enterprise reform has slowed down after 1992. As described above, by 1993 the SOEs had won a large measure of autonomy in making pricing and investment decisions. There are very few products left under price controls and compulsory production contracts with the government. By 1996, barely 5 per cent of SOE output was still sold to the state under the Plan.[25] But when it comes to other types of managerial decisions, especially new investment or major changes in the product mix of the enterprise, old habits refuse to die, and the large enterprises in particular enjoy little autonomy. Decisions filter down to plant directors after they are vetted by a multi-tiered superstructure of state bodies. The State Council, China's highest governing body, is the ultimate owner of all state enterprises. A National Bureau of State Owned Property implements its directives. This sits atop a pyramid of State Asset Supervisory Committees, State Asset Management Bureaus, and finally the State Asset Operating Companies. There is a parallel hierarchy in 57 large company groups under the central government. Within this pyramid conflicts arise regularly because lines of authority overlap or are blurred. In addition, investment decisions have to be endorsed by the central government which has the responsibility to ensure that they conform to the national plan.[26] Needless to say, power gets divorced from responsibility and the type of initiative required to take advantage of market opportunities as they arise is non-existent. State and corporate revenues remain hopelessly intertwined, and the ministries continue to interfere in detailed decision making, especially in the larger SOEs. In 1993, a scholar at the Institute for Enterprise Reform of the Chinese Academy of Social Sciences asserted, during a discussion with the author, that the only way to end the interference was to close down entire departments and eliminate their functions. He referred with approval to a recent decision to close down seven economic departments but pointed out ruefully that five new ones had been created in their place. He and other scholars had been vigorously advocating that the state should be divested of the ownership of public enterprises and not simply of control. But as of 1998 there had been little progress in either direction.

The halfway status of the SOEs was also reflected by the fact that the tax they paid was still not a real profits tax, but a hybrid between a tax and a levy – for they paid a proportion of the operating surplus of the enterprise, even when this was too small to sustain interest and depreciation. As part of a comprehensive new labour code enacted by the National Peoples' Congress in 1994, the government announced another series of reforms of the operation of the SOEs. The primacy of the plant directors was reinforced, while the position of the party secretary in the plant was weakened; taxation and profit retention norms were further rationalised and made uniform; the huge tax advantage enjoyed by the foreign and joint ventures was whittled down; and the government took a conscious decision to retain the 1,000 largest SOEs in the public sector but concentrate on their reform and modernisation, while leaving the remainder to fend for themselves – prosper, merge or perish.[27]

Underdeveloped markets

Markets remain less than fully developed for three main reasons. First, too many pricing decisions remain in the hands of the government. Although price controls on nearly all products were lifted by 1993, the ensuing inflation made the government informally bring a number of them back in the next three years. This played a significant part in bringing about a decline in the rate of inflation in 1996. To some extent, therefore, inflation has been repressed and not tamed.[28] Another way in which the market remains unformed is the continued provision of basic necessities, such as housing, subsidised canteen food, subsidised air and rail fares for approved travel, health and schooling, via the state-owned enterprises.[29]

Last, as described earlier, the state has not separated itself sufficiently from production. This has led not only to a rash of investment decisions that have been taken without sufficient regard for the signals from the market, but, as the consequences have begun to register, to interventions in the market to prevent the sales of products from other provinces and to limit buying to products of local enterprises. These trends are most clearly visible in the automobile industry. Since every provincial authority wanted an automobile plant, by the late 1980s there were as many as 120 plants all over the country. In 1994, the government took steps to consolidate the industry, but provincial governments have fiercely resisted the move because of the prestige attached to producing automobiles and because they are reluctant to lay off workers. As a result, there are still far too many plants. Sales of automobiles touched 1.6 million in 1997, but all but a handful of plants are hopelessly uneconomic. Several, like General Motors' venture in Northeastern China to produce utility vehicles, have produced almost no automobiles in the last few years. As a result several localities have put restrictions on the purchase of automobiles produced elsewhere.

The unification of markets is also far from complete. This leaves a lot of space for favoured middlemen to arrange supplies from their sources for needy enterprises, for a commission. In effect, therefore, China continues to offer insider trading opportunities, to those with connections, that boggle the mind. Huge windfall gains are being made and these are concentrated in the hands of those who were already powerful in the Communist Party, the provincial bureaucracy or the SOEs.[30] This is creating immense differences in incomes and wealth, something that the Chinese had all but forgotten for more than four decades, and that an entire generation was brought up believing to be a cardinal sin. Inevitably, this new moneyed elite is insecure. This has increased the pressure upon it to keep the economy growing at a hectic pace, so that all may benefit to a greater or lesser extent, and to protect the moral foundations of the regime. The tendency to exaggerate the growth rate, especially after Tiananmen, and the periodic execution of corrupt officials can both be traced to these pressures.[31]

Most of these problems had arisen naturally out of the transition from a planned to a market economy. They were clearly understood and extensively debated within the country. There was no lack of clarity about where the policy makers wanted to go, and this was reflected in the continuing reform of labour laws and laws governing the operation of the state enterprises (1994), the banking system and the share market (1994) and agriculture (1993). In 1994 the government began to encourage the mergers of strong and weak enterprises, put a bankruptcy law on the books and declared the creation of a national unemployment insurance scheme to be a national goal. It started open market operation in the share markets in a limited way, raised agricultural prices sharply in 1993 (although this was partly neutralised by a rise in fertiliser prices following devaluation in 1994) and set up wholesale markets all over the country to improve returns to farmers.

But there was a tentative quality in all of the post-1992 reforms. By the end of 1997 barely 1 per cent, perhaps not many more than a thousand enterprises, had initiated bankruptcy proceedings,[32] and nearly all were small in size. An experimental unemployment insurance scheme started with much fanfare by the Guangdong government in 1992, and approved for extension to the entire country in 1993, remained confined to Guangzhou. Overall, between 1993 and 1997 as Deng Xiaoping's health deteriorated, formal changes continued to be enacted but their implementation lagged. Targets were not set, nor completion dates specified. The country seemed to be marking time.

So long as it did so, the losses of the state enterprises, and the non-performing loan portfolios of the banking system, continued to mount. Without breaking the nexus between the two, China's leaders could not resume their journey from the command to the market economy. For so long as the losses had to be funded by the banking system, the banks had to remain under the control of the central, provincial and local authorities. So long as there was no limit on the responsibility of the banking system to fund these losses, the central government was forced to curb the issue of new shares in order to force household savings into the banks. So long as the supply of shares and other financial instruments remained restricted, the stock market remained stunted and highly speculative. And so long as there was any likelihood that the managers of SOEs might use the much greater autonomy they had acquired in 1994 to lay off workers, reduce social security commitments, and stop paying pensions to retired workers, any government in Beijing or the provinces would find it extremely difficult to actually let them exercise their nominal autonomy.

UNEMPLOYMENT –
THE ENDURING CORE OF THE PROBLEM

The only way to cut the Gordian knot was to close down loss-making state enterprises. But that involved throwing workers out of work. This was something that the leaders in Beijing shied away from doing in the uneasy interregnum as people waited for Deng to pass away. For even the electrifying growth that China had experienced during the previous 18 years (1978–95) had not succeeded fully in containing the pressures in the labour market. Although the proportion of the work force made up of rural (i.e. non-urban) labourers had declined from 76.3 per cent in 1978 to 72.2 per cent in 1995, the absolute number had gone up from 306.4 million to 450.4 million, a staggering increase of 144 million. Around 100 million of these had been absorbed into the TVEs, but there were at least 44 million more people living off the land than in 1978. What is worse, the land under cultivation had declined by 4 per cent between 1978 and 1985. It recovered to its 1978 level in 1991[33] but thanks to the rise in rural population by 1995 the per capita availability of cultivated land had fallen by a quarter, from 1.6 Mu per person to 1.2 Mu.[34] As a result in 1995 there were no fewer than 80 million temporary and permanent migrants from the rural to urban areas, of whom 44 million were estimated to be long term or semi-permanent migrants.[35] These 44 million had to be absorbed by industry and the tertiary sector.

To make matters worse, agriculture was not the only area in which unemployment, or more strictly speaking, underemployment, was increasing. Over the previous 17 years, despite the deterioration in their performance, the SOEs had increased the number of workers on their payrolls by 38 million, from 74.5 million in 1978 to 112.6 million in 1995. Thus in addition to the 20 million persons who would enter the labour market every year for the next two decades, China needed to find permanent employment for another 82 million urban dwellers who were underemployed. In addition there were 5.2 million who were officially recognised as being unemployed in 1995 in the urban areas alone. By 1997 this figure had risen to 5.7 million.[36]

On the surface even the 1997 figure did not seem unduly alarming for it was only a little higher than the figure of 5.42 million for 1980; that is, before the reforms began. But it did not tell the entire story. Between 1992 and 1997, an altogether new category of workers had come into being. 'Urban private labour', which had accounted for only 0.98 million workers 1992 and 3.32 million workers in 1994, rose to 26.7 million in 1997. During the same period, employment in what might be termed the organised sector (i.e. SOEs, urban collectives and 'other units') fell by 5 million. These workers became part of the 'urban private labour force' of workers who had no fixed income or employment. This massive casualisation of labour in a newly formed urban informal sector makes comparisons of unemployment between different dates difficult, for it forces one to compare outright unemployment on one date with a mix of unemployment and underemployment on the other. However, if, as seems likely, the retrenched 5 million merely increased an already rapidly growing pool of underemployed labour, it would be safe to say that, in terms comparable to 1992, urban unemployment grew by 5 million more than the statistics indicate.

In 1997, therefore, Chinese urban areas in particular had become a tinder box. Even if only a quarter of the SOEs had to be closed down and other enterprises allowed to shed their surplus staff in an effort to restructure their enterprises and remain solvent, up to 30 million employees of the SOEs, and not just the 15 million officially deemed redundant in 1993, would find themselves out of work in a very short time. These would not be the indigent, politically powerless migrants from the backward areas of the country but the cream of the communist working class. Hundreds of thousands of trade unionists and Communist Party members would find themselves among the victims of the 'socialist market economy'. Laying off several million workers of the state-owned enterprises was therefore simply not a feasible option. The vacuum in leadership made it doubly so.

IS THERE A QUICK FIX?

In the mid-1990s as inflation raged, the losses of the SOEs mounted and Deng Xiaoping's health deteriorated, Beijing was bombarded with suggestions from international organisations and Western think-tanks on how to cut the Gordian knot and disembarrass the banking system of the accumulated bad debts of the SOEs. Most of them urged China to press ahead with the transition to a market economy even faster than before, especially in the reform of banking; bring accounting practices and corporate law in line with international practice; modernise the taxation system; and withdraw subsidies to the SOEs and their workers. The main hurdle was the accumulated debt of the SOEs. Without transferring these or writing them off in some way even the enterprises that stood some chance of becoming viable were likely to perish. One way of doing this was for the state to take over the SOEs' debt and warn them that if they did not break even in the future they would be shut down.[37]

The suggestion seemed to make good sense and the government of

Zhu Rongji made a start in implementing it in 1998. But all it actually amounted to was a transfer of debt servicing from the SOEs' account to that of the government. Unless there was a simultaneous increase in tax or non-tax revenues the true fiscal deficit would remain the same. And unless the transfer was accompanied by, or somehow made possible, an improvement in the profitability of the SOEs, the annual losses of the SOEs would not decline and a new mountain of debt would soon accumulate. There was no certainty that this would happen, for the proposal treated only the symptoms of the disease without tackling the cause. The cause was the failing profitability of the SOEs caused by the slowdown of real growth; the inability of the plant directors to take investment and other managerial decisions on their own; and the unrestricted growth of the urban and rural collectives and the foreign and joint ventures which had snatched consumer goods and other bread-and-butter lines of production from the SOEs and pushed them deeper and deeper into the more difficult areas of technology and marketing.

The vast differential in the burden of taxation between the SOEs and the newer types of enterprises compounded the disadvantage of having to meet large social overheads that the former laboured under and made it especially easy to undercut them in the market. Even after the reforms of 1994, the SOEs continued to pay approximately twice as much tax as the foreign and joint ventures and the TVEs paid no direct taxes at all. These inequalities became accentuated when, behind the frenzied rhetoric of growth and the veil of cooked up statistics, China's growth slowed down in the 1990s. That accounted for the anomaly of a higher rate of growth between 1992 and 1996 going hand in hand with a rapid increase in both the number of loss-making enterprises and the size of their losses. Thus the capitalisation of SOE debt had to go hand in hand with the completion of structural reforms in the SOEs, and the creation of a level playing field between the SOEs and the TVEs and foreign and joint ventures. In terms of the model presented in the Introduction (Table 1.1), China needed the reforms listed in column 3 to even give the SOEs a chance to survive in a market economy. This could not be done overnight. There are thus no quick fixes to the problem of the ailing state enterprises.

INEQUALITY, INSECURITY AND UNEMPLOYMENT – THE DARK FACE OF MARKET REFORMS

Since the middle and late 1990s, reform has become progressively more difficult because, for the ordinary Chinese, the market economy has lost much of its gloss. The belief that switching from a planned to a market economy would leave everyone better off has gradually given way to the realisation that the market creates not only winners but also losers. In the early days of the reforms, nearly everyone benefited from the relaxation of planning and controls. Even the migrant workers, who left their assigned places and struck out on their own, found themselves better off than before. Although they lost some of the benefits conferred on them by the socialist system, notably subsidised food and health benefits, they earned much more than they would have had they stayed in their villages and townships. Better still, for the first time, they felt themselves to be the masters of their destiny. The rags-to-riches stories they heard in the new coastal growth centres became the stuff of their dreams. Not everyone made the transition from socialist dependence to capitalist independence successfully even then, but initially there were relatively few losers and there was a robust belief that these too would soon get swept up by the gale force winds of economic growth.

But by1997 that confidence had been eroded by slowing growth and high inflation. There was a growing awareness among workers that their bargaining power was declining. This created a rising wave of anxiety and what some commentators called a 'job security panic'.[38]

Their declining bargaining power gave birth to a new type of exploitation, dubbed 'sweatshop capitalism'. Sweatshop conditions were originally restricted to some foreign and joint ventures, especially those located in the special economic zones, but soon spread to the Chinese SOEs as they struggled to survive. In the former a kind of Wild West *laissez-faire* prevailed. There were no rules except those that the employers dreamt up; no minimum wages, no right of collective bargaining, and no social security except that which the more enlightened employers provided to their workers. Workers did as a rule earn more than their counterparts in the SOEs, but were totally at the mercy of their employers. Thus their work conditions, and even their take-home pay, depended on the kind of industry they were in and the nature of their employers. The worst off were migrant women workers who had made it into zones such as Shenzen and Zuhai, and worked in the most labour intensive and price sensitive industries such as garments, footwear and toys. They were often subjected to arbitrary and even whimsical punishments, such as being locked up in the factory, or losing a part of their pay for small infractions of discipline, often for breaking laws they did not even know existed.[39]

By 1996 such practices had spread to the SOEs. Sociologists Zhao Minghua and Theo Nichols described in detail the crushing daily routine of 20,000 workers in three textile mills in Henan province, most of whom were women. 'Their situation resembles the plight of most of the workers in the foreign-funded sector: exhausting work hours, no overtime pay, complex work rules, fines for breaking them, ever increasing quotas, draconian sick leave policies, and so on, all under the guise of "scientific management".' Zhao Minghua found that following Deng's tour of the south in 1993, textile factories had reverted from the four-shift system that had been introduced in 1981 to a three-shift system. 'Scientific management' (such as that introduced in the Tianjin factory described above)[40] had led to a preoccupation with productivity and quotas. But superimposed on the top-down communist system this had meant that quotas were jacked up at each level as they permeated downwards, until the entire burden of the managers' ambitions fell upon the shoulders of the bottom rung – the workers on the shopfloor. Even wage malpractice has permeated parts of the state sector. Zhao found that the practice of shrouding pay scales in secrecy, once the preserve of the Asian foreign joint ventures in China, had percolated not only into the SOEs, but the township and village enterprises as well. In this system wages could be, and were, withheld for almost any reason (such as missing a political meeting) on a points system. Accumulate enough points and at the end of the month your 'net' wage could be zero.[41]

As the SOEs found themselves in more dire straits, the system of 'collective capitalism' described in the previous chapter began to break down. In the name of 'scientific management', one after the other the SOEs began to cut back the support systems they had created for their workers. In addition to the 15 to 20 million workers who have lost their jobs or who are on token pay, another 30 million pensioners of these enterprises are in dire straits.[42] The vast majority of enterprises have relinquished responsibility for paying pensions to their retired workers to the provincial authorities, and pay their contributions into a system of pooled pension funds. Since this has broken the direct contact that existed between the retired workers and the enterprise, they are no longer able to safeguard their interests. As a result, the pension contributions are no longer keeping pace with the rise in the cost of living. Since the latter too is underestimated, the real level of pensions also fell sharply in the years after 1992. This fall was only arrested when China was hit by deflation in 1997.

Outright unemployment has appeared in the cities, as has a vagrant population in constant, and often unsuccessful, search for work. In 1996, 5 million people were officially admitted to be unemployed – 3 per cent of the urban workforce. Those who fail to find permanent or semi-permanent employment usually return to their villages. But some stay on and become beggars, or turn to crime. Crime is still very much in its infancy when compared to the major cities of the West, or Latin America. But there are disturbing signs that it is growing rapidly. In

1993, only a few of the more luxurious taxis in Guangzhou had steel partitions between the driver and the passengers, of the kind to be found in the USA. Enquiries revealed that violent crimes against taxi drivers, then among the highest earners in China, had grown to the point where many taxis simply would not take passengers to the suburbs after dark. By 1995, all of even the 10-yuan 'people's taxis' in Beijing had steel partitions.

There has also been a rapid increase in income differentials between the rich and the poor in the cities, between town and country, and between the dynamic coastal provinces overall and the backward north-western ones. In the pre-reform days, all these differences existed but were relatively small.[43] For instance, the director of a state-owned enterprise earned about four times as much as the lowest paid of its workers.[44] Today, directors can legally earn up to 300 times as much as the poorest paid workers.[45] In addition there are innumerable opportunities for insider trading in scarce commodities, of the kind described earlier, and for corruption.[46] As the market system matures, the saving from these vast incomes is congealing into wealth and property. A propertied class has thus come into being. The proliferation of individually owned and private businesses reflects the attempt to reinvest some of this wealth to ensure its future growth.

The urban–rural income gap has also grown at an unhealthy pace. A World Bank study showed that in 36 countries for which sufficient data was available, the ratio of urban to rural incomes tended to be 1.5, and was rarely above 2. In China, in 1995, it had climbed to 4.[47]

Between 1978 and 1985, farmers too went through a honeymoon with reform. Increases in the prices of agricultural produce, reductions in the price of inputs and, after 1981, the introduction of the contract system which privatised agriculture, led to a sharp increase not only in rural output but rural incomes. This narrowed the urban–rural income gap. However, after 1985, agricultural incomes tended to stagnate once more as prices of agricultural produce rose far less than those of industrial products. To make matters worse, in the early 1990s, because of a shortage of money caused in part by the diversion of working capital loans into speculative purchases of real assets, many state enterprises began paying farmers in IOUs instead of cash. In the beginning of June 1993, as prices skyrocketed, the farmers in one of the interior provinces rioted against the practice and insisted on being paid in cash. This, and other signs of growing desperation in the rural areas, sparked the second round of agricultural reforms, with sharply higher agricultural prices and payment to farmers in cash. But much of the improvement in farm incomes was neutralised by a sharp increase in fertiliser prices the next year after the yuan was devalued. As a result in the advanced coastal areas, which are also the richest agricultural areas, more and more peasants are leaving the land and are coming into the towns in search of work. In 1995, scholars at the Institute of Economics of the Chinese Academy of Social Sciences estimated that between 6 and 7 million workers were leaving the farms and flooding into the towns every year in search of work.[48]

What the data on income inequality does not capture is the change in the quality of incomes being earned, and the profound changes in social status that it is bringing in its wake. The losers from the change are those who until recently enjoyed the highest status in Chinese society. These are professors, researchers, and most members of the Communist Party and the bureaucracy, who have not indulged in corruption or insider trading in commodities. What is worse, in a society where status is measured more and more by wealth their social status is on the decline.

Inflation has borne down cruelly on the intelligentsia, the bureaucracy and many professional cadres. The self-employed in the tertiary sector, and to a lesser extent workers in the urban collectives and SOEs, are able to offset this with increases in earnings. Plant directors and provincial bureaucrats, who have access to inside information or are not averse to corruption, are doing even better. Many have amassed large amounts of wealth. But the vast majority of the urban salaried class are finding their real incomes declining year by year. In fact had they not received a good part of their income in kind – subsidised canteen food, housing, health, and education for their children – many would have been driven to destitution long ago. Despite the subsidies and periodic but inadequate increases in salaries, these civil servants, teachers and others live increasingly anxious lives. In a desperate attempt to keep their real incomes from falling they have formed collectives too. Thus members of the All China Journalists Association take foreign journalists around, act as their guides and interpreters and provide a variety of services for sums varying from $40 to $250 a day depending on what the journalists need. The staffs of schools and colleges have formed collectives and lease out the school grounds to those who want to set up shops and factories. The foreign relations departments of the provincial governments have followed in the footsteps of the ACJA.

There is hardly a way of supplementing one's salary that salary earners have not thought of. For instance, one of the perquisites the Chinese government offers to those who return after getting a degree abroad is permission to import a car or to buy one in China free of the heavy internal taxes the government levies on them. Needless to say, no one whose basic pay was Y300 a month in 1993 could think of paying even the insurance on a car, let alone its duty free purchase price. So taxi companies, which have sprung up by the dozen in the large cities, offer them 'loans' to purchase their cars, 'lease' it from him or her, and use the profit made on the taxi to 'repay' the loan it had given to the importer, and give the importer a small income supplement. Everyone gains. The taxi company gets a car at almost half the market price and the 'importer' doubles his income.

This is not only generating social tensions, but causing a drift of the most intelligent and talented young people away from socially more important activities into less important ones. 'Under communism, we built a huge reservoir of talent in science and the humanities. Our best young students wanted to be researchers, scholars and teachers. Today they want to go into the services sector and make money', lamented Dong Fureng[49] in 1993. By 1995, after two more years of high inflation, much of China's intellectual elite had joined the ranks of the new urban poor.

10

China's Undeclared Recession

Deng Xiaoping died in February 1997 after a lingering illness. A year later Li Peng, the conservative prime minister, also completed his tenure and stepped down. He was succeeded by Zhu Rongji, a former mayor and party boss of Shanghai. The new leadership was every bit as committed to reform as Deng had been. Both Jiang Zemin and Zhu Rongji were former mayors of Shanghai. While Shenzen and Zhuhai may have been the first manifestations of China's economic transformation, Shanghai, with its cosmopolitan past and strong mercantile tradition, had always been its nerve centre. It was to Shanghai that Deng had retreated when the conservatives seized hold of economic policy in Beijing after the Tiananmen shooting. With Jiang Zemin as president, and Zhu Rongji as premier, the period of marking time came to an end and China embarked on the second phase of its economic reforms.

At the Fifteenth Party Congress in September 1997, Jiang Zemin unveiled an ambitious blueprint for continued economic reform. By then everyone both inside and outside China knew that the country would not be able to sustain its rapid growth and its transition to a market economy without resolving the problem of the ailing public enterprises. The only question was who would bell the cat? At the Party Congress Jiang Xemin announced that the reform of the medium sized and large enterprises would be accelerated. This would involve laying off a very large number of workers,[1] selling off small enterprises or merging them with larger ones or leasing them to workers and managers.[2] Where these solutions were not available Jiang said that the enterprises would be allowed to declare themselves bankrupt. A short while later, the government announced that it would extend these remedies to more than 10,000 out of 13,000 medium and large scale enterprises.[3] Six months after Jiang's commitment, at the Ninth Peoples' Congress in March 1998, Zhu Rongji announced that China would solve the problem of the money-losing public enterprises and the weak banks within three years. He too committed himself to large scale lay-offs.

But 18 months after Jiang made his commitment and a year after Zhu reiterated it, the government had made very little progress in divesting itself of loss-making enterprises, laying off workers or reducing the losses of the state-owned enterprises. On the contrary, it had been compelled to go back on this commitment over and over again.

The reason was the sharp increase in the losses of the SOEs in 1998. This compelled the government to reinstitute subsidies to reverse losses in China's key industries. Heading the list was the textiles industry where the government, instead of letting the market decide which mills would survive, offered a subsidy of $650,000 for every 10,000 spindles that the enterprises took out of production. In 1997 it also converted $1.2 billion of the debt of 555 enterprises into equity. In 1998 the government estimated that it would convert twice that amount.[4] Zhu also had to go back on his promise to start reducing the number of loss-making enterprises through restructuring, lay-offs and bankruptcy. Instead in 1998 he ordered the banks to lend more to the loss-making SOEs to keep them afloat.[5]

The reason why he was forced to backpedal on his reforms was that even as he and Jiang Zemin made their promises, the economy began moving inexorably towards a crisis. At first sight this might appear a surprising observation, given China's high apparent growth rate, its bounding exports and its rising trade surplus. The 12.7 per cent average growth rate of 1992 to 1995 may have been partly a statistical illusion caused by the difficulties the China Statistical Bureau (CSB) faced in deflating current price GDP figures for inflation. But inflation came under control in 1996 and almost disappeared in 1997 and 1998. This brought the official growth rate down but it still remained one of the highest in the world. In 1996 it was 9.5 per cent; in 1997 it was just under 9 per cent, and in 1998 it was 7.8 per cent. In 1999 China recorded 8.3 per cent growth in the first quarter[6] but ended the year with growth of 7.1 per cent.

China's trade surplus also touched an all time high of $43.25 billion in 1998[7] and foreign direct investment remained firm at $41.07 billion in the first 11 months of 1998 against $45 billion in 1997.[8] China's foreign exchange reserves topped $139 billion, second only to Japan's. But these glowing figures did not prevent Jiang Zemin from remarking that the country faced an economic slowdown,[9] and Zhu from telling the Tenth Peoples' Congress that China faced a grim environment at home and abroad.[10]

THE DISAPPEARANCE OF DEMAND

A closer look at trends within the economy shows that there was little to sustain the claim of a 7.8 per cent growth rate in 1998. Electricity consumption showed almost no change from the previous year. This suggests that manufacturing output, at the very least, was virtually static. Exports declined marginally by 0.5 per cent, against a 20 per cent rise in 1997 – an abrupt reversal of trend that could not fail to have an accelerator effect to depress output. And foreign direct investment was static. Which sector then, experts on the Chinese economy in Beijing wondered, was responsible for this still quite spectacular growth?[11]

Zhu's remark at the Tenth Peoples' Congress was a tacit admission that 7.8 per cent growth in China is not 7.8 per cent growth in a market economy. This became apparent when one looked at the state of demand and supply in various sectors of the economy. The most obvious feature of the Chinese economy in 1998–99 was a slowdown of consumer demand. The evidence for this was both direct and indirect. The direct evidence came from a sharp drop in the sales of consumer goods across the board. Sales of automobiles grew by 4 per cent in January to September 1998 against 26 per cent in the same period of 1997.[12] China's Industry Consultation and Development Corporation estimated that, in 1999, the demand for passenger vehicles would rise by 3.9 per cent and for commercial vehicles by 1.5 per cent. This would give an overall growth in demand of about 2.5 per cent.[13]

Air traffic grew by 30 per cent a year in 1994 and 1995. Then growth slumped to 12 per cent in 1996, 7.5 per cent in 1997 and 6.3 per cent in 1998.[14] This forced the government to ask Boeing and Airbus to postpone the delivery of 43 aircraft that were scheduled for 1999. Declining demand was only one half of the government's reason for asking for the postponement. The other was a growing profit crunch in the buying airlines. This made the government decide to postpone the purchase of the new aircraft (since cancelling the orders was too expensive) until the airlines had sold or leased out 40 of their existing aircraft.[15]

The sales of trucks fell by 2.2 per cent in January to September 1998, and that of motorcycles by 22.4 per cent.[16] The sales of other consumer durables also flattened out or declined, and producers and wholesalers were left with huge stocks of unsold goods.[17] This led to price deflation for the first time in China's post-reform history. To clear their stocks, manufacturers, wholesalers and retailers resorted to price cutting. So widespread was this trend that in October 1998, the retail price index fell for the first time ever, by 0.4 per cent. The decline accelerated in November and by the end of that month, retail prices had fallen by 2.5 per cent.[18] In the first five months of 1999 retail prices of consumer goods were 3.2 per cent below the same period of 1998.[19]

Indirect evidence of the slowdown came from more and more anxious appeals by the government to the Chinese people to spend more. One favoured explanation of the slowdown was that the government's attempt to 'smash the iron rice bowl' had created a hitherto unknown insecurity in Chinese workers, especially after 1997. They had responded by saving more than they did before out of their salaries.[20] In an effort to spur consumer spending, the government cut interest rates seven times between May 1996 and May 1999, from 9 per cent to below 4 per cent.[21] Four of these cuts took place in 1998 with the specific aim of stimulating consumption. The government also reduced the down payment required for the purchase of automobiles and houses to 20 per cent of the sale price.[22] But despite these incentives to spend, the savings rate rose in 1998 too.[23]

The worst hit was the real estate sector. In 1998 Shanghai – where visitors were routinely greeted with the boast that the city had more construction cranes at work than anywhere in the world, where 1,000 skyscrapers had been built since 1990, and 500 more were scheduled to be completed by 2008 – was in the middle of a property collapse. Seventy per cent of the new housing constructed in 1997 had failed to find buyers. In the Pudong commercial area, created in eastern Shanghai specifically as a magnet for foreign investment, 70 per cent of the 13.5 million sq.m. of office space created in the 1990s lay vacant. Not surprisingly, by 1999, rents for office space had fallen by 50 per cent in Shanghai and 40 per cent in Pudong, and were expected to go down by another 20 per cent during the year.[24] Office rents had also fallen by 40 to 50 per cent in Beijing and other cities.

There was a huge mismatch between the housing that was being created and the housing that was needed. In all, 7 million of the 9 million sq.m. of unsold property created in 1997 was residential[25] while the millions of migrant workers who had found jobs in Shanghai had nowhere to stay. Other cities in China were not much better off. After Shanghai, Shenzen and Beijing had the highest concentrations of unsold real estate.[26] In all, according to an estimate by independent economists in March 1998, China had over 70 million sq.m. of vacant housing.[27]

The economic slowdown was also reflected in low or declining capacity utilisation in industry and mounting losses for the state-owned enterprises. Some of the worse hit industries were automobiles and home appliances. But excess capacity was also evident in the beer industry, in machine tools, chemicals and chemical fibres. According to an industrial census in 1995, a year in which China was supposedly enjoying a 10.5 per cent rate of growth, capacity utilisation was below 60 per cent in more than 900 industrial products.[28] And as for the losses of the SOEs, the rate at which bad debts were accumulating had gone up from Y50 to Y60 billion in 1995, to over Y200 billion ($24 billion) in 1998.[29]

The slowdown was hurting not only Chinese enterprises, but had caught many foreign investors flat-footed too. One of the worst affected was General Motors. Undeterred by the poor performance of its sports utility venture in north-eastern China, GM decided to invest $1.57

billion – the largest single investment by a foreign company – in the manufacture of Buick sedans for the luxury market. GM was targeting a very narrow segment of the market, for even with an initial subsidy of Y70,000, the Buick was to roll out at Y300,000 to Y400,000, or twice the price of its main competitor, the Volkswagen Santana. GM's target buyers were the very rich, and senior government officials, who had shown a penchant for luxury cars. But even before the first car rolled out it had become apparent to GM that it would not be able to sell even a fraction of the 15,000 cars it had targeted for the first year. One reason was that the government, which was finding itself in a financial crunch, had strictly limited the levels of officialdom that could buy such an expensive car.[30]

General Motors' experience is one of the more flagrant examples of miscalculation, based on an uncritical acceptance of the growth figures for China put out by the CSB and legitimised by the World Bank. The contract for its Buick plant was signed in the presence of US vice-president Al Gore in 1997. At that time GM was boasting that in 20 years it would be selling more cars in China than in the US. It had announced that in its first five years alone, it would export $1.6 billion of auto parts to its Buick plant from the US. But barely a year and a half later it had already come to the conclusion that it would have to produce a cheaper car.[31]

One does not need to look far to see where GM went wrong. It had simply assumed that China's car market would continue to grow indefinitely at the rate it had recorded in the first half of the 1990s. Even as late as December 1998 this faith still ran strong. As a result, despite the fact that its north-eastern China plant had sold almost no vehicles in the previous two years, GM was doubling its investment in the plant to $230 million. GM's problems are far from atypical. A study of 70 foreign enterprises in China by A.T. Kearney in the early part of 1999 showed that only 40 per cent of them were making profits. Many of the remainder were thinking of pulling out of China.[32]

There are both supply side and demand side explanations for the pervasive excess capacity in Chinese industry. The supply side explanation is that investors – city and provincial governments and SOEs – were carried away by the cheapness of credit and their own lack of experience of markets and went on an investment spree. Competition between these non-market oriented entities, whose managers had not yet forgotten the security and predictability of the command economy, ensured that huge amounts of excess capacity would get created in plants that were too small to be efficient. The truth in this explanation is undeniable, but it is not complete, for it does not explain why foreign investors such as General Motors were also caught flat-footed. The other part of the explanation is that there had been a slowdown in the growth of demand that no one foresaw.

Three reasons have been given for the slowdown in the growth of consumer demand. The first was the Asian economic crisis and the recession in Japan, which put a brake on the growth of exports.[33] The second was a slower growth of income as the growth of employment had slowed down, and an increase in the propensity to save, which had been the Chinese response to growing uncertainty. The third was the saturation of the Chinese market. It was argued that once consumers had acquired all the high-status consumer durables they wanted – the TV, the stereo system, the washing machine, and so on – demand fell to the 'replacement level', which was a great deal lower than the 'acquisition level'.

There is a large element of truth in all three explanations. Export growth fell dramatically from 20 per cent per annum in earlier years to nearly zero in 1998. The government's decision to relieve SOEs of their social overheads, especially health, and to privatise housing forced Chinese workers to start saving towards the purchase of what they had previously taken for granted. Inevitably expenditure on other products came down. The growing insecurity of their jobs, as industry after industry began to be restructured and workers laid off, also increased their propensity to save.

But there is another reason for the extraordinary buoyancy of consumer demand in the early years of liberalisation and the consequent over-investment in almost all consumer goods industries. This relates to the form of China's transition from plan to market in the 1980s and early 1990s. The extraordinarily high initial levels of consumer demand did not only reflect current disposable income but also an accumulation of past savings. As in Russia and the East European socialist economies, during the days of central planning workers were paid salaries that they were unable to spend because of the lack of consumer goods in the shops. Thus at the beginning of the transition from plan to market, there was a large amount of accumulated saving and a pent-up demand for consumer goods in all these countries. In Russia, which went in for shock therapy, the government decided to mop up this saving by removing price controls. The inflation that followed in 1992 and 1993 made these savings vanish in smoke. Not content with that the government also demonetised the currency, causing most of what little had remained to vanish also. By the end of 1993 all Russians, except for the 'new Russians' and the Mafiya, were poor. The pent-up demand for consumer goods had not the slightest impact on production, which fell to half of its pre-'reform' level in just four years.

China had avoided this catastrophe. It had retained price and distribution controls on all essentials; it kept the state-owned enterprises, and assured its workers of employment and basic necessities. At the same time, it allowed foreign and joint ventures and encouraged the establishment of TVEs, and dramatically increased the supply of consumer goods. In effect, therefore, it mopped up the hangover of pent-up demand[34] by increasing output instead of raising prices. And just as the first inflationary shock in Russia started a spiral of rising prices that the government could not control, in China the first demand shock set off a spiral of growing output and income that gave it one of the longest surges in prosperity the world has known. China also benefited from another form of pent-up demand. This was the release of price controls on the output of the SOEs. The rise in corporate revenues that followed led directly to increases in money incomes for their workers. Both individual and corporate purchases rose sharply.

To the investor, whether in a county or urban collective, or in a special economic zone, demand must have seemed insatiable for one had only to produce in order to sell. In that first phase of reform everyone prospered, even the SOEs, for following Say's law the increase in supply created its own demand. This reinforced and prolonged the sellers' market and, consequently, the surge in output. The gradual removal of price controls and increase in the SOEs' share of retained earnings described in Chapter 8 above also increased workers' nominal and real incomes and gave demand another lease on life. But ultimately what Chinese growth was feeding upon was a stock of demand fed from a pool of past savings. Indirect evidence comes from the fact that by 1991, just six short years after the beginning of industrial and tertiary sector liberalisation, 68 out of every 100 urban families had colour TV sets, 49 had refrigerators and 80 had washing machines.[35] This, rather than any cultural difference, is the most probable explanation for why the Chinese, with 1.8 times the per capita income of Indians, bought 40 times as many washing machines in 1996.[36]

Sooner or later that pool had to run dry. This probably happened in the early 1990s, and was accelerated by the Great Inflation of 1993–96. By then the Chinese economy had entered the last, or 'bubble' phase of economic expansion in which the prices of non-traded goods rise more than traded goods, pulling money into non-tradables such as real estate. In Shanghai, fully half the foreign direct investment that came in after 1992 went into real estate.[37] Much of this was money invested by 'red chip' subsidiaries of Chinese companies and provincial and city corporations. The same thing was happening in other cities.[38]

The emergence and growth of a huge real estate bubble could be a part of the explanation for the somewhat anomalous coexistence of high rates of inflation, rising foreign direct investment, and an apparent high rate of GDP growth from 1993 to 1995, with a declining growth of energy consumption and industrial employment, and low capacity utilisation across the entire spectrum of industry.

Massive investments in construction could push up GDP growth without a corresponding increase in energy consumption because construction requires very little energy, in comparison with even agriculture, let alone industry. What is more, when companies, not individuals, account for a large share of consumption, and a part of demand is still being financed from a pool of past savings, a high rate of inflation in non-tradables such as real estate would divert some of these savings from other consumer durables into the purchase of real estate. This would explain the coexistence of a boom in real estate with a simultaneous slowdown in the growth of demand for other consumer durables and a slowdown in employment growth.

DEEPENING RECESSION

Throughout the slowdown the Chinese government, most Chinese economists and foreign analysts clung to the explanation that it was being caused by the Asian economic crisis. But, as has been explained above, the slowdown began well before the Asian crisis in the mid-1990s. This perception was reflected in an editorial article published by the Beijing-based *Economic Times* in November 1997. The paper identified six issues on which future growth would hinge, and frankly conceded that only one of these – the country's large trade surplus and consequently the tendency of the yuan to appreciate – was related to the Asian crisis, as it would affect the competitiveness of China's exports. The other five issues were all structural. The paper noted especially the rapid increase in numbers of redundant workers, and the fact that throughout 1997 investment in fixed assets had shown a declining trend.[39]

A year later, as the recession continued to deepen, such structural explanations became more common. In an article in the *China Daily* Yang Qixian, vice-president of the Chinese Society for Research on the Restructuring of the Economic System, conceded that 'According to some peoples' comparison, China's economic situation in recent years shares some similarities with that of Japan in the 1990s. The root cause of the two countries' problems, they believe, can both be ascribed to the *bubble economy*' (emphasis added).[40] In May 2000, the *China Daily* frankly admitted that half a trillion yuan – $60 billion – of capital goods were lying idle in various government-owned plants all over the country because of the investment spree that these enterprises had gone on in previous years. The *Daily* admitted that this had been made possible by the absence of adequate appraisal systems in banks that had remained too subservient to the demands of powerful provincial officials and party functionaries.[41]

As demand slackened, the sins of poor project appraisal and autarchic investment and lending decisions came home to roost. Within the country, since the government had decided that it could not afford to allow any of the SOEs to go under, the only clear indication of their worsening plight was the rise in their losses. As pointed out in the previous chapter, in 1998 the government poured more than Y200 billion into the SOEs to cover their losses, half of it as bank loans and half through bond issues.[42] This was four times the amount that the enterprises had been losing only three years earlier. However, while the government was prepared to pour billions of yuan into the loss-making SOEs it felt no such obligation to continue bailing out the newer enterprises that had been set up after the reforms began. The fate of these companies thus closely charts the drift towards crisis.

For foreign investors the first unsettling indication of the change in China's economic fortunes was the government's refusal to bail out the Guangdong International Trust and Industrial Corporation (GITIC) in October 1998 and to allow it to go into liquidation. GITIC had attracted $4.7 billion of foreign investment, which was put in jeopardy by the government's decision. Foreign investors got their second shock when the GITIC refused to put them at the head of the list for the repayment of debt when its assets were liquidated. Foreign bankers warned that this would make it difficult for them to extend any more lines of credit to Chinese firms 'as they couldn't explain it to their head offices'.[43] However, Beijing stuck to its resolve and eventually foreign investors in GITIC only recovered 16 per cent of their investment.[44]

Those who had not fully grasped the deterioration in the Chinese economy concluded that Beijing's decision not to bail out GITIC was a part of the Jiang–Zhu team's policy of exposing the economy progressively to the discipline of the market, and simultaneously warning foreign investors to exercise caution in lending to Chinese companies.[45] They therefore cautiously applauded the government's resolve. While this may have been one of the motives behind the decision, a more probable cause was the government's awareness that GITIC was only the first of a long list of state companies and corporations that were on the brink of insolvency. No one knew how many of the 240 ITICs

(International Trust and Investment Corporations) were in trouble, because no one, including their own managers, knew what their assets and liabilities were or indeed in how many companies they had invested. Consequently, no one knew the size of the commitment that the Chinese authorities would be making if they took the decision to bail out GITIC. This caution was soon vindicated. When GITIC went bankrupt, its officials acknowledged that the corporation owned 132 companies.[46] But upon a detailed examination of its records during the bankruptcy proceedings Chinese officials found that it owned 240 Chinese and foreign companies. When GITIC filed for bankruptcy it had assets worth $21.47 billion and liabilities amounting to $36.17 billion.[47]

Once it became clear that the central and provincial governments would not bail out the ITICs if they ran into trouble, a string of other defaults appeared over the horizon. Among the first were the so-called 'red chip' companies – subsidiaries incorporated by the ITICs in Hong Kong – which had incurred no less than $13 billion of foreign debt by the end of 1998.[48] In the beginning of 1999 one of the largest of these companies, Guangdong Investments, found itself unable to keep up payments on $1.2 billion worth of loans. Standard & Poor downgraded its credit rating to CCC minus, the third lowest rating the agency had given.[49] One by one, other red chip companies began to go under. The Guangdong Overseas Chinese Trust and Investment Company failed to make a $50 million payment and the Dalian ITIC did the same, within weeks of each other. Another red chip company, the Yi Fu Trading Company, went into liquidation in January. In the wake of the GITIC collapse, other provincial governments also began to warn companies that borrowed in dollars but lent money in yuan not to expect to be bailed out if they could not meet their payments.[50] The warning was not lost on foreign investors.

Red chip companies were not the only entities in trouble. In December 1998, Moody's downgraded the credit rating of the State Development Bank, the largest of the policy oriented banks set up by the government in 1993 to separate investment from commercial banking activity, from A3 to Baa1. This provoked a strong protest from the bank, which reminded Moody's that 'comprehensive government support in terms of capital, liquidity and various other areas have ensured the bank's healthy financial condition'.[51]

The fact that so many red chip companies, banks, ITICs and domestic companies set up by the provincial governments were facing difficulties in repaying their foreign loans at the same time had nothing to do with China's capacity to pay, for its reserves stood at $146 billion at the end of March 1999. It reflected Beijing's refusal to let them continue eating from the same foreign exchange pot. Their growing non-viability was a direct consequence of the slowdown of the economy and the deceleration in the growth of consumer demand. As the sales projections of the new companies remained unfulfilled, their losses mounted and they found it increasingly difficult to meet their overhead costs. The inability to meet their payments on foreign loans was therefore a byproduct of the more general failure.

Nowhere was the excess capacity more evident than in real estate. As the real estate bubble collapsed it threatened to make vast amounts of investment in other sectors go bad too. By the beginning of 1999 China was caught in the grip of a recessionary vice. Flattening demand had led to growing excess capacity; this had greatly increased the number of unviable companies and increased the number of defaults on loans. But the simultaneous collapse of the real estate bubble had made it less and less likely that the lenders would get their money back. Gradually foreign investors began to grow wary of investing in China. Early in 1998, Moody's investor services downgraded the outlook for nine Chinese banks from 'stable' to 'negative'.[52]

The growing non-viability of Chinese companies casts a different light on the Chinese government's decision not to devalue the yuan in the wake of the Asian crisis. In 1998 Beijing's decision had been welcomed by all major trading countries and by the international financial community as an extraordinary display of responsibility towards the international economic system. Most governments saw it as one more sign of China's self-confidence and attributed it to its growing economic strength. As a major trading nation China no doubt had little desire to take a decision that would further destabilise the crisis-ridden Asian countries and cause another decline of demand for its products. But Beijing also could not afford to devalue. For by then it had realised that most of its ITICs and companies set up by the provincial governments had been borrowing in dollars and lending in yuan. To make matters worse, as they experienced difficulties in meeting their debt servicing commitments, several of the ITICs had begun to take short term loans abroad to service their long term debt.[53] Beijing had no idea how much they had borrowed and what the composition of this debt was. All it knew was that if it devalued it would increase the debt servicing burden in yuan on scores, if not hundreds, of firms and ITICs and hasten their descent into bankruptcy. Since the yuan was not convertible on the capital account, Beijing was able to avoid the mistake that Indonesia and Thailand made. But what the world mistook for strength was in reality a sign of weakness.

By March 1999 nervousness about China's economy had spread

from the banks to Chinese exporters who began to delay the repatriation of their earnings. In order to make them bring their money back, and possibly also to prevent an outflow of investment from China's 'B' listed share market, the Bank of China (which handles most foreign exchange transactions) raised its dollar savings rate from 3.75 per cent to 4.66 per cent.[54]

The economic slowdown also increased the strain on government finances. When the China Construction Bank, following the advice of the central government, tried to set up an asset management company to sell off its non-performing loans at a discount, the Ministry of Finance made the bank put its scheme on hold. Its reason was that it feared that at even half their original value, these debts would find few buyers and the central government would be forced to buy up the rest of the debt.[55] In the same spirit of economy, the government asked Boeing and Airbus to delay the delivery of 43 new aircraft to various airlines until they had made arrangements to sell off, or lease out, 40 existing airliners.[56]

Premier Zhu Rongji made a tacit admission that China was heading for an economic crisis when he initiated a huge programme of deficit financing in 1998 worth over $12 billion (more than Y100 billion) to lift the economy. At the Tenth National Peoples' Congress he announced that infrastructure spending financed by deficit financing would be increased to $18.2 billion in 1999. He justified this by remarking that 'attaining 7 per cent growth will not be easy'.[57] The spurt in infrastructure spending did help to push up the rate of growth. By official estimates, in the first quarter of 1999 GDP grew by an estimated 8.3 per cent, and industrial output by 10.1 per cent. By one estimate a third, if not more, of this growth resulted from the pump priming undertaken by the government.[58] For in the first quarter exports fell by 7.9 per cent – the first significant decline after china's reforms – while imports grew by 11.6 per cent. Both were likely to depress domestic output. Foreign investment also fell by 14.6 per cent in the first quarter.[59] Most observers expected the decline to grow steeper as the year progressed. In March an official of the foreign trade ministry predicted that the decline could be as steep as 56 per cent in the full year – from $43 billion in 1998 to around $20 billion in 1999.[60] This forecast proved too pessimistic. Foreign investment in terms of actual inflows fell by only 11.4 per cent to $40.398 billion. But what was far more significant was the decline in new contracts for FDI. These were barely $840 million higher than the inflows.[61] In short, inflows amounted to 98 per cent of approvals. In the heyday of the foreign investment boom, in the mid-1990s, the ratio had been 25 to 35 per cent. Unless it is reversed, the low level of new commitments presages a sharp fall in foreign investment inflows after a few years.

UNEMPLOYMENT AND SOCIAL UNREST

The most disturbing consequence of China's slowing growth is a sharp rise in outright unemployment and in the number of migrant workers roaming the country in search of work. The second consequence, which might be a direct effect of the first, is a sharp rise in crime and civil disturbances. In 1995 there were an estimated 5 million persons who were overtly unemployed, and an estimated 80 million migrant workers. In the beginning of January 1999, the *China Daily* reported that during the year 16 million persons, or 11 per cent of the urban workforce, would not be able to find jobs. Another 120 million would travel to various parts of the country in search of work. The *China Daily* apprehended a sharp rise in crime as a consequence.[62] Many cities were taking what can only be described as emergency measures to slow down the inflow of migrants from the rural areas, and several were actively trying to force them back to their counties where they faced an uncertain future. In 1995, Shenzen took stern steps to check the inflow of legal migrants. Each provincial authority was allowed to set up an office in Shenzen and was told how many migrants Shenzen could absorb. Those who did not come through their provincial authority were sent back.[63] In April 1999, Beijing city authorities adopted a three-prong strategy to push its 3 million migrant workers out of the city. This consisted of destroying street vendors' stalls, pulling down add-on illegal housing built in the back streets, and putting tight restrictions on the kind of jobs that migrant workers could hold. The pretext was the need to clean up the city for its fiftieth anniversary, but the real goal was to create low-income jobs for its permanent residents, who also included 1.7 million legal migrants.[64]

The increasingly desperate plight of migrants is making them violent. On 1 October 1998 the *Hunan Economic Times* reported that jobless workers had blocked traffic in the city 60 times in the first ten months of 1998.[65] There were five bombing attempts in Chinese cities in the month of January 1999, one of which in Shenzen was foiled. The Shenzen attempt was probably the result of an inter-gang clash, and one in Guangzhou which involved an attack on a policeman was probably in reprisal against the execution of four villagers who had been owed money by a policeman's brother who preferred to kill rather than repay them. But at least two of the remaining three were a product of desperate protest and a botched-up crime brought on by destitution and the impotent rage of laid-off workers.[66]

As China's growth slowed down, there was a rise in crime. Growing

lawlessness in the cities is reflected in the growing security consciousness of the people. In 1993 only luxury taxis in Guangzhou had steel
partitions between the driver and the passengers. By 1995, even the
so-called peoples' taxis in Beijing had these partitions. In 1998 the
police seized 7 tonnes of narcotics. This was more than 19 times the
amount seized in 1997.[67] Smuggling too has reached epidemic proportions. Official estimates put the value of contraband smuggled into
China in 1998 at $30 billion, a little under a quarter of its legitimate
imports.[68]

Crime has not one but two faces. The second is the organised use of
official power by corrupt officials to extort money from the people. In
China complaints against such high-handedness are not new, but in the
middle and late 1990s it scaled new heights and began to pose a threat to
the stability of the regime. In Dalian township, more than a thousand
farmers rioted in the beginning of January 1999 against numerous
arbitrary taxes that were being imposed on them by local officials.
These included school fees, building fees, land use fees and a variety of
licensing fees. More than the fees the farmers were protesting against
the opacity of the levies made on them, the lack of accountability of the
local officials and the absence of any system of redress. In addition, they
were convinced that many of these levies were intended solely to
finance the lifestyles of the county and township officials.[69] The Dalian
riot was reported by the international press because, in the tear-gassing
that followed, one farmer was killed by an exploding tear gas shell and
several others were injured. But it was only one of hundreds of such
demonstrations that were taking place all over the country. At the
National Peoples' Congress in March 1999, Zhu Rongji candidly
admitted that social unrest was rising because of unemployment in the
urban areas and high-handedness and corruption in the rural areas.[70]
After the Dalian riot, president Jiang Zemin cautioned the people that
the country was facing an economic slowdown and stressed the need to
maintain law and order at any cost, a warning he was to repeat more
than once.[71] Anticipating a further increase in social unrest, the
government increased the size of the Peoples' Armed Police by another
100,000 in 1998, to an estimated 1 million. About 730,000 of these
police were primarily charged with maintaining public order.[72]

11

Reform in the Shadow of Recession

The rapid slowdown of the economy in 1998 not only forced the Chinese government to postpone its plans for structural reform: it cast doubt on the very premises of the economic strategy that the government had been following since 1994, and which Jiang Zemin and Zhu Rongji had decided to accelerate in 1997–98. This strategy was based on the assumption that the roadblocks to China's modernisation consisted essentially of the institutions, decision-making structures and laws that were leftover from the days of the command economy. Until as late as September 1997, the leadership believed that all it had to do was restructure the state-owned enterprises and grant them genuine autonomy in management to make them viable, or close them down. If making them profitable required laying off workers and reducing, or even eventually discontinuing, social security benefits, then so be it. The success of its efforts hinged on the continuation of rapid output and employment growth, for only that would enable the economy to absorb the workers who came off the SOEs' payrolls. Until well into 1998, most of China's leaders took this growth for granted. After two decades – in which the economic boom had generated 100 million jobs in the township and village enterprises, 17 million in the special economic zones and countless jobs in the services sector – it is difficult to see how they could have thought otherwise. They were therefore confident that the unemployment created by the drive to make the state sector viable would be transitory and not permanent and the political ripples it generated self-dissipating and not self-reinforcing. Now the economic growth that they had taken for granted and had come to rely upon was threatening to betray them.

The deepening economic slowdown forced China's leaders to make a painful reappraisal of their beliefs. For the slowdown did not originate in the old state-owned sector of the economy but in the new sectors that had come into being as a result of the shift from plan to market. Three facts immediately stood out:

- First, that reform of the SOEs, where most of the losses and redundant workers were concentrated, would become exceedingly difficult if the growth of GDP and therefore of employment were to slow down sharply.

- Second, that while for public consumption it was useful to blame the economic slowdown on the Asian crisis, there were long term, structural causes too that were entirely Chinese in origin. Indeed, there were several parallels between the Chinese experience and that of East and South East Asia. Both had experienced historically unprecedented spells of sustained, rapid growth. In both, this growth had bred complacency and complacency had fostered cronyism. And in both, the final stages of an economic boom had witnessed slowing domestic demand for commodities masked by a boom in real estate. As a result, China had seen the emergence of a real estate 'bubble' every bit as spectacular as those in Malaysia or Thailand.

- Third, China's leaders were aware that, as in the rest of crisis-ridden Asia, the way out of the mess was to complete the reforms they had initiated (to professionalise bank lending); to broaden the savings options before individuals by strengthening the share markets and diversifying financial instruments; to allow the market to impose its own discipline on those who did not read, or chose to ignore, its signals; and to complete the creation of a national labour market by cutting the ties that bound them to state-owned enterprises.

The government's economic policies have been shaped by these perceptions. From 1993, when the Third Plenum of the Fourteenth Central Committee articulated the goal of creating a socialist market economy, until the death of Deng Xiaoping, China's leaders were preoccupied with controlling inflation and content to mark time on structural reform. They therefore concentrated on strengthening the institutions and infrastructure needed for better macroeconomic control and on increasing the market orientation of the economy. The overall purpose was to reduce steadily the role of government in the economy and allow the market to impose its discipline on economic agents.

The central government passed legislation to increase the autonomy of the Peoples' Bank of China, drew up a blueprint for separating government administration from the management of the SOEs by 2000, and passed a new company law to lay the groundwork. It widened and deepened financial markets, introduced stable and transparent tax rates, improved the tax administration and replaced the earlier contract-based revenue sharing with a system that assigned certain taxes to the central government and others to the provinces and established a revenue sharing system for jointly collected taxes. It simplified the administration of the foreign exchange regime by unifying the exchange rate and moving closer to full current account convertibility of the yuan.[1]

It also began to cut back the subsidies it was giving to the SOEs and to encourage their workers to shift to contributory pension and health schemes. Subsidies were reduced from 6 per cent of GDP in 1990 to 4 per cent in 1994.[2] By the end of 1996, according to official statistics, 78 per cent of the workforce had joined pension plans administered by the cities and counties. Seven per cent had also joined state health insurance schemes.[3]

In 1997 it was already apparent that these reforms were being implemented too slowly to solve the central problem of the Chinese economy – that of the loss-making SOEs. In 1993, of an estimated 76 million workers in the SOEs an estimated 15 million were considered redundant. But with every passing year, as the losses of the SOEs mounted and the number that were insolvent grew, more and more of the enterprises became irredeemably sick. Redundancies also increased. The government itself estimated that moving the workers of these enterprises from factory-based unemployment benefit to the state system would take up to 15 years. But in addition the SOEs ran clinics, schools and crèches for their workers and their children. The schools alone accounted for 600,000 teachers and administrators and the clinics employed a third of the country's medical staff.[4] This was the background against which Jiang Zemin announced the government's intention to end the losses of the SOEs by restructuring the large enterprises, and selling off or closing the smaller ones, if necessary laying off large numbers of workers in the process. Six months later, in March 1998, Zhu Rongji unveiled a plan to complete this task in three years.

When China's growth slowed down in 1998, it forced the government to put these plans on hold and to give priority to fighting the deepening recession and preventing an explosion of unemployment. Reforms that involved laying off workers were put on the back burner and premier Zhu Rongji instructed the banks to keep lending money to the SOEs to keep them afloat.[5] This swallowed up a good part of the Y270 billion of refinancing that the government arranged by selling treasury bonds in 1997. In 1999, only months after allowing Guangdong International Trust and Industrial Corporation (GITIC) to declare itself bankrupt, and warning Chinese companies that borrowed in dollars to lend in yuan not to expect to be bailed out in the future, the government was also forced to go back, at least partially, on its resolve to let the market discipline erring Chinese companies and foreign investors. When Guangdong International (Holdings) a holding company set up by the Guangdong government, showed signs of going under and leaving foreign investors with $5.6 billion of investment high and dry, Beijing decided that the impact this would have on the already much alarmed foreign investors, and therefore on foreign investment, was one that China could not cope with. It therefore approved a bail-out plan that would involve selling off a highly profitable water company in Hong Kong that belonged to Guangdong Investments, and to use the money to reduce its debt. Banks and economic analysts based in Hong Kong welcomed the plan which was drawn up with the help of Goldman Sachs, as a sign that the Chinese government would not leave them unprotected, but gave the plan itself at most an outside chance of success.

The government realised, however, that reforms had to be continued despite the recession, for the recession itself was to a considerable extent caused by the incompleteness of reforms. The policies the government adopted therefore attempted to reflate the economy without halting the move from a planned to a market economy. These policies have met with some initial success, but it is far from certain that they will succeed in averting the economic crisis.

Faced with a slowing economy and growing excess capacity, the government adopted that now almost completely discredited Keynesian tool – pump priming through public investment. The route it took was to speed up the implementation of its $1.2 trillion infrastructure development plan. By late June 1999 the government had approved 72 large and medium sized projects involving an outlay of Y124.5 billion ($14 billion). Various state authorities had also approved and were preparing feasibility reports for another 308 project proposals with an investment of Y446.2 billion.[6] The government also released money to speed up the implementation of projects that were already under construction. In September 1998, it issued Y100 billion ($12 billion) of treasury bills to finance the completion of infrastructure projects. In March 1999 Zhu Rongji announced another sale of treasury bonds of $18.2 billion for the same purpose at the tenth meeting of the National Peoples' Congress.

The logic behind this bold decision was irrefutable. About the only time when pump priming, even through deficit financing, is not likely to spark inflation is when the economy is going into a deep slump and prices are falling. Falling prices, moreover, increase the fixed costs of production in relation to sales revenues, and squeeze profits or increase losses disproportionately. Thus at such times pump priming can stimulate economic recovery, and reduce losses or increase profits without incurring the penalty of inflation. In China the case for pump priming was especially strong. The bulk of the products needed by the infrastructure projects – steel, cement, transport and earth moving machinery, transport fuel and lubricants, and a range of chemicals – were produced mostly by the SOEs. These were precisely the enterprises that were incurring the heaviest losses and accounted for most of the bad loans of the banks. If they could not be closed down then it was far better for them to earn the money they needed than to be given it for doing nothing.

This policy yielded several immediate dividends. Investment in fixed assets rose by 22.7 per cent in the first quarter of 1999 over the same period of the previous year. The sharpest rise was in agriculture (122 per cent) followed by transport and telecommunications (46 per cent) and housing (35.5 per cent).[7] GDP growth touched 8.3 per cent according to official statistics in the first quarter of 1999. The driving force was industrial growth, which in value added terms grew by 10.1 per cent in the first quarter and 9.5 per cent in the first five months of the year. Within the industrial sector most of the growth occurred in the heavy industries. In January 1999, when industry recorded a momentary spurt in growth of 17.9 per cent over the same month of the previous year, the consumption of power went up by 10 per cent (against 1 per cent the previous year), the output of cement by 37.2 per cent and of heavy industries by 19.1 per cent.[8] In May 1999 it recorded a growth of 9.7 per cent, while light industry grew by 7.9 per cent.[9] The boost to infrastructure spending also seems to have brought down the losses of the SOEs. In January to April 1999, the profits of the profit-making enterprises went up by 130 per cent to Y30.3 billion while the losses incurred by the loss makers went down by 11.4 per cent.[10]

However, pump priming also has drawbacks, and by the end of 1999 these were becoming self-evident. Perhaps the most important is that it increases domestic demand, which depresses exports and increases imports, and turns the economy inwards. China proved no exception. Exports declined by 5.3 per cent in January to May 1999 while imports increased by 15.3 per cent. The trade surplus therefore narrowed sharply to $7.07 billion.[11] This was less than half the surplus recorded in the same period of the previous year. Reserves therefore grew by only $1 billion. In April the trade surplus shrank further. As a result the reserves increased by only $0.1 billion.[12] The composition of imports showed clearly that they had increased because of the spurt in infrastructure investment, for steel imports grew 38.5 per cent, while machinery and electronic products, and chemicals, increased by 27.7 per cent and 30.5 per cent respectively.[13] But the economic boom in the US and its record levels of imports enabled China to end the year with an export growth of 6.1 per cent. This partly offset an 18.2 per cent increase in imports.[14] Even so China's trade surplus shrank from $40.3 billion to $29.9 billion, and its reserves grew by $15 billion.[15] Had it not been for the spurt of exports to the USA, China might have ended the year with almost no increase in its foreign exchange reserves.

By mid-1999 there were also signs that even the enhanced infrastructure spending was only slowing down the decline of growth. In January to February, the rate of industrial growth was 10.1 per cent. In March it was 9.1 per cent. By May it had slid further to 8.9 per cent.[16] The government itself expected the decline to continue. In April, a spokesman for the state Development Planning Commission (SDC) forecast that growth would average 8 per cent in the first half of 1999 and fall in the second half as various infrastructure projects begun in 1998 were completed. The SDC's reason for caution was the lack of investment in the non-state sector. Against 22.7 per cent in the state sector, investment in the non-state sector grew by only 1.1 per cent in the first quarter of 1999.[17] The government's caution was vindicated. Throughout the year the rate of growth continued to decline. For 1999 as a whole the final tally, according to the China Statistical Bureau official figures, was 7.1 per cent.

The most that pump priming can do, therefore, is cushion the economy's slide into recession and buy the Chinese government some more time. Just how much time will depend upon its ability to keep its exports growing, and prevent a decline in its foreign exchange reserves. In 2000 the continuing US boom enabled China to do this, and therefore continue with its pump priming policies. This lifted its growth rate, according to official estimates, to 7.8 per cent. But a recession in the USA in 2001, a consequent slowdown in the recovery of the Asian economies, and continuing stagnation in Japan could wipe out its trade surplus and cause the first fall in its reserves. If Europe too goes into a recession, a devaluation will become virtually unavoidable. This will have serious repercussions on the viability of the various ITICs and holding companies that have borrowed heavily in the Hong Kong market.

STRUCTURAL REFORMS

The government also pushed ahead with various structural reforms. The industry that has borne the brunt of restructuring is textiles. In 1998 the government retired 5.12 million spindles and laid off 660,000 textile workers. In the first quarter of 1999 it dismantled 780,000 spindles and laid off another 100,000 workers. In all the government expected 2 million spindles to be taken out of production in the first half of 1999.[18] At the Tenth Peoples' Congress in March, Sheng Huaren, the chairman of the State Economic and Trade Commission told the delegates that the government was also in the process of closing down coal mines to reduce the excess of production. This also involved laying off large numbers of workers. The other industries that were being restructured were the petroleum, petrochemical and metallurgical industries.[19]

One of the more important mergers was of three steel plants in Hubei province. These were the Wuhan Iron and Steel complex, the Daye Iron and Steel Company, and the Hubei ISC.[20] Its purpose was not so much product consolidation, for the plants produced different steel products, as a desire to take advantage of the government loans for restructuring to modernise plant and technology and reduce costs. Thus shortly after the merger Wuhan announced that it was replacing its old, energy guzzling open hearth furnaces with modern rotary furnaces. This would cost the company Y650 million but lower the cost of producing steel by Y200 ($23) per tonne.[21]

As part of the restructuring programme the government is also encouraging foreign companies to invest in revamping state-owned enterprises. One of the first such experiments was the purchase of what used to be the Nanjing steel works by a Swiss firm, Glencore Asia Ltd. To make such buyouts attractive, the government allowed foreign managers to hire and fire workers on merit.[22] The government is also encouraging the formation of joint ventures between foreign enterprises and privately owned companies.[23] On 9 March 1999 the Chinese Communist Party also proposed a constitutional amendment offering a measure of protection to the private sector. This had become necessary because the envy generated by private entrepreneurs had made them the prey of arbitrary levies and expropriations by local officials all over the country.[24]

The government has also taken a number of steps to maintain the viability of the banking system in the face of the mounting losses of the state sector. In 1997, it sold Y270 billion of bonds to recapitalise the banks. In 1998 it decided to let the banks set up asset management companies modelled on the American Resolution Trust Corporation that would take over their bad debts and sell them off at depreciated prices. This would enable them to recover some of their capital and reduce their vulnerability. The move has not exactly succeeded because there have been few takers for the depreciated debt, and this has shifted the onus of being the buyer of last resort on the government. The fear that this would happen led the government to postpone the setting up of an asset management company by the China Construction Bank at the last minute.[25] This fear was not unfounded. For the China Construction Bank's expectation that it would be able to sell its bad debt for about half of its face value was excessively optimistic. South Korea and Thailand, which have, intrisically, far more stable economies, had been able to sell only $4 billion out of $11 billion of their bad debts by December 1998, at prices ranging from 21 to 35.6 cents to the dollar.[26]

RETURN TO CONFUCIAN PRINCIPLES

The structural reforms described above were part of a drive to increase efficiency by upgrading technology, improving management practices and making managers accountable for performance, that pervaded every sector of industry from the state sector to the township and village enterprises. One index of the seriousness of the attempt was the fact that in 1998 the government demoted or dismissed no fewer than 48,000 company officials for poor management.[27] But all of these efforts together could not prevent the reform programme from getting stalled by the heavy over-investment in the post-reform industrial sector, mounting losses and the sharp economic slowdown that began in 1997. In 1998 Zhu Rongji had promised that the government would close down or restructure one third of the loss-making enterprises each year until the problem was overcome in 2000. In the first year of that pledge, other than GITIC no other enterprises were allowed to founder and the restructuring programme failed to curb the losses of the state sector.

On the other hand, the attempt to close or pare down enterprises and to lay off staff continued to increase anxiety and unrest in the workers. Chinese commentators expressed anxiety over the impact that the decommissioning of spindles in the textiles industry and the laying off of almost a million workers in the textiles industry would have on society; for the majority of the mills are in the interior and backward parts of the country where alternative job opportunities are scarce.[28] This is also true of the coal miners who are being laid off.

Rising unrest was reflected in the sharp rise in demonstrations, road blockages, riots and criminal acts such as the five bomb blasts in January which were mentioned in the last chapter. The government responded to it by tightening political control on dissent on the one hand and hardening discipline within the state apparatus on the other.

CURBING DISSENT

China's leaders were aware that they had no option but to speed up the process of reform and in particular reform that cut the losses of the SOEs. They also knew that this would lead to more unemployment and greater social unrest. They therefore decided to prepare Chinese society for harder times by steadily restricting the freedom of dissent. They sent the message on 6 December 1998, only six months after President Clinton had called Jiang Zemin a visionary who had ushered in a new period of political openness in China. On that day the government sent six dissidents to jail for trying to start China's first opposition party, the China Democracy Party. The party was registered by Wang Youcai on 25 June, and in just six months had been able to set up preparatory committees in 23 out of 31 provinces. This kind of challenge was the last thing the Chinese Communist Party was prepared to face when it was on the eve of taking highly unpopular decisions. On 21 December the six dissidents were sentenced to up to eleven years in prison.[29] The message was clear, but Jiang Zemin underlined it only three weeks later after the Dalian farmers' riot by observing that 'the country was facing an economic slowdown' and exhorting all state authorities to nip organised opposition in the bud.[30] This was followed by a systematic crackdown on dissidents of all types in the ensuing months.

The government sent out the message a second time when it firmly discouraged the holding of direct elections for township councils. Direct elections had been held for the village councils for several years. But the first election for a township council was held in Buyun, a town in a remote part of central China, on 31 December 1998. Beijing did not countermand the election, but made it clear that this was to be the last such democratic initiative from a local body, at least for some time.[31] It sent out the message a third time when it cracked down on the Falun Gong – a crackdown that was still continuing at the time of writing.

As the number of popular demonstrations mounted, Beijing took steps quietly to increase the numbers of the Peoples' Armed Police by 100,000. Formed in the early 1980s, by 1989, at the time of the Tiananmen demonstrations, it had attained a strength of 600,000. The 1998 expansion brought the number to 1 million, of whom 730,000 were primarily entrusted with the maintenance of public order.[32]

China's retreat from political liberalisation has attracted worldwide attention. It provoked comments by Washington officials and human rights organisations and began a downward slide in Sino-US relations that accelerated sharply when NATO began to bomb Yugoslavia on 24 March. Relations reached a nadir when US jets, using outdated maps, bombed the Chinese embassy in Belgrade and killed three journalists, injuring a score of other staff members and journalists. Chinese leaders, again to the West's surprise and dismay, refused to accept NATO's explanations and apologies and set about carefully fomenting a controlled anger against the West. This was not unconnected to the hardening of the government's political stance at home. With hard decisions in the offing and the communist ideology largely discredited, the government welcomed a chance to fan nationalist sentiments and a induced a degree of paranoia in order to make the people accept greater privation in the months to come.

Where the Chinese government differed from just about every other authoritarian government the world has known was in its awareness that a government that demanded sacrifices from its people had to be worthy of them. Ensuring that this was so became the third component of the government's political strategy. Thus, without invoking them overtly, the Jiang Zemin government fell back on the Confucian traditions that underlie Chinese society. If society had to be organised hierarchically, the leader had to command obedience not by means of terror or brute force but by the power of his or her own personal conduct. The Chinese government translated this maxim into an unprecedented attack on corruption in the ranks of the Communist Party and the bureaucracy, and a drive for openness and accountability in administration. The need for some form of self-correction rose as the grip of the Communist Party and ideology on society weakened and was replaced by the desire for individual self-aggrandisement.

In the city and the provincial administrations this caused a sharp rise in corruption. In the banking system it gave birth to bank fraud that cost the government billions of dollars in payments to fictitious organisations and other types of fraud; and in the state-owned enterprises to asset stripping as managers by collective consent transferred machinery and other assets to newly established subsidiaries and collectives. In the provincial administrations it led to the setting up and financing of corporations that did not appear in the balance sheets of the ITICs and holding companies, and at the village and township level it led to high-handedness, and extortion of the poor.

In 1998 the government's drive against corruption and high-handedness took a quantum jump. According to data furnished to the Tenth Peoples' Congress in March 1999 by Han Zhubin, the chief prosecutor, the number of decisions taken by administrative tribunals and officials that were overthrown by the courts was five times greater in 1998 than in 1997. The number of cases registered against individuals for fianncial 'mismanagement' went up by four times. Han Zhubin conceded frankly that the judiciary and the prosecutor's offices had been tainted with corruption too. The number of judges and their staff who were convicted of abusing their power had jumped from 1,051 in 1997 to 2,512 in 1998. Abuses of power included torture, the illegal enforcement of laws and the arrest of witnesses. Some 70,992 policemen were reprimanded for detaining people beyond the legal limit. Bribes worth $534 million were detected and charges of corruption against 40,000 officials were investigated. More than two-thirds were indicted. Among these were three officials of the rank of provincial governor, 103 provincial department chiefs and 1,714 county chiefs. Overall, the number of persons sentenced for crimes rose by 30.76 per cent.[33] Foreign observers took these statistics as evidence that growing unemployment and slowing growth of incomes had unleashed a crime wave in the country from which the bureaucracy was not immune. But the increase was not so much in corruption and the arbitrary use of power, as in the government's determination to make an example of the transgressors. More than the statistics cited by Zhubin and his aides, delegates at the Tenth Peoples' Congress were impressed by the candidness of the government's tone and revelations. 'They are talking our language', one of them remarked to a reporter.[34]

The government also launched a concerted drive to check smuggling. In January 1999 it announced the formation of a special 10,000-man police force specifically targeted at smugglers.[35] Lastly, narcotics seizures went up by 19 times in 1998 over 1997, to a record figure of 7 tonnes.[36]

This candidness has extended to the airing of people's grievances. In many respects the Dalian farmers' riot proved a turning point. For the newspapers chose to highlight the grievances that brought the farmers to the point where they banded together to challenge the authority of the state. The farmers were driven to desperation by arbitrary levies imposed upon them by local officials – school fees, building fees, land use fees, licensing fees and the like.[37] It is possible that some of these were a consequence of the government's attempt to put its own levies on a contractual basis, but the farmers were not adequately informed and had no legal recourse to a higher authority to seek redress. Decades of carrying out central diktats had made the administration insensitive to the people. The farmers' revolt was another sign that times had changed and a democratic spirit was slowly growing in the people. But unlike the Buyun experiment in direct elections, this was one area in which the government sided with the farmers.

In much the same spirit, while the police remained tight-lipped about the causes of the spate of bombings in January 1999 that killed 29 people, a Guangzhou daily reported on 27 January that one of the bombings had been a revenge killing by relatives of four villagers who had been executed by a policeman whose relative owed them money but was not willing to pay them back.[38] Without some degree of official approval it is unlikely that the daily would have been able to highlight the cause so effectively.

WILL PUMP PRIMING WORK?

In contrast to Russia, where the *nomenklatura*-turned-capitalists have literally gobbled up the state and now have a strong personal interest in opposing the reforms that could save it from disintegration, and contrary to India where for three years the state has not known which way to turn, China's leaders have an extraordinarily clear understanding of the task they face, and the policies they have to adopt. But with all the will in the world the task they face is a truly daunting one and there is no guarantee that they will succeed. For China faces three problems that reinforce each other. First, it is facing a spreading insolvency in the modern sector of the economy, caused by unwise and excessive investment in the past. This has been immensely speeded up by a slowdown in the growth of consumer demand overall and an absolute decline in some sectors like automobiles and consumer durables. Second, growing insolvency is reducing foreign investment and that is further slowing down the growth of demand. Third, demand has been further reduced by the impact of the Asian crisis and recession in Japan, which brought the growth of exports to a halt in 1998. These trends have all the makings of a vicious circle; for each is reinforcing the others and pushing the economy further downwards. The cumulative effect is to slow down the growth of employment and make it next to impossible to absorb those being laid off in the textiles and mining industries, in the urban collectives and the TVEs into alternative employment. China's already daunting problem of labour redundancy and unemployment is therefore growing steadily worse.

The decision to stem the deterioration through pump priming was a brave one. Helped in 1999 and 2000 by the highest growth rate in the USA in 30 years and a small acceleration of growth in Europe, this gave China two more years of a 'soft landing'. But even in 1999 there were signs that pump priming was at best a short term answer. As a result, while the government set a target of 7.5 per cent for 2000, many Chinese economists predicted in mid-1999 that GDP growth would fall to 6 per cent.[39] As of May 2000, pump priming the Chinese economy also had not succeeded in reversing the deflationary spiral in which China found itself. In 1999 retail sales increased by only 6.8 per cent. Since this was 1.7 per cent less than the growth of industrial output, not surprisingly deflationary pressures continued. By the end of December, consumer prices had been falling for 25 months and those of intermediate and capital goods for 44 straight months.[40]

Contrary to the expectations of Chinese economists, exports rallied in the second half of 1999 after falling steadily until June, and ended 5 per cent up on 1998.[41] This was mainly because of the strengthening boom in the US economy and the continued recovery in East and South East Asia. However, imports continued to surge ahead and were a full 18.2 per cent higher than a year earlier.[42] China's trade surplus sank to just below $30 billion.[43] The sharp increase in imports, and the corresponding sharp contraction of the trade surplus in the first half of 1999, meant that a part of the extra money pumped into the economy had gone directly into imports and was stimulating demand in other countries.

In sum, China's ambitious policy of reflation averted a crash, but did not reverse price deflation. But the onset of what might turn into a full blown recession in the USA has led to a slowdown in China's exports.[44] Were the USA to go into a fully-fledged recession, China's trade surplus could disappear rapidly and its balance of payments turn adverse. It will then be forced to choose between fiscal contraction and devaluation. Either course could lead to the crash that it has, so far, so bravely avoided.

Part III
INDIA

12

The Paradox of India's Slow Transition

India's economic transformation has been in many ways the opposite of those of Russia and China. It has been a major contention of this book so far that both countries ran into difficulties because they tried to make the transition too fast. India, on the other hand, has run into difficulties because it has gone too slow. Of the three countries India was best placed to make the transition quickly because it was the only country with a fully developed national market economy. Nor was this a recent creation. A nationwide market for raw materials such as cotton, tobacco, indigo and spices, the finer strains of wheat and rice, and a wide variety of handicrafts, including fine textiles, brocades and jewellery, had come fully into being by the seventeenth century.[1] In the late nineteenth and early twentieth centuries this had been further integrated and deepened by the development of a railway network that connected the furthest points of British India. Parallel to the growth of the market, there had developed a nationwide and highly efficient indigenous banking system. This was gradually marginalised during British rule, but replaced rapidly by a modern banking system that enjoyed the British government's patronage.[2] By 1947, foodgrains, petroleum products, agricultural raw materials, coal, steel and all consumer goods were moving across the country from the ports and the production centres in the interior, and could be bought in the remotest places.

The governments of independent India further consolidated the market by following policies that were deliberately crafted to prevent geographical concentrations of industrial investment close to raw materials sources or major markets. The most important of these was the equalisation of freight charges on foodgrains transported on state account, and key raw and basic materials such as coal and steel, irrespective of the distance they had to be carried. More than four-fifths of the economy, including all of agriculture, nearly all domestic and more than half of international trade, construction, most other service industries and about two-thirds of manufacturing (measured by its share of the output), was in private hands. The public sector had a near-monopoly of infrastructure – railways, ports, major and medium irrigation works, air transport, banking, finance and insurance, about half of international trade, which had to be channelled through state trading companies, and all forms of commercial energy. It also dominated, although it did not monopolise, the heavy industrial sector, especially steel, non-ferrous metals, heavy engineering, chemicals and pharmaceuticals. But all of this accounted for barely a fifth of the national product.

India also had clearly defined property rights, and a well developed system of commercial law inherited from the British. It had both an extensive system of commercial banking, which was extended to the rural sector in 1969 after the government nationalised the major private banks and a number of specialised investment banks. Thus while China and Russia had to create property rights and commercial law, India had only to clear the barnacles that encrusted the judicial system to make both function smoothly and swiftly. While China and Russia had to create commercial and investment banks and a stock market, India had only to make them work faster and more transparently. Perhaps most important of all, while China and Russia had to create an entrepreneurial class, India had a surfeit of entrepreneurs. Not only were there a large number of industrial families that controlled what were, by Indian standards, large and highly diversified conglomerates, but there was a huge number, running into several million, of small and medium sized enterprises and an even larger number of traders, construction bosses and service providers of all sorts. The unorganised sector had at least 14 million establishments.[3] Despite these advantages, at the end of 1997 India looked like the country least likely to succeed in making the transition.

Like China, India had opted for gradual reforms. Like China its partial reforms met with considerable initial success, but created conditions that made further reforms more difficult. Unlike China its leadership lost whatever sense of direction and commitment to structural reform it had ever possessed. And unlike China, it had no Deng Xiaoping to steer it through periods of doubt and indecision. At the end of 1998, when Indian reforms reached their nadir, it had begun to look as if they had run aground.

THE HARBINGERS OF CRISIS

Like China, India abandoned its centrally planned and autarchic economic policies in not one but two stages. Liberalisation came to agriculture first in 1965, 26 years before it reluctantly did so in industry.[4] In retrospect it seems ironic that in 1950 India's leaders were willing to adopt a more or less open industrial economy, but wanted to introduce socialism in agriculture. The industrial policy resolution of

1948 reserved only three industries for the state – defence, atomic energy and the railways. In addition it did reserve the exclusive right to develop key industries. These were iron and steel, shipbuilding, mineral oils, coal, aircraft production and telecommunications equipment. But the right to develop excluded, by definition, the nationalisation of existing private enterprises in these sectors. Nor was the private sector barred from these industries.

It was in agriculture that the government tried to circumscribe the right to private property, by enacting land reforms and introducing cooperative farming. The land reforms were only partially successful, and cooperative farming was a complete failure. The incomplete land reform of the 1950s was roundly criticised by the Left as a surrender to the Kulaks, because instead of giving the land to the tiller it created an intermediate class of small proprietors who became the new legal owners but continued in many parts of the country to lease out their land to tenants-at-will. Fifteen years later, however, this very incompleteness proved to be a blessing in disguise. When, after four years of agricultural stagnation in the early 1960s, followed by two severe droughts in 1965 and 1966, the government abandoned the 'institutional approach' to agricultural development (which stressed cooperative and community farming), and made the private farmer the focus of its development programmes, India had a ready-made class of peasant proprietors with the capacity to raise the capital needed to switch from extensive to intensive cultivation. This accounts, in large measure, for the success of the 'green revolution'.

The relatively liberal industrial policy, which prevailed during the first decade of independence, came to an abrupt end in 1957. Two factors were responsible. There had always been a conflict within the Congress over the issue of socialism. At the Awadi meeting of the party in 1954, the left wing triumphed over the moderates. The party therefore adopted a resolution calling for a 'socialist pattern of society'. At about the same time theories of autarchic economic growth, in which sustained investment in heavy industries was seen as a way of catching up with the industrialised countries, began to gain in popularity. These became the basis of what came to be known as the Mahalanobis model of growth, a four-sector growth model that required the public sector to invest almost exclusively in heavy industry and the infrastructure, while leaving the task of employment generation to a heavily protected cottage and small scale sector. Needless to say, this model required a vast extension of centralised planning beyond the relatively limited first plan.[5]

However, the catalyst for the shift to autarchic industrialisation was a sudden foreign exchange crisis in 1957. Cushioned by what seemed to be huge foreign currency balances built up in pound sterling during the Second World War, the government had followed a relatively open import policy during the first ten years of independence. But the devaluation of the pound in 1949 by about 40 per cent, and subsequent increases in prices, reduced the real value of these balances rapidly. In 1957 the government suddenly realised that the sterling balances were on the point of running out, even while large numbers of import licences taken by importers, who had seen the writing on the wall and indulged in furious stockpiling, still remained to be honoured. By the end of the year it was forced to pull down the shutters. Imports were banned across the board. From this point on the aim of the successive governments for the next 20 years became the attainment of 'self-reliance'.

Self-reliance was not, however, defined as exporting enough to meet one's growing import needs, but simply as the minimisation of imports, at virtually any cost. This gave birth to an enormous bureaucratic machine whose sole purpose was to ensure that only those products would be imported that the government certified were not or could not be produced within the country. The rationale was deceptively simple: it took less foreign exchange to import fertilisers than food; still less to import fertiliser plants than fertilisers; and still less to import the equipment for heavy engineering plants that produced the fertiliser plants. So why import food or fertilisers when one could import heavy engineering plants?

The single-minded focus on minimising imports led to the adoption of an inward looking, heavy industry-oriented strategy of growth which regarded exports as a residual activity, or one confined largely to traditional export sectors like cotton and jute textiles, tea and coffee. One consequence of this approach was that India's foreign exchange balance never ceased to be precarious. Over the three and a half decades from 1956 to 1991, India suffered four more foreign exchange shocks, all of which triggered some rethinking about the advisability of continuing with the autarchic model of growth. But for reasons both external and internal, until the last one in 1991, none of these made more than a transient dent in India's command economy.[6]

The second crisis occurred in 1965 to 1967 and was brought on by a convergence of internal and external shocks. The internal shocks were a three-year stagnation of agriculture that began in 1960–61 and the two droughts of 1965 and 1966. The external shocks were two wars with China and Pakistan in 1962 and 1965, which doubled India's spending on defence. But these were superimposed upon a 'quiet crisis' caused by rapid increases in government investment and consumption, which were not accompanied by any significant rise in exports.[7] On the urging of the

World Bank, India devalued the rupee by 57 per cent, but the failure of the Bank to come up with a large, promised safety net of foreign exchange to cushion the liberalisation of imports left the promised reforms incomplete. The Indian economy survived however, even without the reforms, because the devaluation coincided with the onset of the green revolution. This put an end to the import of wheat for the next few years and allowed the economy to balance its external account once again.

The third crisis occurred in 1973–75, and was once more caused by exogenous shocks superimposed on an internal imbalance. This time the shocks were another drought in 1972, which triggered high inflation and increased imports, and the hike in oil prices in 1973, which caused a sharp foreign exchange crunch. This crisis triggered the first genuine move away from the command towards the market economy. For the first time after 1966, India looked to devaluation to boost its exports. It took the opportunity provided by the US decision to stop backing the dollar with gold, to devalue the rupee steadily. It did this by keeping the rupee linked to the pound sterling at a time when the pound was depreciating rapidly. As a result both the nominal and real effective exchange rates depreciated by 27 per cent between 1972 and 1976.[8] Later, when sterling strengthened, India switched nominally to a basket of currencies but in effect linked the rupee to the dollar. In September 1994, the government gave up its 'low interest rate plus physical control of advances' policy and for the first time raised interest rates for loans to the private sector (but not to the government) to a level higher than the rate of inflation. This curbed speculation in foodgrains and other raw materials, and brought foodgrains prices down sharply. But reforms stopped there, at least partly because there was no foreign exchange cushion to absorb the immediate shock of switching from a closed to an open economy. Not only were the various structural adjustment programmes of the World Bank and IMF a decade away, but the USA cut off its bilateral aid after the India–Pakistan war of December 1971. It was never resumed. India remained an inward-looking economy and exports were promoted throughout the 1980s solely by raising the level of subsidies. When this is taken into account, the real exchange rate depreciated by 49.6 per cent between 1970–71 and 1978–79, as against 38.4 per cent if subsidies are not taken into account.[9]

Had it not been for the 'green revolution', which began in wheat in 1967 and spread to rice, cotton, sugar cane and oilseeds after 1971, it is possible that the inward-looking model of industrialisation would have failed much sooner. But by 1976 India was generating sizeable surpluses of food and raw materials such as long staple cotton and sugar cane. The rise in farm incomes provided an expanding domestic market for industry, while the increase in output made the country less dependent on international trade to obtain the raw materials needed by industry. Even the first oil price hike did not upset India's foreign exchange balance, because in less than three years a gradual decline in real oil prices, and a sharp increase in the inflow of remittances from workers who had poured into the oil-rich Gulf states and Saudi Arabia, enabled it to record balance of payments surpluses once more.

The fourth crisis occurred in 1979–81, and was once again the product of internal and external shocks. The internal was another poor monsoon in 1979. The external was the second oil price increase which took prices up from $13 or $14 a barrel to $35. This made India ask for an extended fund facility loan from the IMF in 1980. The fund agreed to a $5.2 billion bail-out, but laid down what were, by the yardstick of later years, an undemanding agenda of reforms for India to follow. Compliance with these requirements led to two sharp hikes in the price of fertilisers (by 40 per cent in 1980 and another 20 per cent in 1981) in order to reduce subsidies, and the decontrol in stages of the prices of sugar, cement and steel. The next three years also saw a relaxation of industrial licensing strictures. Instead of having to secure a licence to produce each specific product, companies were allowed to produce families of products and to switch production between them within broad ceilings, without having to take the government's permission. What was perhaps more important, 1980 and 1981 saw a relaxation of strictures on the stock markets that had kept them almost completely moribund for the better part of two decades, and forced investors to rely on the banks and long term lending institutions, both of which were, by then, owned by the government. The latter were required by law to convert a part of their loans into equity. Thus any promoter who took a loan to expand their enterprise faced a steady dilution of his stake in the company and a growing risk of nationalisation by the back door if he incurred the wrath of the financial institutions or the government. Few were prepared to run that risk.

The revival of the share market, the development of a host of new financial instruments such as convertible debentures, and the removal of price controls, had a tonic effect on industrial growth. With the help of another round of reforms by Rajiv Gandhi in 1985, which further relaxed industrial licensing and slashed duties on capital goods imports, these reforms pushed the decennial rate of industrial growth up from 80 per cent in 1961–71 and 53 per cent in 1971–81 to 113 per cent in 1981–91.[10] But even after these reforms the economy remained far from open. The partial liberalisation that had taken place was purely of the internal economy, and confined entirely to the product market. Nothing was done to open up the external sector so that it could respond to signals from the world market. As a result the exchange rate remained overvalued – buttressed by very high tariffs and outright import bans or severe restrictions on the import of consumer goods and a wide range of intermediate products.[11] These kept the profit rate on domestic sales two to four times as high as the profit rate on exports. Not surprisingly, exports remained a residual activity, or one that had to be kept alive with regular transfusions of export subsidies. The partial nature of the reforms therefore prevented the rise in industrial growth from being reflected in a rise in exports.[12] The balance of payments gap therefore widened rapidly and had to be covered by borrowing. Thus the spurt in growth in the 1980s within the framework of an autarchic economy itself precipitated the fourth and, until now, last foreign exchange crisis of the Indian economy.

The first indication that structural reform was urgently needed to avoid a future payments crisis, came in a paper submitted to Prime Minister Rajiv Gandhi by his special secretary for economic affairs, Montek Singh Ahluwalia, in the spring of 1989. Gandhi apparently saw the logic of the paper, and the need for a second much more thoroughgoing bout of reforms, straightaway (the first attempt had been in 1985), but felt that it would be wise to leave it until after the next elections, which were then only six to eight months away. With 413 out of 544 members of parliament belonging to the Congress, he never seriously considered that he might not return to power.

In the December 1989 elections, the Congress was defeated and the country entered a period of unprecedented political weakness. A minority government under V.P. Singh was returned to power. Ahluwalia, who stayed on in the prime minister's office as special secretary (economic), submitted an enlarged version of his original paper to the new prime minister. V.P. Singh agreed with Ahluwalia's delineation of the threat. In fact, as Rajiv Gandhi's finance minister, he had himself drawn the attention of the cabinet to the approaching but still distant threat of insolvency, at a specially convened cabinet meeting in March 1986.[13]

However, with only a quarter of the members of parliament behind him, and dependent on both the left wing communist parties and the right wing Bharatiya Janata Party to stay in power, Singh was able to do nothing to avert the oncoming crisis. Then came the Gulf War, the rise in oil prices, the loss of remittances from Indians working in Kuwait and Iraq, and the cost of repatriating 150,000 Indians from Kuwait. This led to an annualised outflow of $4 billion from India. The sudden outflow and the perceived political weakness of the government tipped the scales among international bankers against giving any more short term loans to India. That brought on the crisis.

REFORM AT A TIME OF POLITICAL INSTABILITY

The payments crisis coincided with the fall of the V.P. Singh government in November 1990, and the establishment of the weakest government India has ever seen – that of Mr Chandrashekhar, with a party of 55 in the parliament and wholly dependent on the Congress to stay in power. By December the outlines of the oncoming crisis were visible to everyone and were being discussed in the press almost every day, but the political system remained paralysed. Chandrashekhar was unable to persuade Rajiv Gandhi, the President of the Congress, to extend his party's support for the structural adjustment measures that he proposed to take, and resigned in March 1991, days before his finance minister was to present the budget. For two months the country had a caretaker government and this period was stretched by another month when Rajiv Gandhi was assassinated. All this while the crisis continued to deepen. The fiscal deficit climbed to 8.4 per cent of GDP, the external current account deficit to 3.5 per cent of GDP, inflation nudged 13 per cent, which was double India's historical inflation rate, and foreign exchange reserves slid down to $1.1 billion. Everyone knew that something drastic would have to be done, and secretly every political party other than the Congress was relieved that it would not have to grasp the nettle of reform.

13

The Success of Gradual
Reform – 1992–96

Of the many countries that adopted 'shock therapy', India was among the few that could have carried it off within a time span in which the benefits overwhelmed the costs. By June 1991, when the Congress Party came back to power under Narasimha Rao, the entire gold reserves of the Reserve Bank of India were in London, standing surety for the loans the government was taking week by week to met India's debt obligations. The country's exchange reserves had fallen to $1,136 million, enough to finance 15 days' imports. Beyond that the cupboard was bare. What is more, since India had incurred a large amount of short term debt in 1987, 1988 and 1989, in an effort to roll over loans it had taken earlier, these loans were coming due almost every week. By one estimate, therefore, the country was within 10 days of its first ever payments default.

Shock therapy, to reassure India's external creditors, seemed urgently needed and that is indeed what the IMF had wanted. Had the external payments crisis persisted, the government might well have succumbed. But the economy responded to the first round of stabilisation measures far better than anyone had expected. By 1 March 1992, the foreign currency reserves had risen to $4.1 billion against the IMF's projection of somewhat over $2 billion. By 1 March 1993, they had risen to $6.6 billion, and by 1 March 1994, to $15 billion. The current account balance of payments deficit fell in 1991–92 to 0.7 per cent of GDP, rose to 1.6 per cent in 1992–93 but fell again to 0.3 per cent in 1993–94.[1] As a result, the moment the immediate crisis passed, the Rao government abandoned any notion of rushing the reforms through and began a consensus-building exercise.

This was not part of a grand design, but dictated by two features that put India into a different category from Russia and China. The first was that it was a democracy. This meant that it had not one but two constituencies to serve – an external constituency of alarmed foreign creditors and an internal constituency of equally alarmed voters. What is more, unlike Russia and China, it had a strongly developed entrepreneurial class responsible for the lion's share of industrial production and trade. The government was therefore forced to be mindful not to push reform and the opening up of the economy at a pace that would blow them away.[2] To top it all, the Congress came back to power with only 232 members in a house of 544.

The first task that the Rao government faced was to reassure India's foreign constituency – creditors, bankers and exporters who were holding their earnings abroad rather that repatriating them, and non-resident Indians, who had withdrawn more than a $1 billion between August 1990 and June 1991. Exporters were also delaying remittances to the country. The government had to show that it was taking control of the situation and was serious about reform. It also had to stop the drain of foreign exchange, and to persuade exporters to bring their money back. The only sure way was to devalue the rupee sharply. The first step it took, therefore, was to devalue the rupee by 25 per cent.

Devaluation was not, however, sufficient to loosen the IMF's purse strings, and make it give its seal of approval to India's reform programme. For that, India had to undertake two other sets of reforms – bring down the fiscal deficit and free the external trade regime from its multiple exchange rates, prohibitive duties and quantitative controls. In a nutshell, the IMF wanted India to abandon policies under which for ten years Indian manufacturers had enjoyed the right to import virtually anything they wanted, but came under no pressure, and were offered no inducements (except export subsidies) to export.[3] The economic boom that had been set off by Rajiv Gandhi's partial economic reforms in 1985–86 reinforced the effect of the large fiscal deficits that the government was running, and made the internal market overheat. Manufacturers imported more and more raw materials, but continued to produce goods solely for the home market, where the profit margin was two to four times the profit margin on exports.[4] Thus, deflating the domestic market became an essential part of the strategy to reduce the external payments deficit.

The third essential reform was to lower duties on imports and scrap quantitative controls. This was the best way of increasing the supply of consumer and intermediate goods, and thus mopping up excess purchasing power and ensuring a free supply of world-class inputs to the export industries.

The government adopted a step by step, phased sequence of reform in all these areas. It set itself the target of bringing down the fiscal deficit of the central government from 8.4 per cent of GDP in 1990–91 to 5 per cent. But it first said that this would be done in two years, then three, and finally in five years. The target was not met. In 1995–96 the central government's fiscal deficit was still 5.9 per cent of GDP.[5] The rationalisation and lowering of import duties was not completed over four budgets, although in March 1996 roughly four-fifths of the former task had been completed. Instead of a bewildering number of rates of duty, levied *ad valorem* and by weight or volume, in the late 1980s, the rate structure had been simplified progressively until there were only 12 duty rates left. The peak rate of duty was brought down from 300 per cent before 1990–91 to 50 per cent in 1994.[6] The mean rate of duty fell from 128 per cent in 1990–91 to 38.6 per cent in 1996–7, but the import-weighted rate of customs duties fell more sharply from 87 per cent to 24.6 per cent.[7] Import restrictions on capital goods and intermediates were lifted completely in the first two budgets, but curbs on the import of consumer goods continued, with only a marginal relaxation intended to put a ceiling on the prices of locally made or assembled consumer goods, and to force manufacturers to improve their quality.

The Rao government also made substantial progress in lowering and simplifying domestic indirect taxes (the excise duty). The number of rates was similarly brought down to ten in 1996, all specific duties were replaced by *ad valorem* duties, and MODVAT (i.e. VAT privileges based on existing rates of duty, applicable only to the production of commodities and levied only at the factory gate) were extended to nearly all categories of manufactured goods.[8] The average incidence of the tax, measured as the ratio of its yield to the value of industrial output, was reduced from 10.2 per cent in 1988–89 to 7.1 per cent in 1996–97.[9]

The one area of reform in which the government had almost completed its task by March 1996 was the freeing of the external trade and payments regime. By the time the Narasimha Rao government fell from power in May 1996, India had a single, market determined exchange rate. It had also met all the requirements of the IMF's article 8, for current account convertibility of the rupee. This liberalisation too was carried out progressively over four budgets. However, the government had virtually ruled out capital account convertibility even before the onset of the East Asian crisis. The governor of the Reserve Bank and the finance minister were of the view that full convertibility would have to wait until the fiscal deficit was down to not more than 3 per cent of GDP and inflation had been brought under control.

SOURCES OF OPPOSITION

Indian opposition to the reforms came initially from practically every organised sector of society – a large section of industry, organised labour, farmers and the intelligentsia.

The opposition of the intelligentsia, farmers and organised labour was relatively easy to understand. All consumers are hurt by inflation, but the burden falls most heavily on the fixed income groups. Most of the intelligentsia fell into this category.

The opposition of labour was understandable too, as the removal of protection and internal constraints on competition meant that many firms would fail and their workers would lose their jobs. The opposition was exacerbated by the fact that the strongest trade unions were to be found in the public sector, which was the least competitive, and would suffer the most if the government stopped protecting it from internal and foreign competition.

The third organised interest group that stood to lose from the reforms was the farmers. Over the previous 15 years, the rupee had devalued more and more rapidly in an effort to offset domestic inflation and the competition to India's exports coming from South East Asia and Eastern Europe. Farmers therefore found the price of diesel, fertilisers and power – their three main inputs – going up by leaps and bounds, while their produce, which could only be sold within the country, failed to command a commensurate increase in price. Their political power had, however, enabled them to force the central and state governments not to pass on a part of these cost increases to consumers through annual increases in procurement prices. As these increases were not offset by commensurate increases in the issue price of foodgrains from the public distribution system, food subsidies grew steadily after the early 1970s. The government also subsidised the price of fertilisers, irrigation and power. As a result the subsidies to the farm sector on these three accounts alone had ballooned to about 2.3 per cent of the GDP.[10]

Any attempt to cut the government's unproductive spending would target these subsidies first, and that is in fact what the IMF asked the Rao government to do. The problem was worst in the power sector which was selling electricity to the farm sector at an average of 17 paise (0.6 cents) a unit in 1992, when the cost of generation based on historical cost of investment was Rs. 1.17 per unit (almost 4 cents), and the cost of generation from a new plant was around 6.5 cents.

BUILDING THE CONSENSUS

Broadly speaking, the government neutralised the opposition to reform in five ways:

- First, it slowed down the pace of reforms to give those affected adversely by it time to adjust.

- Second, it sequenced the reforms carefully, implementing first those which would restore balance to the economy, and permit growth to be resumed.

- Third, it deliberately stimulated economic growth as a way of dissolving resistance to the more difficult structural reforms, in the full knowledge that all changes are easier to make when the market is expanding than when it is stagnant or contracting.

- Fourth, rather than close down or privatise existing state institutions straightaway, it decided to strengthen their financial and managerial foundations and give them a chance to compete with a now liberated private sector and foreign investors. If they survived, well and good. If not, their failure would provide the justification for their closure.

- Last, throughout the reform process, the government believed in being not only transparent, but noisy. The finance minister, Dr Manmohan Singh, and others filled the media with declarations of what the government intended to do, but did only a fraction of what they promised. Instead they appointed expert committees to go into every one of the more difficult structural reforms, and produce a report. These reports and statements aroused intense debates in the media and gave everyone a chance to air his or her views. The deliberate use of a strongly independent, vigorous press to get people used to the idea of change, and to evolve a consensus, was another unique feature of Indian reforms. Far from doing things by stealth the government did everything in full view, and proclaimed from the rooftops even that which it did not immediately fulfil.

This strategy was not thought out in advance but developed, little by little, through the constant interaction of economic compulsions with political constraints. For the reasons given earlier, the government simply had to devalue the rupee. But no sooner had it done so than it began to worry about the effect this would have on prices at home. In June 1991 the inflation rate was already 13 per cent, almost twice the average for the previous 30 years. But after the devaluation it shot up to 16.6 per cent at the end of August. In addition to pushing up prices, devaluation also complicated the task of bringing down the fiscal deficit as per the IMF's specifications, because it pushed up the government's expenditure, on imported crude oil and oil products, fertilisers, edible oils and sugar, all of which were being sold at subsidised prices. Now the government had to raise prices not only to eliminate the old subsidy, but also to cover the sharp increase in rupee cost caused by devaluation.

This was too much for a democratic government to attempt. As a result, although the finance minister, Dr Manmohan Singh, made promise after promise in public to bring down the subsidy, the government more or less made up its mind not to make a serious attempt to do so until inflation had been controlled. The government made no attempt to raise fertiliser prices until September 1992, by when the rate of inflation had come down to 9 per cent. A month later as inflation slackened further, the government also decontrolled prices in the oil sector, where the domestic producers had been getting completely unrealistic price for years. But here also, the government showed its political sensitivity by maintaining the cross-subsidy on diesel fuel, needed by farmers, while eliminating the overall subsidy on oil products. In 1991 the only subsidies it eliminated were the ones on exports. Devaluation had made these redundant and the cuts, therefore, politically painless.

However, to reduce the fiscal deficit in line with its commitment to the IMF, the government adopted two other relatively painless courses of action. The first was to reduce the capital component of planned investment (which sent the capital goods industries into a tailspin about 18 months later). The second was to start selling shares in public sector companies, with the objective not of privatising the public sector, but of raising cash. Rs. 30 billion ($1.2 billion) was raised in this way in 1991–92. In 1994–95 the figure was nearer $1.5 billion.

Limiting inflation and not reducing key subsidies on fertilisers and food placated consumers, the intelligentsia, and the farmers. The government neutralised potential opposition by two ingenious means: it enacted domestic reforms that split the industrial class, and it delayed the opening up of the economy to give weaker industrialists time to adjust. The first was achieved by abolishing industrial licensing in all but 14 industries. The removal of industrial licensing was immensely popular with a very large segment of industry consisting of the now very substantial number of large and medium sized companies that had been put on a fast growth track by the rapid industrial growth of the 1980s and the thousands of ancillary enterprises that depended on them. This isolated the enterprises in old, slow growing or heavily protected industries, and poorly managed firms that were in competition with more dynamic firms in the newer industries.

The second political feature of that first budget was the omission of tax reform from the immediate agenda. India had, at the time, one of the most bewilderingly complex and opaque tax systems in the world. Over 80 per cent of government revenues came from indirect taxes, of which just over half comprised domestic excise duties with the balance being customs duties. The actual tax rates varied widely from nil to over 300 per cent for excise duties, and from nil to 225 per cent on imports. New taxes were imposed simply because they were easy to collect, without sparing a thought for their impact on economic development. As a result more and more of the tax revenues came from excise duties levied on intermediate goods such as steel and cement. These cascaded on to the price of the final product in such a bewildering way that no one knew how much of the cost of production was accounted for by these taxes. As if that was not bad enough, no one knew the precise relationship between the excise and customs duties, so that in entire sectors of the capital goods industries there was actually negative protection for the producer behind high nominal tariff walls.

Such a system benefited no one, so making the tax system more transparent was an obvious first step in reform. Its omission was therefore all the more surprising. All that the government did was to bring down the top rates of customs duties from 225 per cent to a maximum of 150 per cent. A handful of items were affected, although even this small change upset the balance between the tariffs charged on imported components and finished products in such a way as to discourage the production of the latter and encourage their import.

Even this small reduction of import duties was made only to reassure the IMF that the government was serious about lowering import duties. The real reason for the delay in tackling the taxation system was that changes here would affect the profitability of hundreds of industries and thousands of producers, which had grown up under the previous system. There was a basic justice behind this reluctance. All that the producers had done was to respond to market signals that the government had set up, through its interventionist policies. It would therefore have been wrong to hurt them for actions that were no fault of theirs. The least that they deserved was to be given warning of where the government was going, and what they could expect in the coming years.

Therefore, instead of making reforms straightaway, the government set up an expert committee under a highly respected economist, who had formerly worked in the IMF, and asked him to prepare a report. The Chellaiah Committee as the expert group was called, issued a report first on the reform of direct taxes, and then on indirect taxes. These were released to the public and extensively commented upon by the press, economists and business associations. In 1993, the government put out a blueprint for fiscal reform that laid out the schedule and the eventual rates of taxation which would be achieved in stages over the next three years. In that way, uncertainty and shock was minimised and business-men given time to change their product mix and investment plans.

PREPARING THE GROUND
FOR STRUCTURAL REFORM

As the reform programme unfolded, with all its fits and starts, it gradually became clear that the government had, without quite intending to, divided the reforms into those that had to be done first, and those that could be delayed until the fruits of the immediate reforms began to ripen. Fiscal stabilisation, tax reform, and exchange rate and trade policy reform came in the first category. Structural reforms could come in the second batch. Thus while it was implementing the first set of reforms, the government set about laying the foundations of the second set. Briefly these are as follows:

Foreign direct investment
In 1991, 34 industries were opened to 51 to 100 per cent foreign ownership. In all the rest, foreign companies could own up to 40 per cent of the equity. A 20 per cent export obligation was set, but at the same time the laws regarding payments of royalties and profit repatriation were made very liberal. To give foreign direct investment a kick-start, the government speedily cleared eight or nine proposals by foreign companies for investment in India, companies including Coca-Cola, Ford, General Electric and several other firms. A Foreign Investment Promotion Board was set up under the prime minister himself, to approve other proposals on a case by case basis. The export obligation was soon given up, and in practice the bulk of the investment proposals began to come through the FIPB, which was very liberal in granting permission. On balance its policy has been to say yes unless there was a good and strong reason to say no. There have been almost no such cases.

Another crucially important signal the government sent out was to allow the multinationals who were already in India but had been forced to dilute their shareholding to 40 per cent or even less, to issue themselves blocks of shares at concessional prices in order to regain control of their companies. By the end of 1994, over 160 companies had done so and the prices at which they issued themselves the blocks of shares ranged from 30 per cent to 8 per cent of the prevailing market price. The government also sold an additional 10 per cent of the shares of its prize automobile company, Maruti, to the Japanese shareholder Suzuki, to enable it to hold exactly 50 per cent of the shares. As is shown below, this did not turn out to be the best of arrangements.

Opening up the capital market

Following a major stock market scam in 1992, the Bombay stock exchange in particular and stock exchanges in general are being vigorously reformed, to cut out malpractices such as delayed registration and transfer of shares. This used to leave large amounts of loose cash in stockbrokers' hands to play around with. Stockbrokers were also compelled to register with the newly constituted Securities and Exchange Board of India (SEBI). These and other reforms were intended to curb, if not eliminate insider trading. The powers the government vested in SEBI were directly at the expense of those that had until then been enjoyed by the boards of the various stock exchanges. This was bitterly resented by the board members and led to several confrontations between the stock exchanges and SEBI. These climaxed in a 'strike' shut down of the Bombay stock exchange, but the government refused to budge. The Bombay stock exchange gave in when it realised that every day it remained closed it lost business and clients to the national stock exchange, which had been created by the government in the 1980s.

The Indian share market was also opened up to foreign institutional investors in 1992, provided they registered themselves with SEBI. A lock-in period of a year was done away with in 1993. By December 1995, 337 foreign institutional investors had registered themselves and were active on the stock market. Two years after reforms began, Indian companies were also allowed to raise capital abroad through Euro-Equity shares. Finally, the government permitted the establishment of an over the counter (OTC) exchange of India.[11]

Banking system reform

In 1991 a committee was set up to propose reforms of the country's nationalised banking system. It did not recommend their outright sale, but recommended removing all restrictions on the expansion of the private banking sector, and the removal of most controls on foreign banks already in the country. For the nationalised banks it proposed financial restructuring, the end of compulsory lending to the government at concessional terms and a phasing out of concessional lending to priority sectors such as exporters, the farm sector and small and marginal farmers, and the handicraft and handloom industries. Financial restructuring and ending compulsory concessional lending to the government have been carried out. The other reforms are being implemented, but slowly. Computerisation and improvement of services has started in most of the banks, but they are far behind the private foreign banks, and if they do not learn how to compete successfully the market will make them waste away eventually.

Privatisation and restructuring

Apart from the state-owned banks, which will not be privatised, at least in the foreseeable future, there are some 262 centrally owned and more than 800 state government-owned enterprises that are prime candidates for privatisation. By March 1996, the central government had not privatised any of them except, to an uneasy extent, the money-spinning Maruti automobile factory. It had decided to close down or restructure the irremediably sick enterprises, which number about 52, and had referred them to an organisation called the Bureau for Industrial and Financial Restructuring, to decide what ought to be done. It had also created a second category of firms, those that were going sick but could be saved, in which it intended to sell 50 per cent of the shares to the private sector, and thus change the board of directors from public functionaries to private shareholders; but this stratagem was not pursued by the Congress or its successors. In 1996, apart from a small number of irremediably sick, over-age textile mills that had been nationalised in the 1970s, and one scooter manufacturing company, not a single enterprise set up by the central government had been sold off, closed or handed over to the private sector, and little has been heard of the three firms in the second category. Thus only one kind of privatisation actually took place – a piecemeal sale of the shares of profit-making public enterprises, 4 or 5 per cent at a time, in order to raise cash to bridge the fiscal deficit. The government announced that it was willing to sell up to 49 per cent of the shares of the public enterprises in the last category of relatively healthy firms. At the turn of the century, that was still a distant goal.

A few central government-controlled enterprises were contemplating selling particular plants or factories to foreign companies. These negotiations had not been completed when, with the weakening of the Congress in 1995 and 1996, their fate became uncertain. However, the privatisation impulse continued to grow stronger in several state governments, including some run by parties to the left of the Congress. More will be said about this below.

Exit policy

The one area in which there has been no change so far is the so-called exit policy – a reform of labour laws to permit enterprises to lay off workers without having to get the permission of the government. Shortly after presenting the first budget in 1991, the finance minister revealed that the government would shortly be announcing an 'exit policy'. This unfortunate phrase became a red rag to organised labour. A bill amending the 1977 Industrial Disputes Act was prepared as far back as in 1992, but the government dragged its feet all through that year. Fresh elections in four crucially important states in November 1993 made the government unwilling to court public displeasure on any score, so the bill was shelved until after that election. In February 1994, after a resounding Congress victory in two of the four states, the bill and another amending the Trades Unions Act of 1927 were brought before the cabinet for approval before being sent to parliament. The cabinet approved the second bill but vetoed the submission of the first. The government, however, did not send the second bill to parliament for enactment either. The reform of trade union law finally took place in 2000.

Despite its fits and starts, the gradual approach to reform paid off. For more than three years, the opposition parties on the left of the Congress had been criticising the reforms initiated by the Narasimha Rao government on the grounds that they had cost India its economic sovereignty; increased the gap between the rich and the poor and were likely to throw millions of people out of work.

Yet, after a series of Congress defeats in elections to various state assemblies between December 1994 and March 1995, when these parties scented victory state assembly in the 1996 elections, they adopted policies in the states ruled by them that showed to what extent the patient groundwork for reform done by the Congress had changed the mindset of the policy makers.

The ball was set rolling in January 1995 by Mr Deve Gowda, chief minister of a newly elected Janata Dal government in Karnataka. The very first decision that his cabinet took after assuming office the previous month was to set up a high-level committee of secretaries that would screen all proposals for foreign direct investment, before submitting them to the chief minister and the cabinet for approval. This reversed the earlier procedure in which projects were approved in principle first, and sent to the concerned ministries and departments for detailed scrutiny later. The change made the concerned ministries and departments active participants in project formulation and cut down delays in implementation.

Mr Deve Gowda also opened up the hitherto closed field of urban development to foreign investors, and awarded the contract to build an international airport at Bangalore to Tatas, India's premier business conglomerate, in partnership with Singapore Airlines and the Raytheon Corporation of the USA on a build, operate and transfer (BOT) basis. In January 1995, Mr Gowda also persuaded Tatas to set up its second steel plant at a coastal location in Karnataka, instead of on the east coast in Orissa. Mr Deve Gowda was not the first Janata Dal chief minister to declare himself unabashedly in favour of reform. In Orissa, the chief minister in 1991, Mr Biju Patnaik, who belonged to the left-of-centre Janata Dal Party, was an ardent proponent of economic reform. In his state he gradually wore down the opposition of many of his own party MLAs (Members of the Legislative Assemblies) to reform, and began to sell off chunks of the public sector to private, and even foreign investors. The most innovative sale of this kind took place in 1994 when the government sold off an almost completed thermal power plant in the Ib Valley to an American consortium. Not only did the buyer boldly announce that it intended to run the plant at 90 per cent of its capacity (against less than 60 per cent for the State Electricity Board) but the State Electricity Board planned to use the proceeds to build a much needed hydroelectric plant which would otherwise have been indefinitely postponed. In 1995 Orissa was all set to get one and a half times as much electricity from the thermal power plant as it would have under the old system, and in addition to generate hydel (hydroelectric) power to meet the peak demand for electricity.

The current of realism was not confined to the centrist Janata Dal, but was equally evident in the decisions taken by the communist-dominated, Left Front government of Mr Jyoti Basu in West Bengal. In sharp contrast to the CPI(M)'s rhetoric even today, Mr Basu began to tilt towards pragmatism in his economic policies shortly after coming to power in 1977, when he made a vigorous though infructuous attempt to attract Indian private investment back to West Bengal. His conversion to the virtues of private management and ownership was completed when he ceded the management of the Calcutta Electric Supply Corporation, which both generated and distributed power, to a private firm and found that power cuts had disappeared in the city almost by magic. He signalled his acceptance of the need to dismantle large parts of the command economy to the rest of the world, in January 1994, when the government of West Bengal underwrote a four-page supplement in the London *Financial Times* inviting foreign investment into the state.[12]

Nor was his conversion skin deep. The West Bengal government hosted the Diamond Jubilee session of the Confederation of Indian Industry in Calcutta, and Mr Basu himself attended five of its sessions. His change of heart attracted the attention of the US government: assistant secretary of state Robin Raphel paid a one-day visit to West Bengal in January 1995, to assess the climate for foreign investment there.

One of the most unexpected converts to reform was the chief minister of Uttar Pradesh (the largest state in the country), Mr Mulayam Singh Yadav. Soon after it came to power in December 1993, this government, composed almost exclusively of previously downtrodden 'backward' and 'scheduled' castes, demonstrated its lack of concern for ideology by selling a number of state enterprises to the private sector outright. Among these was a plant making colour TV tubes set up by the state government in collaboration with Toshiba a decade earlier. In guidelines on private investment in the power sector announced on 16 January 1995, the government assigned power projects amounting to more than 5,000MW of capacity to the private sector and spell out with commendable precision the returns that investors could expect. The guidelines also committed the state government to privatising power distribution. This made Uttar Pradesh the first state to make this explicit commitment.

Why this change of heart, and was it really as sudden as it looked? The answer was that while the central government was putting its own economic house in order, it was putting remorseless pressure on the state governments to do the same. It first urged, and then warned the state governments that if they did not stop running up budget deficits, and did not pay their bills to the public sector for power, electricity and the like, it would simply deduct these sums from their plan grants and cut off credit. Both Mrs Gandhi and Rajiv Gandhi had made such threats before, and the latter had actually carried them out, but never with the single-mindedness and impartiality of the Rao government. The states then found that if they wanted to keep on investing in power and other infrastructure projects, in urban development and other areas of governance, they would have to attract private money, including foreign investors. They would also have to start cutting their huge subsidies to the agricultural sector, and would have to sell off some at least of their state enterprises to cut losses and raise funds for investment. This was an example of how already existing laws, governing the working of a federal democracy, were used to bring one recalcitrant interest group, the state governments, around to the cause of reform and to diffuse the resentment generated in various segments of the population by measures to cut the deficit between many political centres so as not to pose a threat to the stability of the nation state.

GROWTH AS A CATALYST FOR REFORM

The caution with which the Indian government has moved is only half of the story. The sustained opposition of the organised labour movement, underlined by sporadic strikes, continued until early 1994. Powerful opposition, not so much to reforms but to the way the government was enacting them, also surfaced without warning from owner-managers of Indian industry. They had been feeling increasingly insecure that while tariff walls were coming down, new production capacity could be created without hindrance, and foreign companies with superior technology and managerial skills were being allowed in freely, they were not being given the freedoms necessary to meet the increased competition that all this implied. In October 1993, a group of 14 industrialists held a meeting in Bombay and demanded a 'level playing field' in relation to foreign companies. They asked the government to allow them to issue blocks of shares at concessional prices to themselves in order to increase their shareholding in the companies they had founded, or were currently managing, to a majority, in the same way as the government had allowed foreign companies with businesses in India to do. The government denied their request but stopped the practice of allowing them to recapture control of their companies for a song, to which they had taken exception. The industrialists were not mollified, because by then the foreign companies had done what they set out to do. What is more, in the automobile industry, and in what are called 'white goods' – refrigerators, air conditioners and household appliances – they were facing competition from these companies[13] as well as from new entrants, while the absence of any reform of the market for labour and capital, the restrictions on selling land or factories, and the prohibition on laying off workers, made it next to impossible for existing Indian firms to face competition from new Indian and especially from foreign companies. This opposition could have taken a serious turn had it not been for the boom that developed in the economy in 1994.

In sharp contrast to much else that happened to aid the process of reform, this boom was not fortuitous. When the government slammed the brakes on imports in 1991, and cut down its own investment plans, the resulting fall in industrial growth from 9 per cent in 1990–91 to minus 2 per cent caused no surprise, as such a fall had taken place in every country that undertook a financial stabilisation and structural adjustment programme. When industrial growth revived to 4 per cent in April to December 1992 everyone began to hope that the worst was over. Then came the surprise: in January to March 1993, industrial production sank alarmingly by 3.4 per cent over the same quarter of the previous year, and industrial growth for the year as a whole fell to a paltry 1.9 per cent. The index for manufacturing rose even less, by 1.2 per cent.[14]

In February 1993, when the time came to finalise the budget for 1993–94, the government faced a severe problem. Because of the industrial stagnation its tax revenues had not gone up. Instead, because the government had lowered import duties substantially in 1992, and made some marginal reductions of income and corporate taxation, the tax revenues as a share of GDP had actually shrunk. As a result, the fiscal deficit was stubbornly staying wide open. In 1992, while presenting the budget, the government had promised to bring it down from 6.5 to 5 per cent of GDP. In actual fact it was finding it hard to get down to even 5.7 per cent, and although this was the figure eventually given in the budget, the government had had to resort to all kinds of sleight of hand to get there. The IMF was not happy, and although no open rift had occurred, there was a possibility that if the government was not able to show substantial reductions in the fiscal deficit, the extended fund facility loan would get postponed. A sizeable and influential body of opinion in the government was therefore in favour of another dose of deflation. But a minority pointed out that deflation, particularly if it accompanied another round of import duty cuts and the rationalisation of domestic indirect taxation as the country moved towards the value added tax, could easily lead to another decline in the tax to GDP ratio. The fiscal deficit would then refuse to close. It would be like perpetually chasing after a receding goal. This minority, which included the chief economic adviser to the ministry of finance at the time, Ashok Desai, therefore suggested that the government should instead allow the economy to recover its breath, and rely on industrial recovery to fill its coffers. At worst the exchequer would be no worse off, but industry and labour would be happier.

The issue was finally decided in favour of reflation, by the prime minister. In the 1993–94 budget the government cut tax rates in the face of an already high fiscal deficit and increased planned investment substantially. What is more, most of the increases came in the so-called soft sectors – 32 per cent to 70 per cent in health, education and rural employment generation programmes.

Industrial stagnation, however, continued during the rest of 1993. In November the index of industrial production had risen over a year earlier by only 1.8 per cent, with manufacturing once more lagging behind, at 1.2 per cent. It began to seem that there was no end to the tunnel. Revenues continued to shrink, and the fiscal deficit showed signs of going out of control. In the finance ministry, Desai became a pariah, and eventually resigned.

When the time came to formulate the budget for 1994–95, the government found that the fiscal deficit had shot up to 7.7 per cent of the GDP. To its credit, the government stuck to its policies, and refrained from taking any harsh measures to cut the fiscal deficit by reducing subsidies or raising taxes.

It was wise to have done so, because, concealed by a three-month time lag in collecting industrial production data, industry had begun to respond to the reflation package. From December 1993, industry began to show strong signs of recovery. The industrial production index rose by 6.7 per cent in December over a year earlier. This was the highest increase since May 1992. In January 1994 industries making up 82 per cent of the industrial index recorded a growth of 10.2 per cent while in February industries with a combined weight of 52 per cent registered a 16 per cent growth![15]

The resumption of growth seems to have been the final bit of cement that was needed to build the consensus. An expanding market gives weak firms a welcome respite from anxiety, and more time to recover their current investment in the form of profits and accumulated depreciation funds. Thus the death of an uncompetitive industry or sector of industry does not spell death for the individual entrepreneur. It also gives them more time to decide where to invest next. Even the list of profitable investment opportunities grows longer. Needless to say, as the fear of insolvency dissipated, the labour in these plants also softened its stand. In company after company, the unions accepted voluntary retirement schemes, in which the employers gave workers a sum equal to between three and five years' gross salary in addition to all their retirement benefits, if they agreed to quit.

THE SUCCESS OF THE ECONOMIC REFORMS

India's policy of gradual, phased economic reform paid almost instant dividends. 1990–91, which was the year of crisis, would also have been a year of contraction had India not been at the peak of a boom that began in 1986. Growth was therefore vigorous in the first five months, before the Iraqi invasion of Kuwait.[16] Even after renewed curbs were placed on imports in October, production declined only slowly because manufacturers preferred to run down their stocks to meet existing orders. As a result GDP at market prices grew by 5.7 per cent (against

6.6 per cent in 1989–90 and 9.9 per cent in 1988–89), and industrial production by 6.2 per cent. The full impact of the crisis was felt in 1991–92 when GDP grew by only 0.5 per cent and industrial production contracted by 1.3 per cent. The next two years were years of transition. The rate of growth recovered somewhat to 5.4 and 5.0 per cent and industrial production to 4.2 and 6.6 per cent, but growth really took off in 1994–95. In the next three years it attained 8.1, 7.4 and 7.4 per cent (new series, 1992–93 = 100). In 1994–95 and 1995–96, industrial growth rose to 10.4 and 12.5 per cent respectively.[17] Exports also boomed. Between 1993–94 and 1995–96, for three successive years growth in dollar terms exceeded 20 per cent per annum.

In these five years the country moved back rapidly from the edge of the abyss, and improved almost every parameter of economic health in the domestic sector. The external payments gap narrowed: the ratio of exports to imports rose from between 62 and 66 per cent in the second half of the 1980s to 86.7 per cent in 1991–92, 81.2 per cent in 1992–93 and 96.2 per cent in 1993–94, before falling to 72 per cent in 1995–96 despite rapid export growth, under the spur of the industrial boom. Foreign direct investment inflows rose from $150 million in 1991–92 to $2.133 billion in 1995–96. Direct plus portfolio investment rose from $158 million in 1991–92 to an average of $4.5 billion in the years 1993–94 to 1995–96.[18] Perhaps most important of all, the ratio of debt creating capital inflows dropped from 96.9 per cent in 1985–90, to 26.4 per cent in 1994–95 and 17.8 per cent in 1995–96.[19] As a result of these changes, foreign currency reserves rose from $2.236 billion on 31 March 1991, to $17.044 billion on 31 March 1996.

The more important improvements, however, took place in the quality of life. The annual growth of employment, calculated by the Planning Commission, rose from 3.2 per cent per annum in 1991–92 to 7.4 per cent in 1992–93, 5.9 per cent in 1993–94, and 7.9 per cent in 1994–95.[20] Private sector employment in the organised sector, the most coveted form of employment, rose gradually in the early years of reform, but peaked dramatically in 1995–95, when it grew by 5.6 per cent. For the three years of rapid growth the rate of growth of employment in the organised sector was 2.8 per cent.[21] This was almost 1 per cent higher than the rate of growth of population. For the first time in the country's history, young people coming out of schools and colleges found the trauma of trying to find a job lessening. This was reflected in the first ever decline in the number of job seekers on the live register of the employment exchanges, from 36.6 million in 1991–92 to 36.3 million in 1994–95. In the rural areas, agricultural labour wage rates increased in real terms by a little over 5 per cent between 1991–92 and 1995–96.[22] Best of all, the crude death rate fell from 9.7 per 1,000 in 1990–91 to 9.2 in 1994–95.[23]

One index of the success of India's reforms was the rate of growth achieved in the first three years after the crisis. This rate was 2.4 per cent for Kenya, 2.1 per cent for Nigeria, 0.6 per cent for Mexico, 4.1 per cent for Turkey and 5.1 per cent for Thailand. India had achieved an average growth rate of 6.2 per cent.[24]

14

The Congress Defeat
and Setback for Reform

By the middle of 1994, India's smooth and painless transition from a command to an open market economy had begun to attract attention all over the world. It seemed that India too was set to achieve a steady 7 to 8 per cent growth. Getting things wrong in the 1950s and 1960s had condemned it to a 'Hindu' growth rate of 3.5 to 3.6 per cent. Liberalising agriculture had raised it to 4.5 per cent; the first market friendly reforms of industry and finance in the early 1980s to 5 per cent plus; and the second round of such reforms in 1985 and 1986 to over 6 per cent in 1989–90. After a brief transition period, the reforms of 1991 and 1992 had raised growth to over 7 per cent. Most economists therefore concluded that in the absence of any truly monumental blunder or a severe exogenous shock, it would be as difficult to get India off a 6 to 7 per cent growth path as it had been to get India on to it.[1] Unfortunately the honeymoon proved too good to last. As China's experience had already shown, the key requirement for the success of an incremental strategy of economic reform is political stability. In China this had received a severe jolt in 1989, when the Tiananmen pro-democracy demonstrations touched off a conservative backlash against Deng Xiaoping's reforms, that halted the liberalisation process for three years, until he re-established his ascendancy in 1992.[2] In India, that precondition for gradual reform was destroyed by two state elections in December 1994.

These elections were held in the southern states of Andhra and Karnataka, long considered the bastions of the Congress Party. The Congress lost badly in both, its share of the vote falling short of its average vote in the 1980s by a third. The effect this had on the party was like an earthquake. There could have been many reasons why the party fared so badly in the two states. Among these was a lowering of the voting age from 21 to 18 in December 1988. This had ensured that fully one-third of the voters who went to the polls in 1994 were young, first time voters with no historical loyalty to the Congress. A second possible cause was the increasing tendency among voters to vote differently at the national and state levels. But the Congress Party's leaders ignored these and other possibilities and jumped to two broad conclusions. The first was that the Congress had alienated the minorities, especially the Muslims of north India. The second was that economic reforms had alienated large sections of the people.[3]

From that moment onwards, the reformers in the party, including finance minister Manmohan Singh and the commerce minister P. Chidambaram, found themselves on the defensive. The cabinet lost interest in any more structural reforms[4] and everyone who had opposed them began to take potshots at the prime minister and the finance minister.

THE BACKLASH AGAINST REFORM

The attack on reforms came three months later during the run-up to the next state assembly election in Maharashtra, another state that was widely regarded as a stronghold of the Congress Party. The conflict was not so much over ideology as over political control. By 1995, much of the initial opposition to reforms in the orthodox Left had dissolved. The communist chief minister of West Bengal, Mr Jyoti Basu had become convinced that India, and West Bengal in particular, had to embrace radical structural reforms such as privatisation, and to exert itself to change its image and become foreign investor-friendly. But the refrain that India's economic sovereignty was under threat, first voiced by the Left, had been taken up by the Hindu nationalist Bharatiya Janata Party (BJP). In the heyday of the command economy, this party, which was rooted in the middle strata of Indian society[5] had professed a vague economic liberalism, but when the time came to give its stance some substance, it soon became clear that for it, liberalism meant mainly freedom for the trader and small manufacturer from the innumerable imposts levied by local and state governments, and continuous harassment by petty functionaries supposedly overseeing tax, health and safety laws but in reality lining their own pockets. As far as foreign investment was concerned, the BJP proved inveterately hostile to all but investment in infrastructure projects. It professed to admire the Korean/Japanese model of partnership between the government and industry. It was, in short, true to its petty bourgeois origins.

At a meeting of the BJP's national executive in October 1993, a decision was taken to appropriate Mahatma Gandhi's 70-year-old slogan of 'Swadeshi' (be Indian, buy Indian; i.e. be self-reliant) and use it to attack foreign investment, above all, in consumer goods industries. In 1995, sensing the weakening of the Congress, the BJP went in for the kill. The battleground it chose was eight 'fast track' power projects that the Narasimha Rao government had negotiated directly with American concerns in 1992. In 1995 only one of these had achieved financial closure and begun to invest on the ground. This was the 2,095MW gas-based Enron Project at Dabhol in Maharashtra. As a result, during the election campaign in Maharashtra in January to March 1995, the BJP alleged that Enron had inflated its capital costs with the connivance of the Congress Party's leaders, and promised to cancel the agreement for the construction of the Dabhol project if it was returned to power.

Underlying the BJP's 'Swadeshi' slogan was a genuine grievance: by not opening up the consumer goods industries to competition from imports, the Congress government had kept the profit margin in them far higher than it was in the basic, intermediate and capital goods industries. In the late 1980s, a committee set up by the government to probe the causes of sluggish exports, chaired by D.V. Kapur, a technocrat member of the Planning Commission,[6] had concluded that keeping the economy closed had raised the return on sales in the home market to 200 to 400 per cent of the return on exports. By not opening up the consumer goods industries to imports, but opening them up to foreign investment, the Narasimha Rao government ensured that returns to *foreign investors* remained far higher in these industries than the return they could earn on others. What is more, these returns were only available in the domestic Indian market. Partial reforms thus biased foreign investment towards the consumer goods industries, and towards investment that tried to exploit the domestic market, instead of creating low cost outsourcing facilities for products intended for the global market. Such investment brought foreign investors into direct conflict with the indigenous manufacturers, who saw their market being invaded by foreigners who suffered from none of the constraints that bound them down.

The fears of Indian entrepreneurs were heightened by the fact that inadvertently, the opening up of the share markets to foreign portfolio investors in 1993, when superimposed upon the forced dilution of the promoters' shareholding that had taken place under the populist, anti-large industry enactments of Mrs Indira Gandhi in the 1970s (and not formally repealed until the late 1980s), had made them vulnerable to takeover bids from foreign companies or consortia of non-resident Indians.[7] To complete their discomfiture, the government's inability to carry the process of reforms through from the product to the factor markets, had denied them all avenues for responding positively to the challenge from foreign companies. They were allowed neither to sell surplus land to raise cost-free capital or expansion or modernisation; nor to sell off branch companies and factories to make themselves 'leaner and meaner'; nor to lay off surplus workers to cut down production costs.

By later 1993, the playing field had acquired a steep tilt against Indian entrepreneurs. A group of industrialists therefore banded themselves together in what came to be known as the 'Bombay Club'. By 1995 the club had forged firm links with the BJP and the call for Swadeshi had acquired real economic muscle. But all of the BJP's reservations about foreign investment were related to manufacturing and, more specifically, investment in the manufacture of consumer goods. This was captured by its pithy slogan, 'We want computer chips, not potato chips.' Until 1995 the party had never expressed the slightest reservation about foreign investment in infrastructure projects. The reason it switched tracks was that Swadeshi got mixed up with another issue that had little to do with economics. This was a political conflict between the central and the state governments over control of economic policy.

SIGNIFICANCE OF THE ENRON DISPUTE

The Dabhol power project was in every sense a baby of the central government. From the Seventh Plan itself (1985 to 1990) it had been apparent to the Rajiv Gandhi government that the resources at the command of the central and state governments, both from domestic savings and foreign aid, were simply not sufficient to meet the need for additional power-generating capacity in the country. So in 1986, early in his tenure as prime minister, Rajiv Gandhi opened the power sector to the Indian private sector. To the government's surprise, in the next five years it did not receive a single proposal from the private sector for the setting up of a power plant.

The main hurdle was the state governments' monopoly over power distribution. Private power generators could only sell power to the state grids, but the State Electricity Boards could not recover enough to cover the cost of purchase. This was because their monopoly had turned the fixation of electricity tariffs and recovery of dues into a political issue. As a result, the loss incurred on the supply of power to agriculture alone was Rs. 8,384.66 ($2.67 billion) in 1993–94.[8]

By 1992, it had become clear that the country was all set to encounter a huge power crisis a few years down the line.[9] Private investment in power projects was therefore essential, and was needed as soon as possible. The sense of urgency drove the Narasimha Rao government to send out a high powered delegation to talk to power generating companies all over the world and entice them into investing in India. Eight companies consented to come. Enron was the first and largest of these projects.

Enron had first proposed a 2,095MW power plant to be built in a single phase, but the World Bank, which acted as a consultant to the Indian government, pointed out that the western grid, into which the power would have to be fed, could not take such a large input. Enron therefore agreed to implement the project in two phases. The first of 695MW to be run on distillate, and the second of 1,400MW to run on natural gas. The gas would be piped into Bombay from West Asia or brought in as liquefied natural gas in ships. Breaking the project up into two phases raised the costs of the first phase because much of the infrastructure for the second phase – including port facilities, a road link and an LPG re-gasification plant – had to be included in the first phase. As a result, when the first estimates of project costs for the first phase came out, they caused eyebrows to be raised all over the country; for even after various renegotiations, this got pegged at Rs. 42 million ($1.3 million) per megawatt of capacity created. Power was to be provided at Rs. 2.40 (7.7 cents) per unit. Many commentators pointed out that although gas-based plants were usually cheaper than coal-based ones by as much as 40 per cent, the cost quoted by Enron was a good deal higher than the going rate for several coal-based plants being sanctioned at that time. According to the Planning Commission, this was in the neighbourhood of $1.05 million per megawatt.[10]

In a corrupt political system where there was no legal and audited source of the huge sums that political parties spent on elections and day-to-day expenses, the high cost automatically raised the suspicion that Enron had been allowed to get away with gross overcharging because it had paid a 'kickback' to the Congress Party in Maharashtra.

This became the launching pad for the BJP and Shiva Sena's attack on the Congress. When the coalition did come to power in March, its promise to cancel the Enron deal became an albatross around its neck. There is some evidence that despite its pre-election promises, the Shiva Sena was far from enthusiastic about cancelling the deal.[11] However, the matter was taken out of the state government's hands when *Business Line*, an economics daily, published the contract that had been signed by Enron with the Maharashtra government. The cost details it contained gave firm grounds, for the first time, to critics who had been claiming that the project was overpriced. In an analysis of the agreement Kirit Parikh, a well known economist, claimed, on the basis of a comparison with an almost identical power plant set up in Hong Kong, that the project cost was 15 to 20 per cent too high.[12] Parikh also pointed out that the terms of the power purchase agreement were unnecessarily loaded against the Maharashtra government. More specifically, since the Maharashtra State Electricity Board was committed to buying 86 per cent of the power generated by the plant, to fulfil this commitment it would have to give preference to Enron during off-peak hours, over its own power plants, where it could have the power for no more than 60 paise per unit.

Parikh's calculations gave the newly elected BJP–Shiva Sena government a pretext to 'review' the Enron project, before deciding whether it should be allowed to continue or not. But the real damage was done by the economic fundamentalist wing of the BJP, called the Swadeshi Jagran Manch (SJM), which 'unearthed' that a newspaper published a report[13] that in testimony before a committee of the US House of Representatives in January 1995, Ms Linda Powers, vice-president, global finance, of the Enron Development Corporation had admitted that the company had spent $20 million in 'educating' Indians about how to go about securing private investment in power projects. In India, 'educating' immediately became a euphemism for 'bribe'. As is shown below, the statement Ms Powers made was very different from what was reported in the Indian press, but an honest enquiry was the last thing on the SJM's mind.[14]

The purpose of Ms Powers' testimony had been to persuade the US government to make its shrinking foreign aid allocations play a key supporting role to rising private sector investment in developing countries. To do this, she suggested the USA should put its money into the Eximbank, OPIC (the Overseas Private Investment Corporation) and the Multilateral Development Banks, and allow these to provide the loan finance for projects that the private sector was prepared to find the equity for. Her precise words were significant in view of what followed:

> If we are successful, the results are not only the addition of valuable physical assets but the creation of 'commercial infrastructure'. These projects must be put together and financed using standard private sector tools. This process, which for the first round of projects is invariably painful and time consuming, *forces government officials of the country in question to deal with the reforms needed in these key areas* ... [emphasis added]

> Let me give you a real world example to illustrate these points. Just yesterday, Enron reached closing on a $920 million power plant in Dabhol, one of the poorest areas of India, just south of Bombay. ... This is the first privately developed independent power plant in India. Like most such projects it has taken three years to develop the project and arrange the financing. Throughout this process we have worked with the numerous relevant ministries of the government of India and the State of Maharashtra on a daily basis as well as with

the Foreign Investment Promotion Board, the Central Bank [and] the five leading Indian banks. We have had teams of specialists on the ground, addressing each set of issues [electricity sales, fuel supply, environmental requirements, site acquisition from over 600 land-owners, construction arrangements, equipment procurement, financing, foreign exchange requirements, legal and tax issues, relations with surrounding villages, etc.], and working to obtain the nearly 150 different kinds of permits and approvals required.

Working through this process has given the Indian authorities a real and concrete understanding of the kinds of legal and policy changes needed in India, and has given the Indian banks a real and concrete understanding of sound lending practices. *Moreover our company spent an enormous amount of its own money – approximately $20 million – on this education and project development process alone, not including any project costs* [emphasis added]. Thus in only one large project by one US company, we have already spent more money on the educational process than the US could afford to spend in public funds for this purpose.[15]

What Ms Powers was referring to was the cost of converting a legal and administrative system created to serve a command economy, to servicing a market economy. If Enron did pay out bribes, these were most certainly not what Ms Powers had in mind when she spoke so candidly before the US Congress.

The damage however was done. On 3 August 1995, a little over four months after it came to power, the Maharashtra government announced that the project stood 'cancelled'. What followed was an elaborate shadow play. For while the BJP element of the Maharashtra government continued to use Enron to bash the Congress government in New Delhi, in preparation for the parliamentary election that was scheduled for May 1996, the Shiva Sena component, which had no national ambitions began to look for ways of reinstating the project.

THE CENTRAL GOVERNMENT'S RESPONSE

New Delhi could have chosen to oppose the Maharashtra government's decision to cancel the project. It had every right to do so for not one but several reasons. The first was that although the various agreements to set up the Dabhol plant were between the state government and Enron, it had signed a counter-guarantee agreement with Enron to pay Maharashtra's dues if the latter failed to pay. This had effectively made it a party to the entire deal. There were also more basic constitutional grounds. Power was a concurrent and not just a state subject. It had become more and more so as the projects became bigger, as the National Thermal Power Corporation, set up by the central government, began to supply a larger share of the total power generated (in 1995 its share was 30 per cent of thermal power generation), and as the transmission grids became interlinked into regional and national networks. The latter in particular meant that any shortage or breakdown in one state affected several others. This increased the central government's mediatory role. Lastly, it was the government's responsibility to ensure that the actions of a state government did not harm the security of the country. The Enron dispute did pose such a threat because it was apparent from the beginning of the confrontation that the cancellation of the project would severely discourage foreign investment in India. This became apparent when there was a spate of adverse reactions all over the industrialised world. The first was a statement from the US Department of Energy that it viewed with deep concern the attempts to reopen the Enron deal after it had been finalised. The statement expressed the fear that this would affect other projects that were also in the pipeline.[16]

The American announcement aroused the latent xenophobia of a large section of the Indian middle class, and was therefore received with undisguised glee by the BJP. Western governments learned their lesson from this and decided virtually unanimously to refrain from any public statements. But the Japanese suffered from no such inhibitions. The Japanese consul general in Bombay said bluntly at a seminar that the decision would impede future investment in India, because it showed that 'state governments are unreliable'.[17] This was echoed by Masahisa Naitoh, a senior adviser to MITI. Naitoh also made the remark that the cancellation of the deal 'brought into focus Centre–state relations in India'.[18] In subsequent weeks Mitsubishi, Mitsui, Marubeni and Toshiba – companies that had power projects in the pipeline – announced that they would wait to see the outcome of the Enron issue before proceeding further. A Japanese project to build an 'electronic city' in Haryana was also put on the shelf.

The central government was fully aware that if the power crisis in Maharashtra became more acute not only it but also the four other large states linked together in the western grid would be severely affected. In fact by July 1995, power outages, which had been utterly unknown in Bombay were occurring every three months.[19] It therefore had every conceivable reason for stepping in and preventing the cancellation of the project. Within the cabinet in New Delhi, the energy minister, N.K.P. Salve, argued strongly in favour of stepping in and taking over the project. He was supported by the Congress chief minister of Maharashtra who signed the deal, Mr Sharad Pawar. But they were overruled by other colleagues and the prime minister, who pointed out that this would play straight into the BJP's hands, and enable it to reinforce the impression, already strong in the public, that the Congress was trying to hide its misdeeds.[20]

As a result, when the prime minister heard of the cancellation of the deal on 3 August, during a state visit to Malaysia, he told a packed assembly of businessmen and others in Kuala Lumpur that the agreement was between Maharashtra and Enron, and the central government did not come into it. He contented himself with expressing the hope that the BJP–Shiva Sena government would respect the agreements that had been signed by its predecessor. With these few words, the central government threw in its hand.

THE BJP–SHIVA SENA STRUGGLE

Rao's decision turned out to be wise one, for by withdrawing the central government from the centre–state conflict, he forced the BJP–Shiva Sena struggle out into the open. Having milked the allegations of corruption for all the political gain it could get out of them, the BJP began to lose interest in the project. This struggle within the Maharashtra coalition government therefore went eventually in favour of the latter, Shiva Sena.

On 23 September, Joshi made his first public statement that his government was willing to renegotiate the project and repeated it on 5 October. Elements of the Maharashtra BJP continued to fight a rearguard action in the cabinet, but Joshi stood his ground and finally had his way. An experts' committee was set up on 30 October to renegotiate the project; it began its meetings with the Dabhol Power Company representatives on 11 November and took only two weeks to submit its revised project.

Thus, after nearly four months of nerve-racking uncertainty and a quiet but grim war of nerves, the Dabhol Power Project came back to life. The agreement was unusual, if not unique, because both sides emerged as winners. Originally the project was to have been implemented in two phases and only the first phase had been fully negotiated. The renegotiated agreement is for implementing both the phases simultaneously. Thanks to a small change in turbine design proposed by Enron, the overall installed capacity of the plant will go up from 2,015MW to 2,184MW. Despite the increase in capacity, by implementing both phases of the project together, and passing on a fall in machinery prices to the Maharashtra government, Enron was able to reduce the overall cost of the project by $300 million.[21]

A decision to hive off a re-gasification plant and make it a separate venture enabled Enron to lower capital costs by another $450 million, and lower the cost of power from Rs. 2.40 per kilowatt hour for phase one to a level Rs. 1.89 for the entire 2,184MW. This made the Dabhol power plant the cheapest of the large projects under negotiation or implementation. Lastly, a decision to replace distillate with naphtha as fuel in the first phase of the project made it even cleaner than it already was.

The Maharashtra government gained in another way: Enron agreed to sell 30 per cent of its equity (20 per cent more than its original offer of 10 per cent) to the Maharashtra State Electricity Board or its nominee. This was expected to reduce the outflow of dividends from the country in future years by $150 to $170 million a year. Enron did not lose anything either. By combining the two phases the agreement made up a good part of the loss of time that the disruption had caused. At Rs.1.89 per kilowatt hour for the two phases Enron's overall profitability too had not suffered for it expected to earn an estimated 20 per cent return on the entire project, about what it had estimated before the crisis began.[22]

The only loser, eventually, was the country. The Enron dispute led to a hurried retreat by the central government on two issues that the BJP had raised in its campaign against the project. Henceforth, it announced, there would be no more directly negotiated power deals. Contracts for private projects would be awarded on the basis of an open tender. Secondly the central government announced that apart from the eight 'fast track' power projects for which it had already committed itself to giving counter-guarantees, it would give no more such guarantees for future projects. This threw the entire power sector into a turmoil from which it showed no signs of emerging even as late as the end of 1999. In late 1995, when the government of Narasimha Rao changed its mind on these two issues there had been 190 proposals for power projects before the central and state governments. Memoranda of understanding had been signed already for 123 projects to create 55,609MW of power generating capacity. All of these projects had to be renegotiated, and most of the bidders withdrew. As a result, by March 2000 only 56 larger power projects with a generating capacity of 28,849MW had received the government's techno-economic clearance.[23] Very few of these had achieved financial closure. The total power-generating capacity created by the private sector fell well short of 10,000MW.

THE RETURN OF STAGNATION

Once the Congress had managed to convince itself that the economic reforms were unpopular with the people, it began a frantic search for ways in which to limit the damage. The issue on which its leaders felt most vulnerable was inflation. During the crisis year, 1990–91, inflation as measured by the wholesale price index had already climbed to 10.3 per cent. The next year it rose to 13.7 per cent, partly because of the draconian cuts in imports that the crisis had made necessary, but mainly because of a 40 per cent devaluation of the rupee and an indifferent harvest, caused by a poor monsoon season. In 1992–93, the government's fiscal stabilisation policies began to work and the wholesale price index rose by 10.1 per cent. But this was still 3 per cent higher than India's historical rate of inflation in the 1960s, 1970s and 1980s. It was only in 1993–94 that inflation moderated to 8.4 per cent. But by then prices were more than 50 per cent higher than they had been in 1989–90, with still very little to show for it in terms of accelerated growth or increased employment.

In the very next year, the industrial boom that began in the second half of 1994 began to push up the rate of inflation sharply once again, to an annual average of 10.9 per cent.[24] These pressures were augmented by a sharp inflow of foreign capital, which pushed up money supply growth to 22 per cent during the year. In January 1995, the rate of inflation peaked at 12.1 per cent.[25] This was too much for the Congress to bear. After its defeat in the Andhra and Karnataka elections, bringing down the rate of inflation took precedence over growth. But instead of controlling prices by curbing the government's consumption expenditure or selling inert but highly prized assets such as land (and thereby reducing the fiscal deficit), the government took the path of least resistance and tightened its control over the growth of money supply. A sharp reduction in the inflow of foreign investment sharpened the squeeze, and this was further accentuated when the Reserve Bank of India sold dollars in October 1995 in order to stabilise the rupee, which had shown signs of depreciating. Preoccupied as it was with containing inflation the government did very little to offset the drain of rupees from the money market that this entailed. Money supply growth (M3) therefore fell to an all-time low of 7.4 per cent between April 1995 and January 1996.

With GDP growing at 7.6 per cent and inflation, based on the index of wholesale price, still running at an average of 7.7 per cent, the squeeze on the money market was truly fierce.[26] This led to a rise in call money market rates of interest to a peak of 85 per cent in November 1995. Interest rates rose throughout the year, especially in the informal markets. As that happened, investors began to take money out of the share market. As a result share prices began to drop from September 1995 onwards. By March 1996 they had dropped by 9 per cent over a year earlier. The decline continued throughout 1996. By April 1997 the CMIE share price index was 28 per cent below what it had been two years earlier.[27] Rising interest rates and declining share prices conspired to raise the cost of new investment. This caused a postponement of investment plans that was first reflected in the capital raised in the primary share market. This dropped by a staggering 48 per cent in April 1995 to January 1996 over the same period of the previous year.[28] The impact of this postponement was felt a year later.

The Indian economy did not therefore go into recession on its own. The Congress government drove it into recession, albeit inadvertently. The first sign that industry was about to slow down came in June 1996 when the rate of growth of imports slumped dramatically from an average of 30 per cent per annum over the previous 14 months to 2.14 per cent. Over the next six months imports grew by only 1.5 per cent.[29] Since consumer goods imports were largely banned, imports were tied closely with industrial activity. After a time lag of four months, therefore, industrial production, which had been pegging along until October 1996 at a none too impressive 9 per cent, fell dramatically to 3 per cent.

Through most of 1997 the recession continued to deepen. The chief cause was a rapid fall in the output of the capital goods sector. In September 1996 it had risen by 19.1 per cent over the previous year. Its growth declined to an average of 5.1 per cent between January and April 1997. In the five months after April, output contracted by 5.8 per cent.[30] This decline did not occur because of higher imports. On the contrary, between April and September capital goods imports also declined by 14.4 per cent and most of the decline was concentrated in project goods, whose imports fell by 35 per cent.[31] The message was unambiguous. Investors were postponing their investment plans all over the country. Their intentions were also reflected in the fact that in industries not subject to licensing, only 307 IEMs – investors' notification of investment intentions to the ministry of industry – were filed between April and July 1997 for Rs. 28.99 billion ($ 8 billion) worth of investment, against 443 for Rs. 83.78 billion ($26.7 billion) in the same period of the previous year. It was thus clear even in November 1997, when the East Asian crisis first began to affect the Indian economy, that without an increase in investment there would be no economic recovery.[32]

The consequences of the slowdown were most apparent in industry. From 12.8 per cent in 1995–97, growth slumped to 5.6 per cent in 1996–97. It rose marginally to 6.6 per cent in 1997–98, but slumped further to 3.4 per cent in 1998–99.[33] The impact of the slowdown on the growth of GDP was masked in 1996–97 by a 9.4 per cent growth in agriculture. This actually boosted GDP growth from 7.6 per cent in 1995–96 to 7.8 per cent in the following year. But it was fully felt in 1997–98. Industrial growth declined to 5.9 per cent (new series, 1993–94 = 100) in 1997–98 and dipped further to below 4 per cent in the first four months of 1998–99. Exports grew by only 1.6 per cent in the whole of 1997–98, and declined in absolute terms after November 1997. As a result GDP growth in the primary and secondary sectors taken together was a mere 2.5 per cent.[34]

APPRECIATION OF THE RUPEE

The sharp rise in interest rates that triggered recession also killed India's export growth long before the Asian crisis. All through 1996 and until August 1997, India's high real rates of interest and the belief that the economy was still doing well brought money flooding into the country. Reserves rose by $9 billion between August 1996 and 1997. This kept the rupee strong despite a much higher rate of inflation than in its main trading partners in the West. Between January and July 1997 the rupee appreciated marginally from Rs. 35.67 to Rs. 35.62 to the dollar. But since the dollar itself was appreciating rapidly against the European countries and the yen, this, combined with India's 6 to 7 per cent rate of inflation, priced Indian exports out of European and many developing country markets. Steel and chemicals were the worst affected but no sector was spared. As a result the growth of exports fell from 21.1 per cent in 1995–96 to 5.6 per cent in 1996–97. This decline continued into 1997–98, when exports grew by only 1.6 per cent.

All through 1997, as recession deepened, the Indian government made more and more strenuous efforts to deny that anything was wrong. India's economic fundamentals were strong, its spokesmen repeated *ad nauseam*.[35] Eventually they began to believe their own propaganda. But others began to grow wary. In March 1997 Moody's put India on its watch list of countries for downgrading is credit rating. Moody's cited the government's continuing inability to check the growth of its fiscal deficit and the palpable loss of momentum in economic reforms. The government got its first whiff of the growing nervousness of foreign investors in August. The market interpreted an innocuous remark by the prime minister that the Reserve Bank of India would establish an exchange rate band within which it would not intervene when the value of the rupee changed as an admission that devaluation was imminent, and went into a dollar buying spree. The rupee dropped from 35.70 to 36.40 to the dollar. It hovered around Rs. 37 until November and began to fall again, on the back of the second round of the East Asian currency collapse.

15

Reform Grinds to a Halt

THE UNITED FRONT – POLITICS IN THE DRIVER'S SEAT

The Congress succeeded in controlling inflation, but it did so by killing investment and sowing the seeds of a return to stagnation. By January 1996, four months before the next general election, inflation, measured by the wholesale price index, had come down to 5 per cent, and stayed there for the rest of the pre-election period. This did not, however, enable it to recover its popularity. In the May–June elections, it was unable to secure more than 136 seats (out of 544). The BJP fared a good deal better, but with 156 seats it too was in no position to form a government. A new government was finally formed by a 13-party coalition of middle parties, christened the United Front, which was centred on the remnants of the Janata Dal, which had ruled briefly in 1989–90. This coalition was supported by the Communist Party of India (Marxist) from the far left, and the Congress from the centre-right and commanded a comfortable majority of 313 seats. Its only problem was that it had been formed with support from opposed poles of politics, with the sole purpose of keeping the Hindu right-wing BJP out of power. In the sphere of economics it could not muster a consensus on even the simplest and most unavoidable decisions. This became apparent within six weeks of its being sworn in.

Before the United Front took office, it had issued a Common Minimum Programme, in which it committed itself to raising the inflow of foreign investment to $20 billion a year; curbing the fiscal deficit, opening up the economy further to foreign investment, privatising the public sector, and in particular opening up some service sectors, such as insurance, to private investors. Within weeks it became apparent that these promises would be honoured only in the breach.

On 18 June 1996 the new finance minister, P. Chidambaram (who had been minister for commerce in the Narasimha Rao government), unveiled a plan to cut the government's non-developmental expenditure sharply. Two weeks later, faced with rising international oil prices, the government also announced an across-the-board increase in the prices of petroleum products, by 25 to 30 per cent.

Chidambaram's austerity policy was very different from that of his predecessor, Dr Manmohan Singh. While the latter had cut planned investment and sold shares in public enterprises to reduce the fiscal deficit, Chidambaram proposed to freeze future outlays on salaries and allowances in real terms, and make departments reduce the number of employees by not replacing those who retired every year.

The decision to put up the price of nearly all petroleum products in one large step showed a similar readiness to bite the bitter pill of fiscal reform. In the 30 months that petro-product prices had remained unchanged, their cost in dollars had gone up by around 20 per cent and the value of the rupee had fallen by 12 per cent. The resulting losses to the state-owned oil sector had become a huge liability on the exchequer. The only choices before the government were to absorb these in the overall deficit or to raise prices. Wisely, it chose the latter.

Had they been implemented, these measures would have cut expenditure by Rs. 30 billion ($0.85 billion) and increased revenues by Rs. 184 billion. They would therefore have reduced the central government's fiscal deficit from 5.9 per cent last year in 1995–96 to a respectable 4 per cent or less in a single year.

But none of this happened, because the United Front made a historic blunder. Nearly all of its 13 parties faced the Congress as its main electoral rival in their home states. As a result, they were bent upon reducing their dependence upon the Congress at the Centre as far as possible. Mr Deve Gowda invited the two communist parties of India, the main constituents of the Left Front that ruled the states of West Bengal and Kerala, to join the government. While the CPI(M) only agreed to join the United Front's steering committee on policy coordination, the CPI accepted two seats in the cabinet.

The CPI(M) was in the grip of a profound conflict between its diehards, who wanted only to preserve the ideological purity of the party, and pragmatists, such as Mr Jyoti Basu, the chief minister of West Bengal, who had accepted the failure of centralised planning and state ownership and were looking for a viable social democratic alternative to communism. Unable to resolve the dilemma, it compromised by reserving its pragmatism for West Bengal and exporting its ideological diehards to the coordination committee in Delhi.

The ideologues lost no time in flexing their muscles. Within days of the announcement of the austerity measures, they raised a hue and cry that Mr Chidambaram was paving the way to firing surplus government employees. Chidambaram's protest that all he wanted was to shrink the bureaucracy through superannuation fell upon deaf ears. This 'mistake' was intentional, for it gave its ideologues an excuse to demand that the government should first clear all future decisions with the steering committee of the alliance, before announcing them. In one step therefore they sought to replace responsibility to parliament with responsibility to an ideological super-cabinet, not one of whose members had been elected by the voters. Gowda chose to remain silent on this demand, preferring not to precipitate a showdown, but in fact gave in. Chidambaram learned his lesson. His budget for 1996–97, presented a few weeks later, was a lacklustre affair that contained no reference to the privatisation of insurance, a promise included in the Common Minimum Programme only six weeks earlier.

The ideologues got their second chance when the ministry of petroleum announced a 25 to 30 per cent increase in oil product prices. This time the Congress and the BJP joined them. Deve Gowda initially refused to budge, but when some of the chief ministers of states ruled by the coalition partners joined in the demand to reduce the magnitude of the hike, he finally gave in and reduced the increase in diesel prices to 15 per cent. Since diesel accounted for more than 60 per cent of the total consumption of oil products, this retraction left a subsidy of Rs. 9 billion a month that came back to haunt the government a year later.

Chidambaram's 'clarification' and Deve Gowda's retraction on diesel prices would have done less damage if they had followed private discussions among the coalition partners. But from the very beginning the Left's representatives in the steering committee insisted in airing its differences with the rest of the United Front in public. This public discord, followed by policy defeats for the reformers in the United Front, sapped whatever confidence was left in the business community. As a result, share prices, investment intentions and actual investment remained in a slump.

Reforms did continue after a fashion. Rules governing foreign investment were further relaxed, credit was eased, tax rates lowered, and in several areas bureaucratic procedures simplified. But these were all in the nature of fine-tuning. They did not dare to alter the structure of economic policy. They did nothing to tackle the rising fiscal deficit, to open up the market for land, labour and capital – that is, to extend reforms from the product to the factor markets. As a result they left Indian industry, saddled with small, obsolete plants and an excess of labour, and outmoded products. This made them defenceless in the face of foreign companies that were starting afresh with a smaller workforce, new technology and famous brand names.[1] So far had the Left in India moved from radicalism to mindless conservatism that the United Front did absolutely nothing to help the public sector either to become viable or to close down.

BACKSLIDING IN THE POWER SECTOR

The consequences of political disharmony were most evident in the power sector. Until the end of the 1960s the state governments had invested up to half of their Plan funds in the power sector. Approximately half had gone into hydroelectric projects. As a result the balance between thermal and hydro power was a fairly healthy one, with hydel power, which is ideally suited to meeting peak loads, accounting for 43.4 per cent of total generating capacity.

Demand was, however, steadily outstripping supply. As a result India experienced its first power shortages in the early 1970s. To remedy these shortages the central government took up power generation, supplying it to the state grids for the state governments to sell. Since hydel power stations took an average of eleven years to build against the four to five years needed by thermal plants, the central government gave a higher priority to thermal power. The state governments did the same. As a result, by 1990–91 the ratio of hydel to total power generation had fallen to 28.5 per cent.[2]

The concentration on thermal power enabled the government to keep the overall power shortage remaining fairly constant at 7 to 8 per cent of demand. But thermal plants are not well suited to meeting peak power loads. So the peak power shortage rose to over 20 per cent in the early 1990s. After economic liberalisation in 1991, public sector investment fell steeply. The original target for the Eighth Plan (1992–97) of 42,000MW was reduced to 30,000MW because there simply was no money in the kitty. As the Plan drew to a close, it became clear that only 16,500MW of new generation capacity would be created in the public sector.[3] But private investment could not fill the gap. By 1997 private plants had added only 2,500MW of generation capacity, most of it as captive power plants set up by industries starved of power.[4] In 1992, the overall power shortage in the country amounted to 18,000MW of generating capacity. By 1998 the shortage of generating capacity had risen to 30,000MW and industry was meeting fully a quarter of its power needs through captive generation, at prohibitive prices.[5]

The Ninth Plan (1997–2002) therefore set a target of 57,000MW of additional capacity. But the public sector's outlays were sufficient at most to create another 12,000 to 14,000MW of capacity. The sole hope lay in increasing private investment in power generation. Before the Enron crisis there had been no dearth of interest: in July 1995, there were 243 project proposals for a total of 90,368MW. But then came the conflict between the central government and Maharashtra over the

Enron project, and the number of new proposals, especially from foreign investors dropped dramatically. Despite this, on 31 May 1996, 14 new private power projects with a generating capacity of 7,706MW were awaiting the clearance of the Foreign Investment Promotion Board.

The reason was the refusal of state governments to raise the average tariff on electricity to a level that would make power generation viable. For more than two decades the state governments have allowed unprincipled politics to govern the electricity rates they charge from their principal customers – the farm sector. As a result 30 per cent of the electricity the country generated was being sold to this sector at an average of 26 paise per unit, or less than one-eighth of the average cost of power generation. Most of this power was not consumed by farmers but by a host of small industrialists posing as farmers. As if that were not serious enough the distribution staff of these same state electricity boards (SEBs) now routinely strike private deals with consumers to supply them with power without a registered connection or without a meter. Not surprisingly, therefore, a careful calculation of the losses incurred by the state electricity boards, on 'transmission and distribution' and in the supply of electricity to the rural sector showed that in 1998–99 fully 31 per cent of the power generated was not paid for. As a result, the gross subsidy on power sold by the SEBs rose from Rs. 74.49 billion in 1991–92 to an estimated Rs. 379.62 billion in 2000–2001. The loss of revenue to the SEBs from subsidies and theft was of the order of Rs. 540 billion ($13 billion). This was four times the average annual investment in power by the central and state governments together in 1997–98, 1998–99 and 1999–2000.[6]

The state governments tried to cover these losses by overcharging industry, but industry retaliated by setting up captive power plants. There were, in any case, limits to the cross-subsidisation that was possible. As a result, in 1999–2000 the SEBs lost Rs. 312 billion in explicit subsidies, but recovered Rs. 117 billion by overcharging other sectors.

Throughout the 1990s, instead of raising the tariff on power supplied to the rural sector, or stopping the theft of power, the state governments vied with each other to find more and more innovative ways of paying for the electricity they wanted to buy from the private sector without having to raise tariffs for 'agriculture'.

The first expedient was to offer a counter-guarantee to the private supplier of power that if the SEB could not pay its bill, the government would do so out of its general revenues. The central government was the first to offer these counter-guarantees to the eight fast-track projects that it had negotiated, but the state governments followed suit. However, it soon became apparent that the states were in no position to honour such commitments. This was because for years they had not been paying their bills for coal, oil, gas and power to the central public enterprises, and had run up such huge bills that in desperation the central government was already cutting 15 per cent of their central allocations to recover these dues.[7]

The states' next effort was to set up an escrow account scheme. Each project would set up an escrow account into which its revenues would be deposited. This could only be drawn upon by the investor until his dues were met. Only the surplus would be available to the SEB. Again there was a flurry of activity. By mid-2000, 42 small projects of less than 300MW had been commissioned or were under construction, most of them captive units that would also supply power to the SEBs. But following an assessment requested by the Karnataka government from the credit rating agency CRISIL, it became clear that not only Karnataka but virtually all other SEBs were charging so little for the power they were selling that they had either no escrow capacity or had exhausted whatever they had. For private investors these revelations meant only one thing: in 1991–92, a state government counter-guarantee had seemed credible. By 1999–2000 it was not. As a result private investment in power generation came to a halt.

In 2001 the sins of omission by the state governments came back full circle and it was Enron that brought the crisis into sharp focus once more. Enron had brought phase one of its project, with a generating capacity of 740MW, into commercial production in June 1999, had begun to implement phase 2, which would take its generating capacity up to 2,184MW, when the Maharashtra government, now under the Congress Party once more (following an election in 1998) decided it wanted to cancel phase 2 altogether. The reason, it claimed was that against the original estimate of Rs. 2.03 per unit in December 2000 the Maharashtra SEB found itself paying Rs. 7.07 per unit. Maharashtra SEB could buy power from its own stations at Rs. 1.15 per unit, so it did not see why it should pay an extra Rs. 5.94 per unit.

Maharashtra SEB claimed that the power purchase agreement that had been foisted upon it by the state government – first the Congress in 1993 and then the BJP–Shiva Sena in 1995 – was defective. It had fixed the tariff on a cost plus basis, which was an invitation to pad the costs. It further fixed the tariff to be charged in dollars, and it fixed a two-part tariff, in which the first part, intended to cover the capital cost of the plant, had to be paid irrespective of how much power the Maharashtra SEB actually drew. This meant that the Maharashtra SEB had to bear all the exchange rate and oil price fluctuation risks. What was worse, the less it drew, the more it had to pay per unit. Costs had soared in 2000 not only because of a 45 per cent devaluation of the rupee and a trebling of the price of naphtha (the fuel used in phase one until the liquefied natural gas import terminal and re-gasification plant intended for phase 2 were ready). But these were problems faced by all private power plants. The final push to prices was given by Maharashtra SEB's decision to draw only one-third of the power that Enron was capable of generating. The Maharashtra SEB conceded that if it drew 90 per cent of Enron's capacity, the price would fall in October 2002 when phase 2 came on stream, to Rs. 3.52 per unit even at the high energy prices of end-2000. But it could not afford to draw this because its revenue per unit of power generated was far below even Rs. 3.52, and it had little faith in the government's capacity to raise tariffs to the rural sector or check the theft of power. In January 2001 Enron was a bone stuck in the Maharashtra government's throat. It could not cancel phase 2 because cancellation would cost nearly as much as the project, but it could not afford to pay for the electricity that Enron was already generating, let alone what it would generate. This realisation had also made the Maharashtra SEB put two other private power projects under construction, scheduled to add another 1,515MW to the state's generating capacity, on hold. This was despite the fact that Maharashtra's peak power shortage had risen to 2,000MW by December 2000.[8]

RETURN TO *DIRIGISME* 1:
KEEPING PRIVATE TELECOM INVESTORS AT BAY

The weakening of the central government's reformist drive caused a policy vacuum in which the barely suppressed *dirigisme* of the Indian bureaucracy got an opportunity to surface once again. In mid-May 1999, the Department of Telecommunications (DoT) quite suddenly encashed the bank guarantees given by two enterprises that had received licences to operate basic telecommunications.[9] The DoT was legally within its rights to invoke the bank guarantees because both companies had failed to make even a down payment of 20 per cent on the due installment of their licence fees. Representatives of the two companies expressed surprise at the haste the DoT had shown in invoking the bank guarantees, particularly as the government was in the middle of changing from auctioning telecom licences to revenue sharing. Their surprise may have been a shade disingenuous, but the DoT too was not being entirely judicious. Behind its move lay a seven-year story of deliberate obstruction of liberalisation by a determined bureaucracy.

One of the very first companies to come to India after the 1991 liberalisation was Motorola. Motorola proposed seven interrelated projects that included a software company, a major computer chip manufacturing plant, factories for manufacturing or assembling cellular telecom equipment in India and, as a focus for its sales, a single integrated cellular phone system for the four main metropoli. The proposal sought to bypass global tendering but had many advantages. It offered to take India into the cellular phone age in single leap and endow it with many of the hardware-making facilities, such as a chip-making plant, that it had not been able to create on its own for decades. There were, doubtless, catches to the proposal too. But it was only a first offer and could have been refined to fit India's needs and aspirations more closely. A precondition for such negotiations, however, was the willingness of the government to treat Motorola as a partner in the nation-building project and not as a travelling salesman who might be trying to palm off second-hand or export-reject products.

For the DoT, treating a private investor as an equal was inconceivable. At the time when the offer came, it had already floated tenders for cellular telecom services for the four cities. It asked Motorola to enter the bidding like any other company. The long and short of it was that Motorola was shut out, lost interest, took the chip making and other plants to China, and the DoT gave licences to not one but two companies in each metropolis – a policy that it extended to the rest of the country by stages. When the Congress government decided to privatise basic telecom services, the DoT extended the auctioning principle to the award of basic telecom circles too.

The disaster that followed grew not out of the government's initial willingness to make an agreement on the basis of direct negotiations, as was so nearly the case with the Enron power project, but precisely because contracts were awarded on the basis of global tenders to the highest bidders. Between auction and licence fees, bank guarantees and taxes, the cellular phone companies had to pay Rs. 45 billion of the Rs. 75 billion they had invested to the government up front, even before they had generated enough business to break even on running costs.[10] Then it gradually dawned on them that they would never break even. For the high fixed cost imposed on them by the licensing procedure forced them to charge tariffs that made the cellular service prohibitively expensive. As a result, the average phone usage in the metropoli came to Rs. 1,200 a month when, on the basis of equipment prices prevailing in 1995 and 1996, the break-even point was around Rs 3,300. By 1998 most cellular phone companies were deeply in the red and several had already pulled out. While all this was happening in India, China, which had no DoT to contend with, was extending its cellphone network at the rate of 10 million subscribers a year. India, by contrast, had touched 1 million in three years!

The licence auctioning process landed the basic telecom sector in an even greater mess. The government had divided India into 16 basic telecom sectors and allowed competitive bidding for each. Here over-bidding was far more extravagant than in the cellular sector. And the damage was compounded when, by an interesting and possibly not unintentional oversight, the DoT did not put a ceiling on the number of circles a company could bid for. The weaknesses of the auctioning system became glaringly obvious when a fly-by-night Indian company without the statutorily required capital base to qualify for entering the bidding, offered between three and five times as much as anyone else and captured 9 of the 16 basic telecom circles! The company was Himachal Futuristic Communications. Coincidentally, the minister of communications, Mr Sukh Ram, was from Himachal.

The legal mess that ensued, and the arrest of Sukh Ram on various charges of corruption, held up the issue of basic telecom licences for the next three years. By the end of 1998 the entire sector was logjammed and foreign companies were cutting their losses and pulling out in an accelerating stream. Through sheer stupidity, avarice, corruption and shortsightedness, the DoT was within sight of achieving its goal.

That was when Mr Vajpayee got his second wind late in 1999, and took a flurry of economic decisions. Within a matter of weeks the government decided to stop auctioning licences and switch to a revenue-sharing formula for future projects. But the bureaucracy was not prepared to admit defeat so easily.

Had this been part of a more investor-friendly approach to the private sector, it would have extended the same principle to existing projects too. But the concerned ministries were unwilling to give back money collected from the existing companies in any form. So the matter was referred to the attorney general of India, who was still deliberating on it when the Vajpayee government fell in April 1998. By then the DoT had moved into the second phase of its war on the private sector.

In 1997 its departmental offspring, MTNL (Mahanagar Telephone Nigam Limited), announced that it too would enter the cellphone sector. The announcement sent waves of panic through the existing operators. Although the government had kept the option open for itself in the licensing agreements, no one had thought that it would actually take it up. Without a drastic lowering of rates, a third competitor would ensure that none of them would ever break even. Only MTNL would survive because it could afford to cross-subsidise its cellphone system with its land line and long distance revenues. Knowing this, everyone else would sell out. Other companies went to court to bar MTNL but in August 2000 MTNL won that case. One can only surmise what the outcome of the struggle would have been if the Vajpayee government had not been re-elected in October 1999. But upon its return it set about resolving the conflict. MTNL retained its right to enter cellular services but the cellular operators were put on a level playing field by allowing them to enter basic telecom services too and by bringing them speedily under the revenue-sharing system for paying licensing fees to the government..

RETURN TO *DIRIGISME* 2:
THREE CASE STUDIES

The two preceding sections described how policies that were originally intended to promote the opening of the economy either ran aground because of political changes and the lack of a consensus on reform, or were subverted by the resurgence of *dirigiste* sentiment in the bureaucracy when political consensus on reform weakened. This section examines how, by degrees, the opening of the economy went by degrees into reverse gear. Three protracted conflicts between private investors and the central government's bureaucracy highlighted the return to *dirigisme*. The first was the near-termination of the 15-year-old joint venture between the Suzuki motor car company of Japan and the government of India to produce what was until 1996 India's only modern car, the Maruti. The second and third were the abandonment in rapid succession of two projects by Tatas, India's oldest and most respected industrial group. While the Suzuki venture was eventually saved, Tatas abandoned its airport project on 25 June 1998 and its airline project on 3 September 1998. After the Enron dispute the failure of these two projects was the main reason for the decline of interest in India among foreign investors.[11] They deserve to be studied therefore at some length.

The Suzuki dispute
The Suzuki–Government of India dispute began innocuously with a minor misunderstanding at a board meeting in January 1993. The confrontation that ballooned out of this was finally headed off by Prime Minister Inder Gujral in the very last days of the United Front government in 1998. In the intervening years, but especially after the dispute surfaced in 1995, it was represented and misrepresented in a wide variety of ways both by the government and Suzuki. To justify their actions,

spokesmen of the government accused Suzuki of wanting to milk India by indulging in transfer pricing, being niggardly with the transfer of technology and refusing to set up a gearbox plant in India, and a host of other minor sins. On his part the chairman and founder of Suzuki motors, Mr O. Suzuki, accused the Indian bureaucracy of trying to sabotage Maruti's growth and in one outburst went so far as to speculate that they were doing this at the behest of other car majors which were about to launch their own new models on the Indian market.[12]

A reconstruction of the way in which the two partners became estranged over the years suggests, however, that the dispute arose out of a head-on clash between two economic cultures – that of *dirigisme* and a command economy, and that of the free market. This clash took place in the boardroom of Maruti and was so profound that neither side was able to understand the other. The estrangement that followed grew not so much out of mistrust as incomprehension. The allegations came later to serve as a cloak for this clash of cultures.[13]

The seeds of the conflict were planted in 1992 when, at the Indian government's urging, Suzuki increased its shareholding in Maruti from 30 to 50 per cent. This made it an equal partner with the government of India. Equality increased the premium on always being in agreement with each other, for if the two partners disagreed there was no established chain of command. This was too much to ask for. Disagreements began with Maruti's second expansion, which was first mooted, informally, at a board meeting in 1993. At that time the secretary of the ministry of industry was in favour of raising some of the extra capital through a public issue of shares, but it was Suzuki that demurred, preferring to maintain the 50:50 character of its shareholding. Eighteen months later, Suzuki had changed its mind, but there had been a change of personnel in the ministry of industry, and now it was the government that staunchly refused to dilute its shareholding and insisted that the expansion must be financed from internal resources of the company and borrowings alone.

The clash of cultures came out in the open for the first time in a board meeting of Maruti Udyog in March 1995. At that meeting the part-time director appointed by the ministry of industry to represent the government announced baldly that the government expected the remaining four government directors on the board, who were full-time employees of the company, to vote according to its dictates. They were after all, he said, government servants, and expected to uphold the interests of the government of India. He also issued a warning that those who did not toe the line could expect to be replaced. This announcement came as a bombshell to the members of the board. To the Indian directors this was dismally familiar. But the Suzuki directors greeted it with dismay and incomprehension.

The next confrontation took place six months later in September. At that meeting the board had before it three issues. These were how to finance the expansion of the plant, its modernisation plan, and the introduction of new models. At this meeting the industry ministry's nominee proposed that Suzuki transfer the technology for manufacturing the gearbox to Maruti in India. Suzuki's directors claimed during talks with the author that contrary to what has been reported in the press, Suzuki did not refuse the request outright. However, it did point out that a gearbox plant would cost Rs. 15 billion ($0.45 billion) and would soak up all the reserves that Maruti had built up. Maruti would therefore have to choose between it and other modernisation plans. In particular, Suzuki pointed out that the board would have to choose between the gearbox plant and the introduction of a wholly new, more modern, more powerful 800cc model to replace the ageing work horse, introduced in 1984, that was the company's bread and butter product. It was estimated that the latter would cost Rs. 7.5 billion.

The board agreed to shelve the gearbox project but the government director asked for a detailed project report on the new Maruti 800cc project. This request also left the Japanese in dismay because it meant months of delay. Delay was of no consequence in a closed, command economy. As a consequence, the preparation of detailed project reports had become a standard requirement in the Indian public sector even for an expansion plan. By contrast, Suzuki's directors were used to working in a fiercely competitive market where success depended upon identifying and being the first to occupy new market niches. Every day's delay in introducing a new model risked having that market niche taken away by a competitor. Suzuki feared, as it turned out with justification, that in the competitive car market that India was fast becoming, this would allow other companies to introduce much more modern versions of the 'small car' and undercut Maruti's dominance. Despite its misgivings, Suzuki agreed to provide the detailed project report. Preparing one took eight months. And when it came, it was in dozens of volumes that no one, least of all the ministry's nominee, had the time to read.

The next major step in the estrangement took place in June 1996. One of the first files that the bureaucracy submitted to the new United Front minister for industry for signature was for the replacement of two government directors on the board who had not taken the March 1995 warning very seriously and had continued to vote on occasion against the line from the ministry. The minister signed this, but later had second thoughts about the action and promised to restore the two directors by

October. This, however, never happened for it was preceded by the annual meeting of the Maruti board in September 1996, which in a real sense proved to be the turning point in the relations of the government and Suzuki.

At this meeting, the issue of Maruti's expansion and the new model came up again. This time, another part-time director appointed by the government questioned the estimate Suzuki had prepared for the paint shop of the new expanded plant and asserted that it was being overpriced by 30 per cent. When asked by the Japanese to explain his estimate, he said that the Daewoo paint shop, set up in Delhi at the same time, had cost 30 per cent less. The Japanese explained that Maruti's new paint shop was designed for 200,000 cars a year against Daewoo's 50,000, and therefore that the car bodies had to move through the paint shop much faster. This required the installation of higher capacity painting and heat glazing machines.

The government directors accepted this explanation, but the chairman of Suzuki bitterly resented the question and its implications. 'You can ask how we have come to the estimated cost of the paint shop, but how do you arrive at the precise estimate that we are quoting 30 per cent more than the real cost?' he is reported to have remarked.

This was not, however, the end of the conflict. The government-appointed directors also insisted that they would not accept the new 800cc engine until a prototype had been developed and they had checked its performance. It was after all the taxpayer's money, they said, and claimed that they had a duty to make sure it was being well spent. To this Mr Suzuki is believed to have retorted that Maruti's engineers were welcome to visit the company's research facility in Japan where the engine was in the last stages of development. But he very much doubted whether they were sufficiently qualified to form an independent judgement of its capabilities. The end product of these battles was that the new model of the 800cc was not accepted until June 1997. But its implementation was overtaken only weeks later by yet another row, this time over the appointment of the new chairman and managing director for the Maruti-Suzuki company in India. At that point Mr Suzuki threatened to withhold the transfer of any more technology to Maruti. That was when the prime minister's office finally stepped in to save the project. The upshot of the prolonged squabble was that as of April 2000, Suzuki had still not introduced the new Maruti 800. From offering the most modern and fuel-efficient car in the country, which had been its main selling point in the 1980s, it had been forced to rely solely on the cost advantage that its fully depreciated plant gave it over newer and much more powerful and fuel efficient small cars offered by its Korean competitors, Hyundai and Daewoo. Its prestige 1300cc vehicle looked small and jaded before newer competitors, and the slot it had originally filled, as a medium priced luxury sedan had been filled by superior products from Fiat, Hyundai, and above all Honda. Maruti found out when it introduced a new 1.6 litre competitor for this slot, that it faced an uphill battle against Honda.

The Bangalore airport

The Bangalore project was born out of a decision taken in 1991 by a public sector aircraft manufacturer, Hindustan Aeronautics Limited (HAL), to 'take back' the Bangalore civil airport. The airport had been leased originally from HAL. Now HAL wanted it back to test its own aircraft. Following preliminary surveys and the selection of Devanahalli, north of Bangalore, as the site of the new airport, the Karnataka government floated a tender for the construction of the airport on a build, own and operate (BOO) basis in August 1994. In December 1995 the contract was awarded to Tatas and the American construction and armaments giant Raytheon. But in the meantime HAL had begun to have second thoughts. The 1991 liberalisation had hit its finances hard. Like all other public sector enterprises it was under pressure to show profits. Its aircraft design and production business was in the doldrums after the collapse of the Soviet Union. The civil airport on the other hand was booming. HAL therefore became more and more reluctant to close down this lucrative cash cow. It had therefore begun to make noises about continuing to operate the present Bangalore airport. This was too great a danger for Tatas–Raytheon to ignore, as it threatened to make the airport project unviable. The Memorandum of Understanding they signed with the Karnataka government therefore contained the explicit understanding that the present civil airport would be closed once the new one had been built. Based on this, the consortium presented its feasibility study in June 1996 and obtained the Karnataka government's acceptance in principle in November 1996.

But the civil aviation ministry bureaucrats were not prepared to concede defeat and continued to fight a rearguard action to preserve HAL's right to run a second civilian airport, by raising one objection after the other. The first was based on that much-abused ground, national security. 'How', they asked, 'could a private party, and a foreign party at that, be allowed to own an airport? Where, in a time of war, would their loyalties lie?' This nebulous but convenient fear led to a policy change, foisted on the investors and the state government, in which BOO was replaced by BOT (build, operate, transfer). Both Tatas and Raytheon accepted the change, even though it made financing the project more difficult. But they but stuck to their guns over the need to close down the present airport when the new one was opened. This was the situation when in March 1997, Prime Minister Deve Gowda was replaced by Inder Gujral.

Gujral tried to break the logjam and get a number of stalled projects restarted. Two months after he came to power, at the end of May, he quietly transferred the civil aviation secretary, who had thrown the first spanner in the works by raising the issue of national security, to the ministry for rural development and cooperatives. Mr Gujral also carried out a minor cabinet reshuffle and appointed a new a new minister of state under the cabinet minister for tourism and civil aviation, C.M. Ibrahim, who had become one of the main stumbling blocks to the finalisation of the project. This new minister was charged specifically with the task of looking after civil aviation.

Having secured a measure of control over the ministry, Gujral turned to the more substantive issue of whether a private party should own a strategic facility and whether it should be owned by a foreign company. He resolved this by making the Karnataka government a 30 per cent shareholder in the project. Under Indian company law, this was low enough to give Tatas and Raytheon full freedom to run the airport, but high enough to ensure that no change in the stated purpose of the airport was possible without the state government's explicit concurrence.[14]

A tripartite committee consisting of the Karnataka government, the investors and the central ministry of civil aviation, chaired by its secretary, subsequently confirmed in November 1997 that HAL would stop civilian flights once Devanahalli opened. *But the aviation ministry officials never signed the minutes of the meeting.* Instead another meeting of the committee was convened on 17 June 1998, where the central officials again suggested that the present civil airport should also continue to operate. The Karnataka government stuck to its stand, and reiterated its commitment to Tatas and Raytheon. But in the meantime unidentified officials in the civil aviation ministry had planted a story in the media that the HAL airport would not only remain open but be upgraded to operate international flights. That was enough to spook Raytheon and, probably, Tatas as well. The Karnataka government's writ clearly did not run, despite the fact that the airport was to be in Karnataka. In the central government, the prime minister's writ did not run either. It was the bureaucrats' writ that ran. To make matters worse, starting with the Enron and Suzuki conflicts, a succession of Indian governments had shown that they felt no compunction in using *ex post* changes in policy to renege on solemnly negotiated understandings. This was not, therefore, a country that any responsible foreign investor could risk putting $300 million of borrowed money into.

The Tatas–Singapore Airlines project

Tatas' desire to start a private airline in India to serve domestic air travellers had a long, even sentimental history. J.R.D. Tata, who headed the conglomerate for half a century, was a keen aviator and had flown mail to Karachi from Bombay in the 1930s. Tatas and Dalmias were the first private companies to start airlines in India in the 1940s immediately after independence. Tatas' airline, called Bharat Airways, was nationalised by the government in the 1950s after it adopted the Second Industrial Policy Resolution. For the next 30 years, India had only one airline – Indian airlines, whose timings were inconvenient, service poor and accident record among the worst in the world, thanks mainly to the poor quality of the airports to which it was compelled to fly. In the late 1980s, in the second wave of partial liberalisation initiated by Prime Minister Rajiv Gandhi, air services were partially thrown open to the private sector. But the bureaucrats who made the rules were the ones who ran Indian airlines. What they finally permitted was 'air taxi' services. Initially these were to have been allowed only on routes that Indian airlines did not fly. But within a very short period of time, by means of a reasoning that remains entirely obscure, the air taxi companies were able to fly on all the four prime routes of the country – between Delhi, and Bombay (Mumbai), Madras (Chennai) and Calcutta. These routes generated four-fifths of Indian airlines' revenues, and within a few years the air taxi companies had taken almost half of the existing traffic through better service alone. (A condition of the licence was that they would not charge less than Indian airlines.)

Within a decade of being formed, all but two or three of the air taxi operators had gone broke. Apart from managerial failings one reason was that when they asked for permission to become scheduled airlines they were given it provided that they flew a certain proportion of non-economic routes. This lowered their profits. But the main cause was the steep devaluation of the rupee in the 1990s. From 1984–85 to 1987–88 the rupee was fairly stable, for it depreciated barely 9 per cent against the dollar. In the next four years, it lost 38 per cent of its value. In the next six years it lost another 50 per cent. Unlike Indian airlines, the private operators had leased their aircraft. The devaluation of the rupee made the lease rates uneconomic. Most of them defaulted on their payments. In the end only two important private players remained. The larger was Jet Airways. This was a company with a non-resident Indian promoter, registered in the Channel Islands and funded entirely by Arab money. This was reflected in the composition of its board of directors, all of whom were Arabs.

Tatas floated the joint venture with Singapore Airlines International (SIA) in March 1995. India's reforms were then in full swing, and foreign investors were showing a rising interest in the country. SIA was in the forefront of businesses wishing to invest in India. It needed a stopover/refuelling point on the London–Singapore route and wanted to make it a regional hub. The large and rapidly growing Indian market made Bangalore an especially attractive location. Both the domestic airline and the Bangalore airport project developed out of these longer term global plans. Tatas were an excellent choice as a collaborator. The twin projects were thus a true offspring of globalisation, and precisely the kind of foreign investment India needed to become integrated into the global economy. But the same handful of officers and the same secretary to the civil aviation ministry sabotaged both. And like the airport project, the airline project was also sabotaged by means of appeals to national security.

Since the foreign investment promotion board had already approved of the project during the Narasimha Rao government, other ways had to be found to stop the project. The main argument was, when even the USA did not allow foreign airlines to lift purely domestic traffic, why and for that matter how could India do so? Thus for SIA to operate within India a change in airline policy was first needed. The Congress had announced that it would adopt an 'open skies' policy. The United Front had proclaimed its support for it in principle. But when it came to the crunch, the civil aviation ministry demurred. Tatas and SIA were told to wait until the new airline policy was announced. After a lapse of several months when the policy was announced, it explicitly reneged on the open skies commitment. The government told Tatas that it could set up the airline provided SIA was not an equity shareholder. So Tatas found financing from a consortium of banks and investors, and SIA, which had helped to arrange the funding, agreed to be a technical collaborator.

It then became apparent that Tatas had not one but two enemies – not just Indian airlines, but Jet Airways. And so far as wielding influence in the government was concerned Jet was far ahead of Indian airlines, for its connections were with the political strata. This became apparent when a group of 58 members of parliament protested that the new consortium of investors was simply a cloak for SIA, and demanded complete disclosure of the identities of the investors. Tatas complied with this too. But the MPs were not to be mollified. In August 1998, 40 MPs wrote to the government accusing Tatas of withholding information about their investors and demanding a thorough investigation. That was enough for the ministry of civil aviation to defer a decision once again. That was also sufficient for Tatas to pull out of the project.

16

The Second Crisis and False Dawn

By September 1997, the United Front government had been in power for 16 months, and its inability to overcome its internal contradictions, and in particular to manage the Left, were apparent to all. It could not control the fiscal deficit, the root cause of the premature end of the boom of 1993–96. It could not prevent the Left from publicly sabotaging structural reforms such as the opening up of the insurance sector of the economy, or the amendment of India's patent laws to bring them in line with the requirements of membership of the World Trade Organisation. It could not repeal the 1976 Urban Land Ceiling and Regulation Act to give enterprises the freedom to buy and sell land, or amend the 1977 Industrial Disputes Act to enable it to hire and fire labour without the prior, and rarely given, permission of the government. Indian industry therefore remained denied the freedom of managerial decision making that it needed to compete with the foreign investors who were entering the domestic market. It could not prevent a resurgent *dirigiste* bureaucracy from sabotaging prior commitments made by the government. It could not even take decisions in pursuit of previously enacted policies, such as raise oil product prices, to ensure that Indian oil companies were not forced to sell these at prices below their cost of imports.

All the United Front government could do was to pretend that reforms were 'on course' and that that India's 'economic fundamentals were sound'. It conceded that there were a few clouds on the horizon: exports grew by less than 5 per cent in 1996–97 compared to 20 per cent between 1993–94 and 1995–96; and the rate of industrial growth fell from 11.7 per cent[1] in 1995–96 to 6.7 per cent in 1996–97.[2] But this was a consequence of the exceptionally tight credit policy adopted by the Congress government in mid-1995 to control inflation, and was being corrected rapidly by lowering the cash reserve ratio, and thereby increasing the supply of bank credit available to the commercial sector. All in all, the government claimed, the economy was likely to attain a 6.7 per cent rate of growth in 1997–98. This was not far short of its performance in the previous four years.

As was pointed out in the previous chapter, this picture was utterly misleading. The rapid decline in industrial output in November 1996 was the beginning of a recession that was to go on for the next five years, and had shown no signs of lifting even in April 2001.[3] Industrial growth fell from 12.7 per cent in 1995–96 to 5.6 per cent in 1996–97, rose slightly to 6.6 per cent in 1997–98 and fell to an all-time low of 3.4 per cent in 1998–99. It rose to 6.5 per cent in 1999–2000, but slumped once more to below 5 per cent in 2000–2001.[4]

THE FISCAL CRISIS OF 1998

Trade cycles do eventually reverse themselves. Thus if the downturn had been solely cyclical, it should have ended in 1998 or at the latest by 1999. Its prolonged duration showed that the slump in industrial growth was not caused by cyclical factors but by a structural imbalance in the economy. That imbalance was the country's growing fiscal deficit – the excess of its recurring expenditures over its income – and it was steadily getting worse.

The failure to curb the fiscal deficit did not start with the United Front. On the contrary it reflected the weakness of the consensus in favour of reform in India whose causes were analysed earlier in this section.[5] In 1991 India had to choose between reducing its bloated fiscal deficit by cutting its non-development expenditures or by reducing developmental outlays. Dr Manmohan Singh tried initially to do both. In standby agreements with the IMF and the World Bank the government readily accepted time-bound targets for the reduction of the fiscal deficit. The IMF and Bank for their part made the release of successive tranches of their loans conditional to achieving these targets. But unfortunately for the country, its foreign exchange reserves bounded back to comfortable levels far more rapidly than anyone had anticipated. The sense of peril dissipated, and Dr Singh received very little support for austerity measures within the cabinet.

At the Centre it rapidly became clear that the government would not be able to reduce subsidies on food and fertilisers to any appreciable extent, to shut down and sell off loss-making public enterprises, or to reduce the colossal subsidy on higher education. All that it was prepared to do was to sell some of the shares of public enterprises in order to raise revenue, without allowing them to go into private hands. As a result all the cuts in government spending fell on planned investment in new projects and other developmental expenditures. This sharply reduced new investment in the public sector. Whereas capital expenditure had made up 33 per cent of the central government's total spending in 1985–90, in 1998–99 its share had fallen to 22 per cent.[6] Since by the end of the Seventh Plan the bulk of central government investment was going into the infrastructure, the attenuation of the Plan caused an especially sharp fall in the rate of creation of new infrastructure facilities. The worst hit was the power sector, where the annual outlay fell from about 4,400MW worth in the Seventh Plan to a mere 2,000MW worth in the Ninth. Another crucial area that also felt the axe was defence. Outlays fell from 3.5 per cent of GDP in 1988 to 2.2 per cent in 1996–97.

But the fall in capital spending did not reduce the fiscal deficit for it was more than offset by a sharp increase in central government consumption expenditure. The share of the revenue deficit in the government's gross fiscal deficit rose from an average 32 of per cent (a not very healthy figure) in 1985–90 to 53 per cent in 1998–99.[7]

Throughout the reform period, the states too were no more eager than before to cut the huge subsidies they had been handing out to the farm sector on nearly free power and token irrigation dues, and to the rural population as a whole in the form of subsidised bus services. Worst of all, while the central government was at least trying to freeze the size of its bureaucracy, no such effort was visible in the states.[8]

The one change that economic reforms did bring about was a noticeable hardening of the central government's resolve not to fund state government overdrafts. But this too boomeranged with devastating effect. With their capacity to finance fiscal deficits by borrowing and taking overdrafts severely curtailed, the states took to using their public enterprises to borrow funds on the open market and pass them on to their parent departments to finance their recurring consumption expenditures. They also began to use the central government-owned infrastructure companies as lenders of the last resort. They did this by simply refusing to pay their coal, electricity and telecommunications bills. This left the enterprises no option but to treat these dues as 'accounts receivables' on their balance sheets.[9] More and more of the grants and loans that the states were getting from the central bank and the commercial banking system, also went into meeting the deficit. Not surprisingly, in absolute terms, the states' revenue deficit rose fivefold between 1992–93 and 1998–99. This rate of increase far outstripped the growth of revenues. As a result, while the revenue deficit ate up 39 per cent of these receipts in 1992–93, in 1998–99 the ratio jumped to 73 per cent.[10]

The states responded to the hard budget constraint in another, even more damaging way. Caught between their ballooning consumption expenditures and the central government's fiscal severity, they too chose the soft option of cutting down developmental spending. Only in their case the cuts bit much, much deeper. In addition to curtailing capital spending, they were also forced to make 'economies' in the maintenance of previously created capital assets, and on health, education and shelter programmes. Taking the central government and the states together, the decline in developmental spending (this includes both money spent on creating new assets and money spent on maintaining existing ones) was little short of catastrophic. From a fairly healthy 22.1 per cent of GDP in 1989–90, the last year of Rajiv Gandhi's government, it fell to 15.7 per cent by 1994–95, in just five years.[11] Judging from the steep rise of revenue deficits at the central government and the states since 1994–95, this may have fallen to 12 per cent of GDP by 1998–99. If this trend were to continue, in a few years most of the capital assets created over the past half century will become derelict.

The full extent to which the finances of the Indian state have deteriorated since 1989–90, the year before the economic crisis, is the sum of the rise in the consolidated fiscal deficit of the central government and states, the increase in its borrowing through the public enterprises to meet consumption expenditures, the fall in defence spending, and the decline in developmental expenditure. In 1997–98, taken together these amounted to over 9.5 per cent of GDP![12]

THE *COUP DE GRÂCE*

This was the situation when, in September 1997, the United Front government decided to increase the salaries and pensions of all central government employees. The hike resulted from its decision to accept the recommendations of the Fifth Pay Commission. Under the Indian constitution pay commissions are set up every ten years to bring salaries in line with the cost of living. Since government salaries are protected against inflation by a 'dearness allowance' pegged to the cost of living index, in previous decades the Commission's award had only created a temporary cash crunch that eased within a year or two as revenues rose with growth. However, in the more than a decade that had elapsed since an earlier government accepted the recommendations of the Fourth Pay Commission, two developments had greatly enhanced the averse effect of another salary increase. The first, mentioned earlier, was a rise of 4 million in the number of civil servants. The second was the decision of nearly all state governments to match the salaries of their employees with those of the central government.

In the 1970s and 1980s there had been a sharp deterioration in both central and state government finances for other reasons. As a result, state governments recorded the last of their revenue surpluses in 1981–82 and went consistently into the red thereafter. The central government's fiscal deficit rose rapidly in the 1980s until it hit 7.7 per cent of GDP (8.7 per cent by the old calculation of GDP with 1980–81 as base year) in the crisis year 1990–91.[13] As has been described above, the financial condition of neither central government nor states improved during the reform years. The Fifth Pay Commission therefore took this into account and recommended that to cushion the shock of the salary increases the government should raise the retirement age by two years (thereby postponing the payment of retirement benefits) and reduce the number of its employees by 30 per cent over the next ten years. The Congress government accepted the award in January 1996, but deferred details of its implementation until after the election. The task of implementing the award therefore fell upon the shoulders of the United Front.

But the United Front was united only in name. None of its constituents wanted to grasp the nettle of reform. None even expected to remain in power long enough to have to face the consequences of accepting the recommendations. As a result, five of the six members of the committee it set up to discuss the wage awards with the employees competed with each other to find ways of going beyond the Pay Commission's recommendation, and gave in to every demand made by the central government employees' unions. Not only did they add a further 30 per cent to the Pay Commission's salaries and pensions, but they also agreed not to raise the retirement age and not to reduce the size of the bureaucracy. The sixth member, finance minister P. Chidambaram, who was the only person in the committee who could have reined in the enthusiasm of the other five, took himself off to Chennai (formerly Madras) in the middle of the meetings and inexplicably failed to return to Delhi until they were over. Enquiries revealed that he had been commanded by the leader of his party, the Tamil Maanila Congress, to stay away from the meetings on pain of expulsion. The TMC leader, G. Moopanar, did not see any reason why his party should be the one to run foul of the powerful 3.6 million-strong central government employees federations when none of its partners in the United Front was willing to do so.[14]

As Table 16.1 shows, the effect of these decisions, which were taken in September 1997, was devastating. Between 1996–97 and 1998–99 the consolidated gross fiscal deficit rose by 2.3 per cent of GNP. However, this was before the states had fully met their obligation to raise salaries, and before either the central government or the states had made provisions to pay the increased pensions decreed by the Pay Commission.

Over the two years in which the salary increase was implemented, the central government's salary bill rose by 76 per cent in absolute

Table 16.1
Deterioration of state and central government finances

Year	1993–94	1994–95	1995–96	1996–97	1997–98	1998–99
GNP*	7869.97	9303.25	10897.54	12721.77	14132.31	15799.92
Centre: revenue deficit (%)	4.1	3.3	2.7	2.6	3.3	3.8
Centre: gross fiscal deficit (%)	7.5	6.2	5.5	5.2	6.3	6.6
States: revenue deficit (%)	0.5	0.6	0.8	1.3	1.4	1.7
States: gross fiscal deficit (%)	2.6	3.0	2.9	2.9	3.6	3.8
Consolidated revenue deficit (%)	4.6	3.9	3.7	3.9	4.9	5.5
Consolidated gross fiscal deficit (%)	10.1	9.2	8.4	8.1	9.9	10.4

* GNP at factor cost (1993–94 = 100) (Rs. bn)
Source: CMIE, *Public Finance, February 1999*, pp. 178, 516. GNP figures are taken from *Economic Survey 1998–99*.

terms, a sum of Rs. 140 billion or just over 1 per cent of the GDP.[15] But the central government employed only 3.6 million employees whereas the state governments employed 9.7 million employees in state and local government in addition to about 6 million in quasi-government bodies. When they finished their calculations the states found that they would have to pay out another Rs. 352.66 billion or 2. 2 per cent of the GDP.[16] In all, this single act of largesse increased the fiscal deficit by 3.2 per cent of the GDP!

ST PATRICK'S COLLEGE LIBRARY

FALSE DAWN

The salary increases awarded to central and state employees ensured that the fiscal deficit would not come down below 10 per cent of the GDP, no matter how hard the central government tried to control its own expenditure. As a result, public borrowing continued to crowd out private, to push up real interest rates, and prevent a revival of investment. After two years of unremitting decline, in virtually every respect, the Indian economy reached its nadir in October 1998. The growth of industrial production touched zero (compared to the same month of the previous year); foreign currency reserves fell from $25.9 billion in March 1998 to $22.3 billion at the end of September;[17] thanks, in part, to the Asian economic crisis, exports declined in absolute terms by 3.3 per cent in the first half of the year, against a rise of 4.4 per cent in the first half of 1997–98. Most serious of all, inflation, as measured by the consumer price index for industrial workers, was running at 13 per cent, and nearly the whole of this was caused by a phenomenal increase in the prices of primary articles, such as foodgrains, fruit and vegetables, and dairy products.[18]

In March 1998 the ramshackle United Front government had finally fallen because the Congress no longer felt it had anything to gain by supporting it from the outside. The elections that followed brought the country's first overtly right-wing government to power. Called the National Democratic Alliance, it was headed by the BJP. One of the first actions of the new government was to deepen the financial and economic crisis by conducting five nuclear weapons tests on 11 and 13 May 1998, barely two months after it came to power. This immediately brought down economic sanctions upon the government's head and a sharp cut in both bilateral and multilateral foreign assistance. It also led to a fall in foreign direct investment, and for some months a decline in exports as buyers abroad imposed their own sanctions to show their displeasure.[19]

The government met the immediate decline in inflows of foreign exchange by floating a new series of bonds in the New York market, called the India Resurgent Bonds. These netted $4.7 billion and gave the country the cushion it needed. But the convergence of sanctions, a decline in public and private capital inflows, and a decline in exports caused in part by the Asian crisis, made the government extremely sensitive to any outflow of foreign exchange and caused it to raise interest rates to check these outflows at the slightest pretext. One such increase in January put an end to a mild industrial recovery that had begun in 1997. A second hike in interest rates for the same reason in August 1998 dealt another blow to industrial investment. A third in July 2000 put an end to another mild industrial recovery that had begun in 1999.

Finally, in October and November the National Democratic Alliance government, which had initially also sung the United Front's tune that the economy was fundamentally sound and a recovery was around the corner, decided that it could pretend no longer. In the budget for 2000–2001, economic reform at last got its second wind. The change was presaged by the tone of the economic survey for 2000–2001. In sharp contrast to its predecessors the survey cast aside all pretence that India's economy was doing well. On the contrary, in dispassionate, dry statistics it conceded that the economy was in a deep slump and that the cause was structural.

The data it presented were damning. They showed that the growth of GDP (at factor cost) came down a full 1 per cent from 7.1 per cent between 1993–94 and 1996–97, to 6.05 per cent between 1997–98 and 2000–2001.[20] Even the latter growth rate, the survey hinted, was inflated by the vagaries of national income accounting. While the growth in the first period was concentrated in industry (9 per cent) and agriculture (4.5 per cent), in the second it was concentrated almost entirely in the services sector (9 per cent). As a result, while service sector growth was 1 per cent higher in the first period than the growth of GDP (8.1 per cent) it was a full 2.95 per cent higher in the second (9.1 per cent).

The survey left readers in no doubt that a good part of the latter growth was purely statistical. While service sector growth in the first period was concentrated in what might be termed 'productive' services – trade, tourism, hotels, transport and financial services, all of which are directly linked to the volume of real business being done in the other sectors of the economy – growth in the second period was concentrated almost entirely in community and personal services. This was a direct result of the more than 40 per cent increase in salaries and pensions to civil servants described above, and the fact that by a quirk of the UN system of National Income Accounting, any growth in money incomes in this sector is treated as a growth of real product. As a result, from 1997–98 to 1999–2000 community and personal services grew by an average of 11.1 per cent!

The economic survey for 1999–2000 had estimated that this had inflated the overall GDP growth in 1997–98 and 1998–99 by 0.7 per cent.[21] By pointing out that service sector growth was expected to come down by a full 4.2 per cent, and the growth rate by a full 0.4 per cent in 2000–01, because the salary hikes by the central and state governments

Table 16.2
Deceleration of growth (all figures are percentages)

Structure of GDP	1993–97	1997–2001
GDP *of which:*	7.1	6.05
Agriculture	4.5	1.6
Industry	9.0	5.2
Services *of which:*	8.1	9.0
Community and personal	5.2	11.1
Adjusted GDP	7.1	5.4

had been fully absorbed, it implicitly put a figure for GDP inflation caused by the salary hikes in 2000–01. After allowing for these the adjusted growth rate in these three years was as low as 5.4 per cent.

INDIAN DEFLATION

The economic survey also left readers in no doubt that the spurt in the sale of consumer durables and the resulting mild industrial recovery in 1999–2000, when growth in this sector rose from 3.4 to 6.5 per cent, was fuelled mostly by the spending of the arrears of the salary and pension hikes, and only peripherally by an agricultural recovery in 1998.

In 2000–01, as in the following year, the evidence of a slump in demand was unmistakable. First there was the data on prices: although the wholesale price index had risen by over 8 per cent year-on-year in January 2001, if one excluded a 29.6 per cent rise in fuel and energy prices, the wholesale price index of all other commodities had risen by only 2.4 per cent. The same exercise for 1999–2000 showed an increase of only 1.5 per cent. The consumer price index also rose by only 2.7 per cent until the end of November before the rise in administered price of petroleum products kicked in, against zero per cent in the previous year. (In India, ever since the early 1950s the normal increase in prices has been of the order of 7 to 8 per cent a year.)

Table 16.3
Structure of government finances (%)

Central government finance	1990–91	1996–97	1999–2000
National debt	pre-reform	46.4	51.8
Fiscal deficit	pre-reform	4.1	5.5
Interest/GDP	3.8	4.6	4.7

Source: Compiled by the author from data in the *Economic Survey*.

Private consumption growth decelerated to 4.2 per cent even in the 'recovery' year of 1999–2000, from 7.2 per cent in 1998–99. At the time when the economic survey came out, there were no estimates available for 2000–2001, but sectoral trends showed that it declined further; for while there was a small revival in the sale of basic consumer goods, there has been a whopping decline in sales, ranging from 6 to 16 per cent in consumer durables. Clearly India had been having its own milder version of the Chinese deflation of 1997–2000, but unlike China no one in government had grasped its significance or wished to adopt the pump priming measures that China so resolutely undertook.

The survey minced no words on where the problem lay. This was the fiscal deficit, which stood, in spite of the government's optimistic estimates of GDP growth in 2000–01, at 10 per cent of GDP. This relentless dissaving, the survey said, had turned an East Asian private saving rate (over 33 per cent) into a miserable gross saving rate of 23 per cent and was mainly responsible for the decline in public investment, the crowding out of private investment and the consequent stagnation in overall investment and economic growth.

Significantly, most of the deterioration occurred after 1996–97 – during the period of political instability at the Centre. The national debt grew from 46.4 per cent in 1996–97 to 51.8 per cent in 2000–01; the central government's fiscal deficit has risen from 4.1 to 5.5 per cent; and the ratio of interest on the public debt to the GDP had risen from 3.8 per cent of GDP in 1990–91 to 4.7 per cent in 1999–2000.[22] An index of the crowding out of private investment was given by the finance minister during his budget speech: he said that while real interest rates had seldom exceeded 3 per cent between 1980 and 1998, in the past three years they had risen to between 6 and 8 per cent.[23]

And at long last, the economic survey conceded that the way to tackle the fiscal deficit was not to tinker with it, but to eliminate administered pricing altogether and concentrate on identifying and precisely helping the weaker target groups that really needed help. To this end it suggested completely deregulating pricing and sales of petroleum products, fertilisers and sugar, making labour laws more flexible, and lowering interest rates.

The economic survey for 2000–01 was not the first to have told home truths about the state of the economy. On the contrary, it had become a settled practice in the government to allow the survey to appraise the needs of the economy while the budget handed out political sops often with scant regard for what the survey had said. This time, however, the survey proved to be an accurate pecursor to the contents of the budget.

In his budget speech, finance minister Yashwant Sinha conceded that the economy was facing not one but three interrelated challenges. These were to bring down the fiscal deficit; to revive growth in agriculture and industry (as opposed to services); and to initiate the long-deferred structural reforms without which the country would not be able to fulfil its pledges to the World Trade Organisation to eliminate quantitative restrictions on imports and bring tariffs down progressively.

REVIVING INVESTMENT

The budget sought to boost investment by reducing the prime real rate of interest and reviving the primary share market. Interest rates were brought down by an average of 1.5 per cent. In order to increase the equity component of new investment the budget lowered the tax on distributed dividends from 20 to 10 per cent, and exempted capital gains on shares sold in the secondary market from taxation if the proceeds were reinvested in the primary share market (i.e. in new shares). The three measures together were expected to lower the cost of borrowed funds and increase the equity portion of new investment. Together these measures were capable of lowering the fixed cost of borrowing for investment by up to 4 per cent (i.e. reduce it by a quarter).

REDUCING THE FISCAL DEFICIT

In December 2000 the government had introduced a Fiscal Responsibility and Budget Management Bill in the parliament that would bind the Centre to reducing its fiscal deficit to 2 per cent of the GDP within a period of five years. The Bill received a cautious welcome, not because its contents were in any way objectionable, but because no one believed that the government could do it. But Mr Sinha confounded his critics, for the budget was all that anyone could have hoped for.

The main tools were the reduction of interest rates; the deregulation of petro-product pricing; the deregulation of fertiliser pricing; and the curtailment of food procurement.

The absolute amount of reduction in the deficit needed to achieve the target set in the Fiscal Responsibility Act depends upon the rate of growth of the nominal GDP. If this continued to grow at the historical rate of 12 to 14 per cent, then to attain a 2 per cent fiscal deficit the government would have to bring down the fiscal deficit from Rs. 1.1 trillion in 2000–01 to Rs. 800–850 billion in 2005–06.[24] A close analysis of the budget shows that this reduction is entirely feasible. Indeed, if the growth of GDP in real terms were to pick up as a result of the deficit reduction and other measures announced in the budget, the target could easily be surpassed.

The measure with the most immediate impact was the 1.5 per cent cut in the prime interest rates. This will save the government around Rs. 45 billion in annual interest payments, but when the interest rate reduction percolates through the economy, it will enable the government to roll over its national debt and reduce the burden of interest payment on national debt by up to 2 per cent. Overall, the saving in interest payments could be of the order of Rs. 200 billion to Rs. 220 billion.

Another key reform will be the deregulation of petroleum product pricing. In 2000–01 the subsidies on various petroleum products amounted to Rs. 80 billion.[25] Deregulation, even with some cross-subsidies will therefore increase revenues by this amount. In addition the budget began a process of consolidating taxation rates on petroleum products around a single VAT of 16 per cent that will add another substantial amount to the government's revenues. Overall, the deregulation and harmonization of taxes is likely to increase revenues by Rs. 250 billion.

In the same manner the deregulation of fertiliser prices will eliminate Rs. 130 billion of subsidy by 2006–07.

Lastly, the government announced a change in its procurement policy on foodgrains with an immense potential for fiscal saving. From 1951 until this year it was committed to buying all the foodgrains that farmers offered to it at the announced procurement prices. From 2001 it reduced its commitment to buying only as much was needed to maintain a buffer stock against drought and famine. This will mean a reduction in purchases from an average of 30 million tonnes to between 15 and 20 million tonnes.[26] Every tonne cost Rs. 5,000 to transport, store and distribute, and the entire cost was being borne by the central government. Thus bringing down the buffer stock to 20 million tonnes will therefore save Rs. 125 billion at today's price.

Overall, therefore, the budget contained the potential to reduce the current fiscal deficit by Rs. 700 billion. If this could have been done in a variant of shock therapy, the fiscal deficit would have dropped to between Rs. 400 billion and Rs. 500 billion in 2001–02. But stretching out the changes over two to five years will add interest payments on the additional debt that will be incurred in these years. The fiscal deficit may therefore fall only to around Rs. 900 billion, or a fraction more than 2 per cent of GDP, in 2005–06.[27]

STRUCTURAL REFORM

The most significant element of the 2001–02 budget was the start it made in changing the structure of the economy. In agriculture the decision to buy only as much foodgrains at the official support prices as the government needed to replenish its buffer stocks, meant that farmers would be forced to bring between 10 and 15 million tonnes more to the market every year. This would inevitably lead to a sharp decline in market prices. As a result farmers would no longer have the assurance of covering their costs of production and making a minimum return on their produce and would have to actively explore what the market demanded before sowing their crops. In effect this would lead to a sharp acceleration of a shift away from foodgrains to cash crops and perishable produce such as fruit and vegetables.[28] The finance minister sought to mitigate the resulting uncertainty by simultaneously removing curbs on the inter-state movement of foodgrains. This led to a rise in the price offered to farmers in grain surplus areas by traders, and unified the national market for foodgrains.

The second structural change was the freeing, at long last, of the market for labour. Ten years after the reforms began the Vajpayee government has finally enacted an 'exit policy' for labour. By freeing all establishments employing less than a thousand workers from the need to get government permission for laying off workers, it opened the labour market for 96 per cent of industrial establishments and 89 per cent of industrial labour. The government also began the long-delayed process of creating a safety net for the retrenched workers and a national unemployment insurance scheme. The budget decreed that those who were laid off would get their accumulated provident funds, 45 days of separation pay for each year of service and a year on unemployment insurance at 30 per cent of the last pay drawn. The government also freed investment in 14 key products which had previously been reserved for the small-scale sector. Eleven of these were leather goods and three were toys that accounted for a large part of the exports of the small-scale sector. Dereservation opened up the possibility of increasing size and upgrading technology to international levels.

The freeing of the labour market has been severely criticised by trade unions and the Left, but it is not by any means obvious that giving employers freedom to retrench will increase unemployment in the country. This is because it will make it possible for managements to close down sick enterprises, sell the remaining assets, pay off loans and, above all, pay workers their accumulated dues. This would free a large amount of capital for new investment that would create jobs. Much of the threatened loss of jobs was in any case illusory, because employers who had not been allowed to close loss-making plants on the grounds that this would involve laying off workers, had for decades been simply pulling down the shutters, putting padlocks on the factory gates, and paying lawyers to keep them out of jail. According to the economic survey there were 306,000 small enterprises in the country in March 1999 which had taken loans amounting to Rs. 43.13 billion from banks and then declared themselves sick.[29] But these account for only a fraction of the sick units in the country. In 2000, there were more than 3 million small units, of which not more than 15 to 20 per cent had access to bank credit. One expert has estimated that 30 per cent of these small units are sick.[30] This amounts to over a million units whose closure will release at least Rs. 100 billion of capital for new investment. Another 30 per cent were existing on the margin of sickness.[31] Freedom to shed surplus labour and to sell their land could save many of these and consequently the jobs of their employees.

TOWARDS POLITICAL STABILITY

Mr Vajpayee's National Democratic Alliance came to power after the fall of the United Front government in March 1998. Why did it take two full years to come to grips with the task of completing the economic reforms that Narasimha Rao had begun? The answer is that not until October 1999 did it acquire sufficient political stability and self-confidence to believe that it could last its full five years and therefore afford to take hard decisions.

As was pointed out in Chapter 13, Narasimha Rao was forced to begin the process of economic reform without a majority in parliament. He was therefore forced to carry out a delicate balancing act between India's domestic lobbies and its foreign creditors. His government therefore attempted only the easier reforms – those of the product and foreign exchange markets. When his government fell in 1996 virtually nothing had been done to reform the factor markets. As was pointed out in Chapter 15 the political instability that followed prevented any meaningful reforms, and allowed a resurgence of *dirigiste* sentiment in the bureaucracy. Despite this the remorseless logic of Indian democracy was paving the way for a return of political stability. The elections of 1996, 1998 and 1999 saw a steady movement towards a bipolar (or binodal) political system. In its essence this system, when it stabilises fully, is likely to replace the dominant party democracy that Indian had enjoyed under the Congress, with brief interruptions, from 1947 to 1996 with two coalitions of political parties, each consisting of a powerful all-India party joined by a number of overtly ethnic parties with strong bases in a single state. The transition from Congress dominance to this binodal system is far from complete, but it is being brought about by two opposed pressures, that have operated in the Indian political system from the very beginning. The first is India's federal constitution and more specifically the ethnic distinctness of its federating states. The second is the simple majority, or 'first past the post' voting system.

The first has created strong ethno-national parties in almost every state of the country. The second has consistently rewarded the largest party by giving it a higher proportion of seats than votes, and has penalised the smaller parties by doing the opposite; thus the simple majority voting system has exerted a relentless pressure towards political consolidation. Over half a century, this has led to the emergence of stable two-party or two-coalition political systems in all but one or two states. But the very same voting system that has promoted the development of a two-party system at the state level has yielded as many as 37 recognised and 139 registered but unrecognised parties at the Centre.[32] This is because ethnic parties command strong loyalty in their home states. This has enabled each of them to capture a handful of seats in the national parliament. In these circumstances a stable national government could only emerge when these parties gravitated into stable coalitions at the Centre also. Since no ethno-national party could form a coalition at the Centre with the political party that was its principal rival in its home state, political stability required the fulfilment of three conditions. First, the emergence of two major parties at the national level. This required the erosion and eventual disappearance of any 'third force' or party with national aspirations. Second, that in its home state the ethno-national party should face only one dominant national party. This will automatically make it gravitate to the other at the national level. Third, where there are two competing ethno-national parties, they should ally themselves with the rival national parties.

Viewed against this model, the development of a binodal democracy to replace the dominant party democracy that India has known, is clearly visible. In the 1991 elections the National Front, led by former prime minister V.P. Singh, brought together a large number of ethno-national parties and all secular national parties except the Congress and projected itself as a national alternative to the BJP. The purpose was to supplant the Congress. Had Rajiv Gandhi not been assassinated, this front might well have secured more seats than the Congress, but in the aftermath of that tragedy, the Congress gained from a large sympathy vote and ended with 232 seats and the National Front sank to 131. The era of alliances had begun but this was masked for the next five years by the skill with which the Congress president and prime minister, Narasimha Rao, managed a tacit coalition without having to concede any cabinet seats to other parties.

The 1996 elections saw the Congress reduced to second place with only 140 seats out of 544. The BJP forged into the lead with 161 seats, but a motley collection of 13 centre-left parties won 171 seats, formed a hurried coalition and got the Congress to agree to support it against the BJP from the outside. As was described in Chapters 14 and 15, the resulting 'United Front' was paralysed by its own internal contradictions. In 1998, a disgusted electorate halved its numbers from 171 to 98. Both the Congress and the BJP-led front gained from the attrition of the United Front, the former increasing its strength to 141 and the latter to 252. This time the BJP and its allies were close enough to a majority to form a government.

The 1998 elections made it clear that the Congress and the BJP would be the future 'poles' of national politics. This fulfilled the first of the three conditions outlined above. The second condition also had been fulfilled gradually over the previous decade and a half. Since the Congress had been the dominant party, with powerful units in every state, ethno-national parties came up naturally in opposition to it. This was the genesis of the National Front which was formed in 1989 and captured power briefly that year under V.P. Singh. Since then, as the 'third force' has been whittled away, more and more of its members have made alliances with the BJP. In the same way, local or remnant national parties that find themselves opposed or threatened by the BJP have begun to gravitate to the Congress. This trend was not as clearly developed as the movement of regional opponents of the Congress towards the BJP, but gathered momentum in 1998 and 1999. Finally, in the one state, Tamil Nadu, where national parties had been reduced to third and fourth place by two powerful competing ethno-national parties, the DMK and the AIADMK, by April 1999 these had aligned themselves with the BJP and the Congress respectively. Thus by mid-1999 India was well on the way towards meeting all the three conditions for the emergence of a binodal political system.

Part IV
CONCLUSION

17

State and Market
in Economic Reform

It is now possible to compare the three countries' experience of economic reform in the 1980s and 1990s with the model presented at the very beginning of this book.

RUSSIA

Russia had the longest road to travel but tried to do so in the shortest possible time. As a result, Russia's economy was reduced to a shambles. Its GDP declined by more than half. In 2000, at least 35 per cent of its people were living in absolute poverty, and overt unemployment, unknown in the Soviet Union, was rising rapidly. Its population was declining, and the average life expectancy of Russian males had fallen by five years. In a classic vindication of the theory of underdevelopment, its economy had been torn in two: while exports, which consisted almost entirely of minerals and raw materials, were booming and the country was chalking up higher and higher trade surpluses, the domestic economy had regressed to barter and subsistence.

The rise of the barter economy destroyed the tax base of the country. The ratio of tax revenues to GDP therefore declined by almost two-thirds in six years. Employees' contributions to the four other welfare funds, which constituted the mainstay of the socialist economy, declined by the same proportion. Since the GDP too fell by more than half, this meant that in absolute terms the revenues of the state fell by five-sixths in absolute terms. This forced the state to choose between printing more money to meet its expenses or resorting to borrowing. Until 1994 it printed money. After that it borrowed money. That led directly to the collapse of August 1998.

The collapse of the tax base was both an effect and a cause of the erosion of the state. The state can remain a seat of authority and a source of legitimacy, only so long as it has an assured source of revenue sufficient to discharge its obligations. Russia lost its revenue-raising capability when it privatised the state-owned enterprises. It thus gave away its only revenue base – the socialist equivalent of the 'Royal Domain' of the Crown – to the first comer, free of cost. In theory the privatised state assets should have yielded taxes and, being better run, should have swelled the government's revenues. But Russia privatised its economy and thereby lost its 'socialist domain' without putting an effective alternative system for raising revenue – in the form of direct and indirect taxation – in place. By 1998 therefore the state had lost most of its legitimacy and was well on the way to disintegration.

In sum the adoption of 'shock therapy' in a non-market economy came close to destroying not only the economy but also the state. Communist Party leader Gennadi Zyuganov's 1996 accusation that Russia had fallen victim to the 'neutron bomb of monetarism' was not just accurate, but in view of what happened in August 1998, extra-ordinarily prescient.

CHINA

China had a considerably shorter distance to travel from plan to market. In 1978, only 500 products were under central planning against 20,000 to 60,000 (depending upon the definition of product) in Russia. Twenty per cent of total industrial production took place even then outside the state-owned enterprises (SOEs) and was therefore outside the centrally planned system of production and distribution. A nascent local market existed, and was supplemented by a growing and increasingly complex system of barter of 'above plan' output between SOEs, in semi-annual buyers' conferences that had all the characteristics of an emerging national market system. China also made the changeover very much more slowly than Russia. It recognised that competition was the essence of the market system and that those who succeeded in the market had to be allowed to profit from their success. But it introduced competition from the edges of its economic system – by encouraging the develop-ment of township and village enterprises, and by encouraging foreign and joint ventures. As most of the joint ventures were allowed to sell their products in the domestic market, and did in fact sell just under half within China, the SOEs came under pressure to modernise and become more market oriented from both directions at once. At the same time, by lifting controls on output and prices in stages, and simultaneously increasing the share of earnings an enterprise could retain and distribute as wages and social benefits, it allowed SOE workers to profit from output and price decontrol and made them increasingly profit minded. Their rising salary packets disarmed the workers and removed the main potential hurdle to reform.

But in retrospect it can be seen that the pressure on the SOEs from these two directions was allowed to grow too rapidly. In 1985 the non-SOE industrial output was 34.1 per cent of the total when measured in current prices. In 1995 its share had risen to 66 per cent. The township and village enterprises and joint ventures worked in an environment where there was freedom not only of the product markets but to a large extent of the factor markets as well. The foreign companies worked in special economic zones where they could hire and fire workers, and were not burdened down with pensions, and a host of other social security obligations. The infrastructure facilities in these zones was of a higher quality than those available to the SOEs, and their managers did not have to get decisions endorsed by a state bureaucracy. They could change prices and the product mix at will. They could also close down a factory, or relocate with relatively little trouble. The township and village enterprises were similarly free of the burden of dealing with a massive state bureaucracy. The county or city to which they belonged bore many of the overhead costs of the workers. As a result wage rates were often less than half of what the SOEs had to pay and they changed their products so frequently that it was difficult to make constant price estimates of the value of their output.

By contrast, the SOEs were grudgingly awarded the freedom of the product markets in incremental stages but never acquired freedom in the factor markets. Without it they could not take major investment decisions, hire and fire labour, divest themselves of social security obligations, or sell off surplus land to raise capital for modernisation. In particular, ten years was far too short a time to change the mindset of bureaucrats who manned the National Bureau of State Owned Property, or the institutional framework in which the SOEs had to operate. Thus the larger enterprises remained bound down by the multi-tiered state bureaucracy under the NBSO, which effectively prevented them from taking managerial decisions on their own; and all of them had to spend a large part of their earnings on meeting social commitments that lay at the heart of the 'Socialist market system with Chinese characteristics'.

In effect, therefore, incremental reform from the edges towards the middle had the unintended consequence of creating two levels of managerial freedom. As a result while the edges of China's industrial structure thrived, the core sickened and its losses mounted. As the managers of the SOEs realised that they were going nowhere, the temptation to strip their enterprises of financial reserves and physical assets in order to set up new collectives or joint ventures free from the crippling restrictions of the state sector became progressively harder to resist. That speeded up the spread of sickness in the state sector of industry.

Until 1997 China's problems appeared serious but manageable. So long as growth in the new sectors of the economy remained brisk, workers laid off by the SOEs could be absorbed in new enterprises. It even seemed possible to close down entire enterprises. But in 1997 it became apparent that the new sectors of the economy – the enterprises that were the darlings of the market – were in trouble. The trouble had been brewing for some time and had been visible in the slowing growth of employment in the non-state sector. But in the aftermath of the Asian economic crisis it became apparent that every undesirable feature of the East Asian growth model was present in an exaggerated form in China. Thus there was huge over-investment in the 'pillar' industries without proper techno-economic feasibility studies. Bank managers who were still halfway between the command and market economy in their mentality, and for whom therefore the word of a prominent state official was far more important than the signals of the market, furnished the capital for the investment. And they did so at unrealistic interest rates, partly because the official estimate of the rate of inflation was too low, and partly because they had not broken the habit of listening to the dictates of powerful provincial bosses.

Other weaknesses of the Asian Tigers have also reproduced themselves in China. ITICs and holding companies set up by provincial governments have raised loans in foreign exchange and lent in yuan; borrowed short and lent long – both recipes for disaster. Lastly, China has developed a real estate bubble as spectacular as that of Malaysia. In sum, China's gradual reform has not been gradual enough. The pace of change from plan to market – from socialism to capitalism – has been too fast and has not allowed the institutional framework of capitalism – its market-based production and finance systems – to develop. As a result, China has rapidly developed its own variant of Asia's crony capitalism, and as growth has begun to flag, the pigeons have come home to roost

INDIA

Of the three countries, India had the shortest way to go to become a fully-fledged market economy. India's transition to industrial capitalism began in the 1860s, shortly after the construction of the railways by the British. India's national market was even older, going back to the days of Mughal rule. India also had a flourishing modern financial sector. Its commercial banks covered every corner of the country, and its investment banks were familiar with the procedure for vetting new project proposals. It had a well developed although poorly administered system of property, contract and corporate law and inadequate but usable laws on bankruptcy and foreclosure.

In India, therefore, economic conditions on the eve of reform were precisely what the framers of the Washington Consensus had imagined them to be in all countries at all times. The market existed. All that the government had to do was remove the hurdles that it had itself created to its efficient functioning. India was therefore the best possible candidate for shock therapy. But instead it too opted for gradual reform. What was worse, Indian reforms were excruciatingly slow. As a result, with the shortest distance to travel, India has also travelled the shortest part of that distance.

SOME LESSONS FOR THE FUTURE

Five lessons emerge from the above analysis. *The first and most important* is that structural adjustment programmes can work only if there is a market system already in place. It has unpredictable effects and can fail miserably when there is no market. *The second* is that the creation of a market economy has not one but two facets: the creation of the markets (defined as places or systems that bring together a large number of buyers and sellers), and the creation of regulatory institutions that will make them work smoothly. The neglect of either can lead to severe setbacks to the economy and complicate the transition from plan to market. *The third* is that since in practice no country can create the institutions needed to govern a market in the absence of the market itself, the two must go hand in hand. This requires a careful sequencing of the reform measures to keep pace with the enactment of laws and the development of the capacity to implement and enforce them. *The fourth* is that the speed at which the transition can be completed depends on the extent to which the institutions that collectively make up the market already exist when it is attempted. This virtually rules out shock therapy, except as a remedy at one fringe of the range of strategic options. *The fifth* and final lesson is that economic reform creates a paradox: while the sheer complexity of the transition increases the demands on the state during the transition period, and therefore requires a strong state, the economic reform tends to generate forces that weaken the state at precisely this moment. This is particularly true in the realm of government finance.

In terms of the model given in Chapter 1 (Table 1.1), Russia's economy collapsed, and the state very nearly disintegrated because instead of carefully sequencing the ten reforms listed in column 1 and allowing them time to have the effects listed in column 2, Russia tried to carry out all of the column 1 reforms virtually simultaneously. The result was that the effects listed in column 2 never occurred, or did so in odd, often unrecognisable ways (such as the creation of that most primitive of market economies – the barter economy). The emphasis laid by the IMF and Western liberal economists on the creation of the regulatory institutions listed in column 3, and their diagnosis in 1997 and 1998 that the economic reforms were failing because of Russia's failure to do so quickly enough therefore acquired a growing tinge of unreality. For they hid the fact that having started from the false assumption that the state had only to vacate the realm of economic management for the market to appear spontaneously, they neither understood what was going wrong, nor had any useful suggestions left to make.

China followed the sequence of reforms laid out in column 1 and succeeded in creating a market economy by stages as laid out in column 2. But it lagged far behind in creating the regulatory institutions listed in column 3. This prevented its budding market economy from becoming self-regulating. As a result investment went out of control and the resulting overproduction brought China to the brink of crisis.

India already had the market economy outlined in column 2 and most of the regulatory financial and legal institutions listed in column 3. It needed to carry out the reforms listed in column 1, and because the institutions listed in columns 2 and 3 already largely existed, it was in a position to carry out the column 1 reforms all at once, by shock therapy. But it dawdled endlessly over them, preferring instead to fine tune institutions such as stock markets and the banking system. These reforms, which were characteristic of the phase of unstable federal governments that followed the fall of the Congress in 1996, became in a sense pointless because the column 1 reforms which alone would have created the conditions in which these reforms became needed, kept being postponed.

THE TRANSFORMATION OF THE STATE

The transformation of a planned to a market economy requires not just new economic institutions, but a profound reorientation of the role of the state as well. In Western Europe the mercantilist state was unabashedly interventionist and its goal was not the maximisation of welfare but the augmentation of state power. It regulated domestic trade, and treated international trade as an adjunct to its capacity to wage war. Accordingly, it maximised exports and curbed imports to create a trade surplus, and used the gold it obtained as settlement to finance a professional army and navy. It strove for self-reliance in food and a monopoly of technology. It banned the emigration of skilled artisans and, in the early years of the Industrial Revolution, tried its best to prevent the export of machines from Britain to the Continent. The Industrial Revolution made it necessary to create the self-regulating market. But this was only possible if the state ceased to regulate the market. Thus the demolition of the mercantilist state and its replacement with the liberal state, which defined its functions in minimalist terms, was a necessary requirement for the success of industrial capitalism.

Socialist and *dirigiste* economies faced a similar need to redefine the goals and functions of the state. Castells has described the change as moving from statism to capitalism.[1] A 'statist' economic system is one oriented towards maximising state power while a capitalist system is oriented towards maximising profit. Partly because of the circumstances of its birth and the bitter hostility that it faced throughout its existence, and partly because of the internal logic of communism and centralised planning, the Soviet Union proved to be a statist economy *par excellence*. But China was only a few steps behind. India, along with most countries that gained their freedom after the Second World War, also adopted statist policies in order to speed up industrialisation and 'catch up' with the West. They were not to know in the early 1950s that 'convergence' required open and not closed economies.

In statist economies every major interaction between economic agents is mediated to a greater or lesser degree by the state. This makes decision-making lines run vertically instead of horizontally. Every decision is handed down and every response sent back up along a chain that runs vertically from economic agencies to government and back. This is the antithesis of a profit maximising (i.e. competitive) economy, where to ensure the maximum speed and flexibility in decision making, the lines of interaction must run horizontally between consumers, middlemen and producers with no intermediation by the state. The shift from vertical to horizontal economic linkage therefore requires not one but two profound changes in the role of the state. The first is that it has to take itself out of the economic decision-making chain. This involves a vast diminution of its role and functions. The second is that it has to develop, administer and enforce a complex framework of rules and regulations designed to ensure the smooth functioning of the market. This involves a vast enlargement of the state's functions and therefore of its administrative capability. The transformation from a planned to a market economy does not therefore involve weakening the state. On the contrary it requires a strong state – a state with unquestioned authority to promulgate new laws and considerably enhanced administrative powers to enforce their observance. When the withdrawal from direct intervention and the development of regulatory functions are synchronised, the transition is smooth. It runs into trouble if one runs ahead of the other.

Unfortunately while liberal economists readily acknowledged the importance of the state regulation in advanced market economies, they adopted a wholly neo-liberal distrust of the state when it came to prescribing policies for countries on the way to the market. The seductiveness of shock therapy made them put their weight behind the lowering of import tarriffs and domestic taxes, and the privatisation of state-owned enterprises, and forget that even if markets could somehow mushroom overnight, the institutions that were needed to make them function effectively – a central bank, a corpus of property, contract and corporate law and the judges to administer them, and a tax administration – would take years to create. Not one devoted any thought to what would happen in the interregnum. The result has been disastrous. In Russia, which followed this advice faithfully, the net effect was to gravely weaken the state, to the point where it endangered the unity of the country. The USSR began to dismantle its centrally planned production and distribution system when it adopted its first Law on State Enterprises in June 1987, and completed it at a stroke when it adopted shock therapy in January 1992. But it did this when it had only the rudiments of a market system, no marketable surpluses, in effect no central bank, and had not even begun to build the myriad economic and regulatory institutions needed to make a market economy function smoothly. It then pushed aggressively ahead with privatisation, literally giving away the assets built up by the state, in the mistaken belief that privatisation was an end in itself when it was only a means to an end – making the economy more efficient and competitive. Since a precondition for competitiveness was the existence of a market, the enterprises that catered to the world market thrived and their new shareholders became very rich. But enterprises that catered to the domestic market were beggared or driven into barter, and their shares became worthless. Both ways, the state ended up getting next to nothing. This was reflected by the paltry dividends earned by the state from its 5,000 privatised enterprises, and the decline in its revenues from 22 per cent of GDP in 1992 to 8 per cent in 1997.

China, by contrast, did not ask for and did not follow the advice of the World Bank and IMF. It kept the central planning and distribution system in place, and reduced its scope by degrees over a period of a decade and a half. It did this both by lowering the planned output requirement in each commodity and by reducing the number of commodities under the centralised procurement and distribution system. It also adjusted prices in stages before decontrolling them. Price controls were also lifted a few items at a time to minimise the inflationary impact of the change. But in the end China too dismantled the planned economy before it was able to put the regulatory economy in place. For instance, if the government felt (as its leaders proclaimed) that shifting workers from enterprise-based social security and health plans to contributory plans administered by the provincial governments would take 15 years, it should have protected their sales and revenues by continuing with planned output and distribution for another 15 years. China also failed to regulate the growth of the non-state sector. Since the new enterprises in this sector were not prevented from going into any industry, and since they were burdened with neither the inherited costs of the state sector nor its lack of managerial autonomy, the outcome of competition between them and the state-owned enterprises was a foregone conclusion.

But in the final analysis, it is not the state but the non-state sector whose declining viability is pushing China towards a crisis. This is because China did not get the time it needed to build the institutions and enact the laws it needed to prevent gross over-investment and the emergence of a bubble economy.

Attempts to hasten the shift from plan to market without building the institutions of the market, therefore weaken the state. The near-collapse of the state in Russia in 1998 captured worldwide attention, but what has escaped notice is that there has been a hollowing out of the Chinese state for precisely the same reason. Having surrendered what might be termed its 'socialist domain' and therefore its automatic right to a share of the national output, and unable to make good the loss by raising tax revenues from an economy reduced to barter, the Russian state borrowed its way into a debt trap. Stripped by insolvency of its power to fulfil even its most basic obligations to its people, let alone the extended commitments of the socialist state, it has lost its authority. Today, Moscow's writ runs only fitfully in the farther regions of the country.

China's economic liberalisation has also reduced the state's share of the output of its 'socialist domain' – the state-owned enterprises – without being able to tax the newer sectors of the economy. As a result, the revenue to GDP ratio has fallen from 35 to 11 per cent, a decline that is almost as steep as that in Russia. China therefore does not have the cushion of revenue surpluses that it needs to absorb the losses of the SOEs without incurring fresh debt, or to take over their past losses and their social overheads and enable them to make a start on a level playing field. The state is thus being pushed inexorably towards the third and sole remaining option – to allow the lay-off of workers, merge or close down plants, or sell them off to foreign buyers. All involve permanently

Table 17.1
Tax to GDP ratio, 1989–90 to 1998–99

Year	1989 –90	1990 –91	1991 –92	1992 –93	1993 –94	1994 –95	1995 –96	1996 –97	1997 –98	1998 –99
Tax revenue (Rs. bn)	776	877	1031	1142	1220	1478	1753	2011	2376	2490
GDP (Rs. bn)	4086	4778	5528	6308	7991	9434	11032	12853	14267	16150
Tax to GDP ratio (%)	16.9	16.1	16.5	16.2	15.3	15.7	15.9	15.6	16.7	15.4

Source: Public Finance Reports; Ministry of Finance, *Economic Survey 1995–96* and *2000–2001*.

retrenching millions of state employees. The further and faster the government goes down this road, the more will it erode the remaining legitimacy of the Communist Party and the state.

Although India has been the slowest in its reforms and had the fewest structural problems to cope with, the reforms have also reduced its tax to GDP ratio marginally from 16.9 per cent in 1989–90 to 15.4 per cent in 1998–99. A far more telling indicator of the weakening of the state is its inability to control expenditure – either its own or those of the state governments. Tables 17.1 and 17.2 reveal this deterioration.

This deterioration in finances is not irreversible but it has brought the state governments, in particular, to the edge of bankruptcy and has severely eroded the central government's capacity to play a mediating role between the states that are attracting the bulk of domestic and foreign investment and those that are getting left behind, by investing in infrastructure and communications in the backward states to increase their attractiveness to investors.

In the pre-1991 command economy, the central government had a substantial degree of control over the direction of investment. On an average between 1952 and 1989, it was responsible for approximately half of the total fixed investment in the country, through its five-year plans. It took care to distribute this fairly evenly across the country. It

Table 17.2

Deterioration of state and central finances (% of GNP at factor cost)*

Year	1993 –94	1994 –95	1995 –96	1996 –97	1997 –98	1998 –99
Centre: gross fiscal deficit	7.5	6.2	5.5	5.2	6.3	6.6
States: gross fiscal deficit	2.6	3.0	2.9	2.9	3.6	3.8
Consolidated gross fiscal deficit	10.1	9.2	8.4	8.1	9.9	10.4

* 1993 = 100.

Source: CMIE Public Finance Reports, February 1999 and March 2000.

also adopted policies, such as the equalisation of freight rates for the transport of raw materials and food across the country to prevent the emergence of locational advantages that concentrated industrial growth in a few locations in the country such as close to sources of raw materials and sea ports. These measures did not yield a uniform rate of growth but did limit inter-state disparities in economic growth. As a result, between 1981 and 1991 the rates of growth recorded by the 14 major states of India (which contain 95 per cent of the population) varied from a low of 3.6 per cent to a high of 6.6 per cent. After economic liberalisation, however, between 1991–92 and 1997–98, the inter-state disparity in growth rate rose from a low of 2.7 per cent to a high of 9.6 per cent.[2] There was also a significant increase in inter-state income inequalities. This was reflected in a rise in the Gini coefficient from 0.15 to 0.23 between the two periods.

A close analysis of the reason for the increase in disparities showed that it was caused by a simultaneous decline in public investment and a sharp rise in private investment. But while the former was spread more or less evenly across the country, the latter was heavily concentrated in the states that already had the best infrastructure and most educated labour force. These differences had existed even during the pre-reform days, because of sharp differences in the quality of governance between states. But they became severely accentuated in the 1990s.

The three states that have fared worst in the post-reform period,

Bihar, Uttar Pradesh and Orissa, comprise more than one-third of the population of India. The slow growth of employment opportunities in these three states has, over the decades, led to a strong outflow of labour to other, more industrialised states in search of work. This has not so far created inter-state tensions. But were the flow to increase it well might. The progressive weakening of central finances has made remedial investment in education and infrastructure in the states that have fallen behind increasingly difficult.

Notes

1. INTRODUCTION. FROM PLAN TO MARKET: FORCING THE TRANSITION TO CAPITALISM

1. Karl Polanyi, *The Great Transformation* (Boston: Beacon Press, 1957), chapter 4, p. 43.
2. Joseph Stiglitz, chief economist of the World Bank from 1997 until 1 February 2000, made precisely this criticism of the IMF and the American treasury. In an interview given to the *International Herald Tribune* (*IHT*) he said that the West assumed that a rules-based legal and financial infrastructure would emerge spontaneously and that 'all we needed to do was privatize'. *IHT*, 27 January 2000.
3. Eugene F. Rice Jr. and Anthony Grafton, *The Foundations of Early Modern Europe, 1460–1559* (London and New York: W.W. Norton and Co., 1994), 2nd edn, p. 53.
4. For a detailed explanation of how these worked see Polanyi, *The Great Transformation*, chapter 4.
5. Polanyi, *The Great Transformation*, chapter 5: 'The evolution of the Market pattern'.
6. Herman Schwartz, *States Versus Nations* (New York: St Martin's Press, 1994), chapter 1: 'The rise of the modern state: from street gangs to Mafias', esp. pp. 24–30.
7. Rice and Grafton, *Early Modern Europe*, chapter 4.
8. When Louis XII was preparing to invade the Duchy of Milan, he asked one of his Italian commanders what was needed for success. 'Money, more money, and again more money', came the reply.
9. Rice and Grafton, *Early Modern Europe*, p. 119.
10. A good example is the World Bank's publication *The East Asian Miracle* (Washington DC, 1995). It points out that there were two models of integration into the world market in Asia – the 'pro-active' East Asian and the 'passive' South East Asian – and goes on to criticise the former and praise the latter.
11. Polanyi, *The Great Transformation*, chapter 6.

2. A SOCIETY IN TORMENT

1. Marshall I. Goldman, *Lost Opportunity: Why Economic Reforms in Russia have not Worked* (New York: W.W. Norton and Co., 1994), pp. 140–1.

2. An interview with first vice premiere Oleg Soskovets, reproduced in *RIA Novosty* Daily Review of the Russian Press (Daily Review), 2 April 1996.

3. The 4 per cent estimate is a subjective one. It comes from a survey of the mood of Russians today, carried out in March 1996. Four per cent of the respondents believed that their standard of living was better than the national average. If they are prepared to concede this it must be sufficiently above the national average to make denials unconvincing. Natalia Pliskevitch in *RIA Novosti*, Panorama no. 10, Daily Review, 14 March 1996.

4. Ibid.

5. Stephen Handelman, 'The Russian Mafiya', *Foreign Affairs*, March/April 1994, p. 95.

6. Marc Fenouil, 'The Russian Riviera', *International Herald Tribune*, 24 July 1998.

7. On 1 January 1998, 1,000 old roubles became one new rouble.

8. These prices prevailed in June 1996.

9. 'How to bring Russia's living standards closer to European average', by Professor Vladimir Groshev. Summarised in *RIA Novosti*, Panorama no. 12, Daily Review, 29 March 1996.

10. Enquiries by the author in Moscow, June 1996.

11. 'Russia's Standard of Living'. Paper translated from Russian, citation unknown, p. 70.

12. According to Goskomstat 5.8 million were out of work or were actively seeking a job in September 1995. In addition another 3.4 million were wholly or partially laid off. Forty per cent of these were receiving no financial compensation whatever.

13. Albert Valentinov, 'Russia's hard-up R&D establishment needs more money', *Rossiiskaia Gazeta*, 1 March 1996.

14. 'Russia's Standard of Living'. Paper translated from Russian, citation unknown, p. 73. The Economist Intelligence Unit (EIU) estimates the fall in Russian per capita income in purchasing power parity terms as being somewhat less sharp, from $7,710 in 1990 to $4,573 in 1994. EIU country report for Russia, fourth quarter 1995, appendix C. It fell further after the second crash of the rouble in August 1998.

15. EIU country report for Russia, 1995.

16. Quoted by BBC in an election-eve television programme on Russia on 13 June, 1996.

17. Joseph Stiglitz, speaking at the Annual Development Conference of the World Bank in Washington, June 1999.

3. THE FAILURE OF PERESTROIKA

1. Manuel Castells, *End of Millennium* (Oxford: Blackwell, 1988), vol. 3, pp. 50–1. 'The last Communist Perestroika was a top down process, without any

participation by the civil society in its inception and early implementation ...
It was aimed at rectifying internal failures from within the system, while
keeping unscathed its fundamental principles: the Communist party
monopoly of power; the command economy and the super power status of the
unitary Soviet State ... The stop-go policies that derived from such
half-hearted reform literally disorganized the Soviet economy ...'

2. Despite devoting 30 per cent of its investment and 30 per cent of its labour
   force to agriculture, the Soviet Union failed to achieve self-sufficiency. The
   main reasons were collectivisation, a systematic underpricing of agricultural
   products in relation to industrial (itself a product of the ultimately unsustain-
   able policy of subsidising urban consumption) and waste. Ibid., pp. 58–60.

3. Friedemann Muller in J. Echeverri-Gent, Richard E. Feinberg, Friedemann
   Muller and others, *Economic Reform in Three Giants: US Foreign Policy and
   the USSR, China and India* (New Brunswick: Transaction Books, 1990), p.
   47.

4. Ibid., p. 222, table 9.

5. Ibid., p. 57.

6. Mikhail S. Gorbachev, *Perestroika: New Thinking for our Country and the
   World* (Fontana Collins, 1988 paperback edn), chapter 1, pp. 18–21.

7. See Chapter 9 on China, 'Enterprise autonomy – the core of economic
   reform'.

8. Echeverri-Gent *et al.*, *Economic Reform in Three Giants*, p. 146.

9. Castells, *End of Millennium*, pp. 10, 12–13.

10. Muller in Echeverri-Gent *et al.*, *Economic Reform in Three Giants*, p. 56.

11. Ibid., pp. 55–6.

12. Ibid., p. 146.

13. Ibid., pp. 57, 150.

14. Alexander Yevlakov, 'Zigzags of stabilisation', *Passport*, May/June 1996, p.
    70.

15. L.V. Nikiforov and T.E. Kuznetsova, 'Utilisation of private financial for
    investment purposes', *Studies in Russian Development*, 7 (3), 1996, p. 238.
    According to a survey quoted by the authors, 48.8 per cent of Russians keep
    their savings in cash, 10.7 per cent in rouble accounts, and 38.1 per cent in
    hard currencies.

16. Ibid., p. 76.

17. The expectation was absurd. Germany, which was forced to adopt shock
    therapy in its eastern region in 1990, planned to complete the change in 12–15
    years. This assessment is based on the number of years for which Bonn plans
    to make massive infusions of capital of between DM100 and DM200 billion a
    year.

18. Gorbachev spoke readily about his party leaders' fears, but did not readily
    admit to his own. In July 1990 he told visiting Indian prime minister V.P.

Singh, 'My party members are afraid of the market. After 70 years of socialism they have no experience of it. I tell them that the market existed before capitalism and will exist after socialism, but they are not reassured' (told in the author's presence).

19. Marshall I. Goldman, *Lost Opportunity: Why Economic Reforms in Russia have not Worked* (New York: W.W. Norton and Co., 1994), pp. 176–8.

20. World Bank, *China: Reform and the Role of the Plan in the 1990s* (Washington DC, 1992), p. 36.

21. This system was extensively discussed at a conference organised jointly by the World Bank and the Institute of Economics of the Chinese Academy of Social Sciences, at Beijing in August 1985. A subsequent book containing some of the papers presented there was published by the bank, edited by Gene Tidrick and Bill Byrd.

22. Goldman, *Lost Opportunity*, p. 13.

23. Joseph R. Blasi, Maya Kroumova and Douglas Kruse, *Kremlin Capitalism: Privatising the Russian Economy* (Ithaca: Cornell University Press, 1997), p. 25.

24. Goldman, *Lost Opportunity*, p. 146. When the centrally mandated 'State orders' were reduced in 1988, these ministries issued their own 'state orders' which often pre-empted the enterprise's entire productive capacity.

25. Stephen Handelman, 'The Russian Mafiya', *Foreign Affairs*, March/April 1994, p. 95. The Mafiya had enjoyed a symbiotic relationship with the Russian bureaucracy right through the communist years. This continued in a new form in the era of reform.

26. The budget deficit reached 30 per cent of GDP in 1991! Anders Aslund, *How Russia Became a Market Economy* (Washington DC: Brookings Institution, 1995).

4. DESCENT INTO CHAOS

1. GDP, which had fallen by 2.1 per cent in 1990 for the Soviet Union, fell in Russia alone by 12.9 per cent in 1991. Inflation, which was 5 per cent in 1990, rose to 92.6 per cent in 1991. These figures, compiled by the Economist Intelligence Unit (EIU), are at sharp variance with those given by Marshall I. Goldman, *Lost Opportunity: Why Economic Reforms in Russia have not Worked* (New York: W.W. Norton and Co., 1994). Goldman says that Yeltsin and Russia were confronted with a collapsing GDP (down 20 per cent) and an inflation rate of 1,100 per cent. These are the figures for 1992, i.e. the result of shock therapy, and not for 1991, the last year of perestroika (ibid., p. 96). The EIU gave the fall in GDP as 18.5 per cent and inflation as 1,356 per cent in 1992. EIU country report on Russia, 4th quarter, 1995.

2. Goldman, *Lost Opportunity*, p. 99.

3. Ibid.

4. Yevlakhov, 'Zigzags of stabilisation', p. 70.

5. Ibid.

6. Taken from Joseph R. Blasi, Maya Kroumova and Douglas Kruse, *Kremlin Capitalism* (Ithaca: Cornell University Press, 1997), table 2, p. 190.

7. UNU/WIDER.

8. Goldman, *Lost Opportunity*, p. 102, quoting Oleg Bogmolov.

9. In an interview given to the author in June 1996, Arkady Volski, chairman of the Russian Union of Industrialists, who was a close aide of Gorbachev, and with him when he resigned on 25 December, quoted Bismarck to express his feelings about the simultaneous adoption of shock therapy and dissolution of the USSR: 'It was worse than a crime. It was a mistake.' Volski claimed that during the entire period between 25 December 1991 and 2 January 1992, he desperately tried to persuade Yeltsin and the prime minister, Burbulis, not to go in for shock therapy but wait until the dissolution of the Union had been worked out. He could as well have argued the opposite, had the dissolution not already taken place, having been Gorbachev's last act before resigning.

10. Goldman, *Lost Opportunity*, pp. 107–9.

11. Ibid., pp. 107–8.

12. In 1987 the GDP of the USSR was $2.375 trillion, so that of Russia would have been around $1.5 trillion. By the first two months of 1996, the annualised GDP had sunk to R2,000 trillion (old), or $400 billion. With a population of 148.3 million, this amounted to $2,670 per capita. The 1987 estimate is from the US Central Intelligence Agency, *Handbook of Economic Statistics 1988* quoted by Muller in Echeverri-Gent, *Economic Reform in Three Giants*. The 1996 estimate is from official estimates published in the *Rossiiskaya Gazeta*, 23 March 1996. The estimate of the Gaidar institute of per capita incomes in June 1995 was even lower at $1,320.

13. EIU country report on Russia, 4th quarter, 1995.

14. *Rossiiskaya Gazeta*, 23 March 1996, 'Russia's economy in figures'.

15. Ibid.

16. Ibid.

17. EIU, 3rd quarter 1998, table: 'economic structure', p. 5.

18. Ibid.

19. Ibid.

20. Ibid.

21. Analysis by Alexander Potyomkin, deputy chairman of the Bank of Russia, *Finansovye Izvestia*, May.

22. Information provided to the author by the State Committee on Privatisation, June 1996. According to the calculations of Blasi, Kroumova and Kruse, by the end of 1995 some 17,937 medium and large sized businesses, 105,111 small shops and 12.118 million apartments had been privatised. In addition a total of 794,889 small businesses had been started. Joseph R. Blasi, Maya

Kroumova and Douglas Kruse, *Kremlin Capitalism: Privatising the Russian Economy* (Ithaca: Cornell University Press, 1997), p. xix.

23. Ibid.

24. 'Russia suspends Eurobond sales', *International Herald Tribune* (*IHT*), 31 July 1998. These sales were suspended on 30 July 1998, days before the second crash of the rouble which occurred on 17 August.

25. EIU annual country report, 1996.

26. Because of the long, harsh winters Russian farmers feed their cattle with grain for much of the year.

27. EIU annual country report, 1996.

28. Goskomstat.

29. EIU 4th quarter report 1995, p. 29.

30. The output of fuel fell by 18 per cent, of processed foods by 24 per cent, of the engineering industries by 27 per cent; of timber, paper woodpulp and cellulose by 29 per cent; of steel, alloys and other metallurgical industries by 30 per cent, and of chemicals by 38 per cent.

31. EIU annual country report 1996.

32. A. Yevgeniev, 'Inflation rate steadily falling', *Rossiiskaya Gazeta*, 23 March.

33. EIU 4th quarter report 1995, p. 24.

34. This was more through a set of exceptions to policy than policy itself. See below.

35. IMF, Washington DC.

36. Ruskomstat.

37. Konstantin Baskayev, 'Russian fuel and energy sector remains mainstay of economy', *Finansovye Izvestia*, no. 31, 25 March 1996.

38. EIU 3rd quarter report 1998, p. 5.

39. The first figure is based on the estimate given earlier in this chapter that the GDP of the Russian federation was around $1.5 trillion dollars in 1987. The second figure is taken from the World Bank, *World Development Report 1997*, tables.

40. Stephen F. Cohen, 'Look what's happening to Russia under reforms', *IHT*, 21 August 1998.

41. Susan Eisenhower, 'Strains from Russia's crisis put the federation at risk', *IHT*, 2 September 1998.

42. Svetlana Lolayeva, 'Russian Finance Ministry moves to fight tax evaders and illegal cash transfers', *Segodnya*, 13 March 1996.

43. Andrew Higgins, 'Russia is forced to barter its economic future for survival', *Asian Wall Street Journal*, 28 August 1998, p. 12.

44. Sharon LaFraniere, 'An enemy of the Russian economy: Barter', *Washington Post* service, in *IHT*, 4 September 1998.

45. Higgins, 'Russia is forced to barter'.

46. LaFraniere, 'An enemy of the Russian economy: Barter'.

47. For 1992 and 1998: Charles Wyplosz, 'Formula for Russia: pay your dues or go to jail', *IHT*, 25 August 1996. For 1994 and 1995: Executive and Legislative newsletter no. 12, 'Budget '96: Increase revenues, streamline expenses', *RIA Novosty*, 26 March 1996. A report quoting the finance minister.

48. Executive newsletter no. 12, 'Budget '96'.

49. Ibid. According to the EIU (3rd quarter 1998), the federal budget deficit in 1995 was 5.4 per cent of GDP, or 85.59 trillion old roubles.

50. Lolayeva, 'Russian Finance Ministry'. In January and February accruals amounted to 18 trillion old roubles, against an expected 54 trillion. In march the finance ministry expected 12 trillion against the budgeted 36 trillion.

51. Ibid.

52. Vladimir Radyuhin, 'Yeltsin's woes', *The Hindu*, Madras, 4 January 1998, p. 15.

53. Jonas Bernstein and Matt Taibbi, 'Security official to head Sports Fund', *Moscow Times*, 25 May 1996, p. 4.

54. Executive newsletter no. 12, 'Budget '96'.

55. Vladimir Kucherenko, 'Non payments can wreck the entire Russian state', *Rossiiskaya Gazeta*, 12 March 1998.

56. Marina Kryuchkova, 'Yeltsin signs programme to protect investors and shareholders', *Rossiiskiye Vesti*, 26 March 1996.

57. Estimate of the Academy of Sciences Institute of Sociology, 1995. Quoted in Blasi *et al.*, *Kremlin Capitalism*, p. 115.

58. The threats the Mafiya makes are cited by Kucherenko, 'Non payments can wreck the entire Russian state.'

59. Ibid.

60. Ibid.

61. 'Russian economy still suffering from wage and other non-payments', *Delovoi mir*, 21 March 1996.

62. Interview given to Andrei Kolesnikov, *Rossiiskiye Vesti*, 23 March 1996.

63. Higgins, 'Russia is forced to barter'.

64. LaFraniere, 'An enemy of the Russian economy: Barter'.

65. Andrei Kolesnikov.

66. BBC report.

67. David Hoffman, 'In Moscow and Beijing, search is on for investors and fakes', *IHT*, 8 June 1998.

68. Hoffman, 'In Moscow and Beijing'.

69. Daniel Wiliams, 'IMF reaches $12.5 billion deal with Russia', *IHT*, 13 July 1998.

70. Michael Wines, 'Russian markets spiral down as buyers vanish', *IHT*, 14 August 1998, p. 17.

71. Dimitri K. Simes, 'Chernomyrdin looks like Russia's best chance', *IHT*,

29–30 August, p. 6.

72. John van Schaik and Geoff Winestock, 'If the dam bursts …', *Moscow Times*, Business Extra, 25 August 1998.

73. Alexander Velichenkov and Vladimir Kucherenko, 'Anti crisis measures dictate their logic', *Rossiiskaya Gazeta*, 18 August 1998.

74. Schaik and Winestock, 'If the dam bursts …'

75. Steve Liesman and Mark Whitehouse, 'More debt threats looming in Russia's future', *Asian Wall Street Journal*, 14 September. According to the Bank for International Settlements, at end of 1997 the claims outstanding by banks from the US, UK, France, Germany, Italy, Austria, the Netherlands and Japan totalled $56.5 billion. German banks alone had lent $30 billion. Of this $56 billion, the restructuring and moratorium had caused a loss of $7 billion. $29.4 billion was covered by government guarantees and hard currency exports. The fate of $17 billion was uncertain.

76. *IHT*, 4 September 1998, p. 1.

77. Quoted by L.V. Nikiforov and T.E. Kuznetsova, 'Utilisation of private financial savings for investment purposes', *Studies in Russian Development*, 7 (3), 1996. The survey also showed that 40 per cent of all respondents had deposits in the banks, 8.1 per cent had invested in stocks and securities. Of the 48.8 per cent that kept their savings in cash, 10.7 per cent kept it in roubles. Thus, in all, 59 per cent of Russian families have lost a significant part of their savings in the crash after 17 August.

78. Celestine Bohlen, 'Russia smolders as world waits', *IHT*, 2 September 1998, pp. 1, 8.

79. Andrei Kushnerenko, of the ministry of foreign economic relations and trade, to Interfax, *IHT*, 5–6 September 1998.

80. Reuters, 'With the Ruble's fall, foreign retailers' sales sag', *IHT*, 31 October to 1 November 1998.

81. Michael Wines, 'Russians brace for lean times as food and goods vanish from shops', *IHT*, 5–6 September 1998, p. 7.

82. Report by Brunswick Warburg published in *IHT*, 5–6 September 1998, p. 1.

83. Interview with Mikhail Delyagin, by Anatoly Velednitsky, 'Not by money alone; it is the amount that matters', *Trud*, 18 August 1998.

84. Kathy Daigle, 'Bleak economic figures released by government', *Moscow Times*, 7 October 1998.

85. Ibid.

5. THE UNMAKING OF RUSSIA

1. *International Herald Tribune* (*IHT*), 24 June 1998, 'Yeltsin sounds financial alarm: Implores Duma to adopt new tax code urgently'.

2. For convenience of analysis, Ronald Suny has identified nine major ethnic nationalities in the Soviet Union: Belorussians, Lithuanians, Azerbaijanis,

Ukrainians, Estonians, Latvians, Georgians, Finns and Armenians. But this does not even begin to describe the ethnic complexity of the Russian state. For instance, neither the Tatars nor the Chechens are mentioned. Today 23 of the 89 'regions' that make up the Russian federation have a distinct ethnic identity. See Ronald Grigor Suny, *The Revenge of the Past: Nationalism, Revolution and the Collapse of the Soviet Union* (Stanford University Press, 1995), chapter 2.

3. Ibid., pp. 21–7.
4. Ibid., p. 87.
5. Ibid., pp. 102–6.
6. 'Russia's balance of payments 1997' and other newspaper reports already cited. Russia had by the end of 1997 received $12.5 billion in standby credits from the IMF; $2.5 billion from the IBRD; and $3.6 billion from the sale of Eurobonds. In 1998 it floated another $2.5 billion of Eurobonds, and finally received $450 million from the IMF's $6 billion credit before the crash cut off further funds. Russia was also able to reschedule $28 billion of Soviet-era debts. This gave a further undetermined amount of relief.
7. The main lacuna was agriculture. Here the Duma had fought a bitter rearguard action against privatisation, preferring an enlargement of family plots and other half-measures. In 1996, 10.5 million agricultural workers had benefited from these half-measures, but another 40 million, in over 26,000 state and collective farms, and some of the key services, like transport and health, remained within the public sector. Joseph R. Blasi, Maya Kroumova and Douglas Kruse, *Kremlin Capitalism: Privatising the Russian Economy* (Ithaca: Cornell University Press, 1997), p. 26.
8. See for instance Maxim Boycko, Andrei Schleiffer and Robert Vishny, *Privatising Russia*; and Blasi *et al.*, *Kremlin Capitalism*.
9. Blasi *et al.*, *Kremlin Capitalism*, pp. 26–7.
10. The following extract from a study of privatisation highlights what followed: 'The Russian General Director is similar in authority to the chief executive officer (CEO) of a capitalist company, but the terms are not completely interchangeable because the Russian factory director was never answerable to a board of directors ... Let us consider a General Director Mr Smirnov ... In the past a Soviet Ministry could hire and fire him. Once Gorbachev removed cabinet supervision ... the only formal authority over his enterprise was a distant state bureaucracy that was itself spinning out of control ... Smirnov was probably tempted to treat the company as his personal property ... Certainly the gap between the prices charged for goods in Russia and the prices they could fetch if they were shipped across a border gave the Smirnovs in the system many opportunities to privatise wealth informally. (The difference was itself the product of another Gorbachev half-reform, the devaluation of the rouble for international trade only.) ... Before a factory

was privatised the top managers would also start related corporations and joint ventures ... before they had a board of directors looking over their shoulders, they began the simple physical transfer of equipment to those daughter companies. They sold them goods and services at low rates and used their financial accounts to transfer funds to them. Managers and their families now own significant parts of these new corporations... It is hard to quantify the property that was stolen and appropriated, but managers did sell equipment and products at ridiculously low controlled prices to friends, associates and family who then resold them at higher prices or exported them ... Managers abused their personal expense accounts. They paid friends, relatives and cronies for services to the enterprises and received kickbacks. Many oil and mineral products and types of machinery and equipment could be "honestly" sold for far less than the world market price. The temptation was enormous and the line between legal and illegal dealings very fuzzy' (ibid., pp. 33–4)

11. The details of this scheme have been described in several books and need not detain us here. Only the broad principles are therefore given. See for instance Boycko *et al.*, *Privatising Russia*, and Blasi *et al.*, *Kremlin Capitalism*, chapter 1.

12. Blasi *et al.*, p. 43.

13. Ibid., pp. 39–49.

14. Marina Kryuchkova, 'Yeltsin signs programme to protect investors and shareholders', *Rossiiskiye Vesti*, 26 March 1996. According to this report, more than 2,100 Russian investment companies and banks were not paying any dividends to their investors. According to Kryuchkova, about a quarter of all Russians had lost their money to various kinds of investment funds, mortgage banks, pawn shops, private pension funds and insurance companies.

15. Ibid. The official concerned was a senior functionary of the State Committee on Privatisation.

16. Conceded by first deputy economics minister in an interview with Andrei Kolesnikov and Yuri Rytov. *Rossiiskiye Vesti*, 23 March 1996.

17. Interview by the author with an official of the State Committee on Privatisation in June 1996.

18. Blasi *et al.*, *Kremlin Capitalism*, chapter 3, pp. 89–96.

19. Ibid., table 3, p. 192.

20. Perhaps the best known of these is Yeltsin's longest lasting prime minister, Victor Chernomyrdin. Chernomyrdin and his family are widely believed to have taken advantage of his position as general director of the oil and gas giant Gazprom, to corner no fewer than 10 per cent of its shares.

21. 'We shall not abandon reform', interview given by vice-premier Oleg Soskovets to Natalya Konstantinova, *Nezavisimaya Gazeta*, 12 March 1996.

22. Jonas Bernstein, 'Victory of reform', *Take 2 Moscow Times*, Friday 14

November 1997.

23. Jonas Bernstein and Matt Taibbi, 'Security official to head Sports Fund', *Moscow Times*, 25 May 1996.

24. Andrei Piontkovsky, 'Modern day Rasputin', *Moscow Times*, 12 November 1997.

25. Ibid. Piontkovsky cites an autobiography by Alexander Korzhakov, written after his fall from power, for this information.

26. Bernstein, 'Victory of reform'.

27. Andrei Piontkovsky, 'Modern day Rasputin'.

28. Vladimir Radyuhin, 'Primakov's move to curb separatism', *The Hindu*, Madras, 6 October 1998.

6. AN UNCERTAIN FUTURE

1. Gary Peach and Matt Bivens, 'Primakov's six weeks magically confused', *Moscow Times*, 24 October 1998.

2. Interview with Andrei Ilarionov, *Argumenty i fakty* no. 34, 24 August 1998.

3. Andrei Piontkovsky, 'Season of discontent', *Moscow Times*, 1 October 1998.

4. Obtained and published by *Kommersant*, 16 September 1998.

5. This phrase was used, ironically, by Chubais.

6. Andrei Piontkovsky, 'Season of discontent: Oligarchs gun for Zadornov, Kamikaze style', *Moscow Times*, 8 October.

7. Sujata Rao, 'Cabinet approves plan for the economy', *Moscow Times*, 3 November 1998.

8. Sujata Rao, 'Strengthening Rouble defies logic', *Moscow Times*, 7 November 1998.

9. Rao, 'Cabinet approves plan for the economy'.

10. Even Maslyukov is a part owner of no less than five companies. Piontkovsky, 'Season of discontent'.

11. The Economist Intelligence Unit (EIU), *Second Quarter Report 2000*. Even in 1997, the best year Russia had known under the Yeltsin–Gaidar–Chubais–IMF dispensation, GDP had grown by only 0.8 per cent. In 1998, the GDP shrank by 4.9 per cent.

12. Anders Aslund, 'The Russian economy shows signs of improvement', *International Herald Tribune*, 19 January 2000; EIU, *Second Quarter Report 2000*, p. 23.

13. Alexander Levinsky, 'Some Russians like it cheap', *Moscow News*, no. 47, 8–14 December 1999, p. 7.

14. EIU, *Second Quarter Report 2000*, p. 25.

15. International Moscow Bank (IMB), Research Papers, vol. 3/7, July 2000, p. 3.

16. From 6.4 per cent at the end of June 1998.

17. IMB research paper, p. 2.

18. Survey of Industrial Entities by *Russian Economic Barometer*, quoted in IMB

research paper vol. 3/7 and by EIU *Second Quarter Report 2000* p. 33.

19. IMB research paper, vol. 3/7, p. 2.

20. The estimate was ascribed to Andrei Ilarionov. John Thornhill, 'Step back from the edge of the abyss', *Financial Times* Survey of Russia, 10 May 2000, p. 1. An estimate by Sergei Glaziev, chairman of the Economic Committee of the Duma was even lower at 4.2 per cent. In its report for the second quarter of 2000 the Economist Intelligence Unit predicted a slowdown in industrial growth during the quarter, and pointed to a decline in he rate of growth in April as proof that it had already begun. The acceleration of growth in the second quarter did not dispel the Russians' deeply ingrained pessimism. In an interview to Patrick Gill of the *Russia Journal* (19–25 August 2000) Sergei Prudnik (an economist) and an investment firm, Troika Dialog, said that they expected a deceleration in the rate of growth in 2001. Another investment firm, Renaissance Capital, called the recovery 'superficial' and predicted that it would peter out without 'structural reform'.

21. Catherine Belton, 'Lessons of August 17 crash not learned', *Moscow Times*, 17 August 2000.

22. The widening of the tax base as the main reason for the rise in tax revenues was noted by the EIU, *Second Quarter Report 2000*, p. 23.

23. IMB research paper, vol. 3/7, p. 5.

24. While the volume of fuel exports grew by only 11.6 per cent in the first half of 2000, that of ferrous metals grew by 28.3 per cent, of copper by 15.1 per cent and nickel by 17.4 per cent. From IMB research paper, vol. 3/7, p. 4.

25. Ibid., p. 1.

26. Among these is Otto Latsis, a well known journalist and columnist for the *Moscow Times.*

27. Alexander Bekker, 'Cabinet suggests plan to curb inflation', *Vedomosti*, 4 July 2000.

28. K. Lyubov: 'Geraschenko, the chief editor of money', *Izvestia*, 6 July 2000.

29. The real effective exchange rate adjusts the nominal exchange rate for differences in the rate of inflation.

30. EIU, *Second Quarter Report 2000*, p. 29, table.

31. Calculated from IMB research paper, vol. 3/7, p.1, table; and from EIU, *Second Quarter Report 2000*, p. 29, table.

32. John Thornhill, 'Step back from the edge of the abyss'.

33. I am indebted for this and much of the following analysis to Andrei Ryabov, scholar-in-residence at the Carnegie Moscow Centre, Carnegie Endowment for Peace. The conclusions, however, are entirely mine.

34. John Lloyd, 'Sounding the retreat from Russia's rule of wealth', *Financial Times*, May 2000.

35. Marina Shahina, 'Moscow Diary', *RIA Novosti*, 4 August. The author is a political analyst and columnist for *RIA Novosti*.

36. Z. Alexeyev, 'No one loves the Oligarchs', *Vedomosti*, 3 August 2000.

7. HOW FAST IS CHINA GROWING?

1. World Bank, *China 2020* (Washington DC, 1996), table 1.1.
2. *China Statistical Yearbook* (*CSY*) 1996 (data from the *CSY* is reproduced by the World Bank as tables attached to its annual country studies and to *China 2020*).
3. World Bank, *China 2020*, p. 2.
4. R. Summers and A. Heston, 'Penn world tables (mark 5): An expanded set of international comparisons, 1950–1988', *Quarterly Journal of Economics*, vol. 2, 1991, pp. 327–68. Also World Bank, *China 2020*, chapter 1.
5. Angus Maddison, *Monitoring the World Economy* (Paris: OECD, 1995).
6. Ibid.
7. Kim Jong-il, and Laurence Lau, 'The role of human capital in the economic growth of the East Asian newly industrialised countries', *Asia-Pacific Economic Review*, 1–3, 1995, pp. 235–71.
8. *CSY 1996*, p. 203, and *CSY 1994*, p. 193.
9. Quoted in *The Economist*, 16–22 March 2002. 'China: How Cooked are the Books?' p. 35.
10. World Bank, 'China, the energy sector', annex 3 to *China: Long Term Development Issues and Options* (Washington DC, 1985).
11. *CSY 1996*, p. 203.
12. *CSY 1994*, p. 193.
13. World Bank, 'China, the energy sector'.
14. Ibid., pp. 22–6 and p. 33, especially table 2.1 on p. 26 and table 2.5 on p. 33.
15. Ibid.
16. *CSY 1994*, p. 32 and *CSY 1996*, p. 272. GDP at factor cost in constant 1990 prices.
17. Prof. Dong Fureng of Beijing University, a member of the standing committee of the National Peoples' Congress and vice-chairman of its financial and economic committee, revealed some of the weaknesses in the statistical base of Chinese estimates during a discussion with the author in 1993.
18. Prof. Dong Fureng explained that China used to have two estimates of agricultural output – one prepared by the ministry of agriculture, and the other by the ministry of commerce. The first was as a rule too high, and the second too low. More recently the China Statistical Bureau (CSB) added a third estimate, which was based on sampling in various parts of the country, and was reasonably accurate. The CSB had been publishing the ministry's estimates but, in 1993, the Chinese government 'abolished' the ministry of commerce figures.
   Measuring the output of the township and village enterprises (TVEs) in

constant prices has proved difficult because the TVEs do not keep sophisticated accounts and are therefore unable to supply the information that is needed to derive constant price data. As a result the constant price indices compiled at least partly contain a great deal of information in current prices. Another reason why it is nearly impossible to untangle constant and current price figures is the very rapid change in the composition of the TVEs' output. This makes it difficult to create a constant price series of estimates of output. The end result has been that most of the data furnished is a mixture of current and constant price data. To the extent that supposedly constant price data contain current price figures the rate of inflation gets underestimated. This inevitably exaggerates the increase in output in real terms. Prof. Dong Fureng also said that there were difficulties in estimating the real growth of consumer durables output, once again because it was not easy to keep track of price changes in an area where new products were being introduced at a very rapid pace.

For similar reasons, the measurement of the output in the tertiary sector is even more difficult than for the TVEs. Even in mature market economies the estimation of the product of the tertiary sector is far from easy. Some Western economists are arguing that the slowdown in GDP growth in the mature industrial economies after the early 1970s is an illusion created by the fact that over 70 per cent of their output now originates in the tertiary sector, where mind-boggling increases in quality and efficiency brought about by the revolution in information technology are not being reflected in the indices of output. In China this indeterminacy is compounded by the fact that enterprises are small, accounts sketchily kept and new enterprises are starting up and going out of business all the time. Making constant price estimates is even more difficult than for the TVEs, and one should assume that much of the data being supplied is in current prices. Since the TVEs and the services sector together account for 45 per cent of total output, the scope for underestimation of inflation and therefore overestimation of output is considerable.

The table opposite reflects this inability. In 1985, 1988, and consistently from 1992 to 1995, sharp peaks in the index of consumer prices in the urban areas coincide with similar peaks in GDP growth. In 1992–95 the growth rate traces the same curve as the inflation rate.

Until 1995 the CSB published data that showed a marked decline in the rate of growth of energy consumption. Overall from 1988 to 1994, energy consumption grew at 4.3 per cent, against 4.8 per cent for the period 1978–88. However, the CSB 1996 has changed these figures drastically upwards, beginning in 1993. No explanation is given. The possibility that the figures have been sanitised to avoid the anomaly of a sharp jump in growth with a sharp fall in energy consumption, cannot be ruled out. The figure in brackets is an older CSB estimate, before the corrections were made.

Rates of growth (%) of GDP, consumer and retail prices and energy consumption, 1978–95

Yr	79	80	81	82	83	84	85	86	87	88	89	90	91	92	93	94	95
1	7.6	7.9	4.5	8.5	10.2	14.5	13.5	8.8	11.6	11.3	4.3	3.8	9.2	14.2	13.5	12.6	10.5
2	1.9	7.5	2.5	2.0	2.0	2.7	11.9	7.0	8.8	20.7	16.3	1.3	5.1	8.6	16.1	25.0	16.8
3	2.0	6.0	2.4	1.9	1.5	2.8	8.8	6.0	7.3	18.5	17.8	2.1	2.9	5.4	13.2	21.7	14.8
4	2.6	2.9	-1.5	4.5	6.2	7.4	8.2	5.4	7.0	7.4	4.2	1.9	5.2	5.2	6.2	5.8	5.1
																	(1.6)

1 = percentage increase in GDP over previous year
2 = percentage increase in consumer prices in the urban areas
3 = percentage increase in overall retail prices
4 = percentage increase in energy consumption

19. Bian Hongwei, 'Accurate statistics essential', *China Daily*, 21 January 1999.
20. Roderick MacFarquhar (ed.), *The Politics of China* (Cambridge University Press, 1997, 2nd edn). MacFarquhar, introduction pp. 1–4 and Richard Baum, 'The road to Tiananmen' pp. 340–471.
21. Joseph Fewsmith, 'Chinese politics since Tiananmen', in MacFarquhar, *The Politics of China*, pp. 472–531.
22. 'No letup in economic overhaul, China pledges', *International Herald Tribune*, 6–7 March 1999.
23. In 1996 SOEs accounted for 96 per cent of the oil industry, almost 70 per cent of the logging industry, and about 60 per cent of the coal, electricity, gas, steel and alloys industries. Only in the cement industry (which was not classified separately) was the SOE presence relatively small. *China Statistical Yearbook 1996*, quoted in World Bank, *China 2020*, p. 31.
24. Estimated from World Bank, *China 2020*, table 4, p. 24 and table 27, p. 147. Source of data: China Statistical Bureau.
25. Neil C. Hughes, 'Smashing the iron rice bowl', *Foreign Affairs*, July/August 1998, p. 76.
26. Derived from the current price data for industry given in World Bank *China 2020*, table 26, by applying a sectoral GDP deflator for industry. This was derived by comparing the current price data for 1990 and 1995 in table 26 with the constant price data for 1990 given in table 2.
27. World Bank, *China 2020*, box 3.3, p. 20.

28. Ibid.

29. Even the 5.5 per cent rate of growth of energy consumption in 1990–95 is suspect. The figures given by the *China Statistical Yearbook 1996* are at odds with those given a year earlier, which showed a decline in the rate of growth of energy consumption from 4.8 per cent per annum between 1978 and 1988 to 4.3 per cent between 1988 and 1994. This data was revised upwards from 1993 onwards, in the *China Statistical Yearbook 1996*, but the cause of the revision, which coincidentally was made only from the year that saw the onset of the great inflation, was not mentioned.

However, the *CSY 1996* estimate of the growth of consumption of energy for the period 1990–95 is belied by its own statistics for the production of the various sources of primary energy. The weighted average of the growth of energy production between 1990 and 1995, was 4.325 per cent. Thus unless there was a sudden and very large jump in the energy China imported, amounting to a fifth of consumption, it is safe to assume that consumption too did not grow by much more than 4.3 per cent per annum in the 1990s. The decline in energy consumption thus reinforces the validity of the estimates of GDP growth made above by adjusting the official statistics for industrial output by the growth of employment.

30. Seth Faison, 'China economy's class act: High growth, low inflation', *New York Times*, 14 November 1996.

31. Nicholas R. Lardy, 'China and the Asian contagion', *Foreign Affairs*, July/August 1998, p. 79.

32. World Bank, various publications. Quoted by Hughes, 'Smashing the iron rice bowl', p. 73.

8. FROM PLAN TO MARKET

1. World Bank, *China: Reform and the Role of the Plan in the Nineties*, Country Study 1992, pp. 37–42.

2. For intance Prof. Dong Fureng conceded that 100–200 million of the more than 440 million workers in the rural areas were underemployed. Interview cited in previous chapter, note 16.

3. World Bank, 'Reform and the role of the plan', pp. 37–42. The Bank makes the same point but more obliquely. Pointing out that China was not impelled into reform by a deep macroeconomic crisis, it ascribes the reforms to 'dissatisfaction with the "extensive" growth model that had generated overall growth *but little if any improvement in productivity*, and required increasing levels of investment to be maintained'.

4. This was discussed at some length at an International Symposium of State Enterprise Management Systems, organised by the World Bank and the Chinese Academy of Social Sciences, in Beijing in August 1985, in which the author participated. Some of the papers presented were published as Gene

Tidrick and Chen Jiyuan (eds), *China's Industrial Reform* (World Bank, 1987).

5. By the end of 1991 in a prosperous enterprise producing Chinese herbal medicines (the Jingxiutang Pharmaceutical Company in Guangzhou, which the author visited in 1993) a third of all the worker were contract workers.

6. Gene Tidrick, 'Planning and supply', in Tidrick and Jiyuan, *China's Industrial Reform*, chapter 8, p. 176. The difference in number, however, is deceptive, because it reflects the much less detailed classification of goods in China than Russia.

7. Ibid., chapter 10, by William A. Byrd, pp. 262–3.

8. Ibid., 'Supply and marketing', by Tang Zongkun, p. 225.

9. Ibid., Tidrick, 'Planning and supply', p. 176.

10. Ibid., p. 177.

11. Ibid., chapter 10, by William A. Byrd, p. 237.

12. World Bank, *Reform and the Role of the Plan in the Nineties*, p. 40.

13. World Bank, *China 2020* (Washington DC, 1996), p. 28.

14. Ibid. The SOEs need to be distinguished from the urban and rural collectives. While both are not strictly speaking privately owned, the SOEs are directly owned and operated by the state. The collectives by contrast may have been financed and set up by a state-owned enterprise, but are as a rule not directed by the state and enjoy more or less complete freedom to engage in business, fix prices and determine output.

15. Profits are defined as the operating surplus of the enterprise less the actual expenditure incurred on the replacement and maintenance of the capital stock – what the Chinese economists call the simple reproduction of capital.

16. UN World Investment report, 1999.

17. See below in main text.

18. Interview with the director of the county by the author in May 1993.

19. There is an unavoidable imprecision about many statistics when it comes to China or the former Soviet Union. In a 1992 publication (*Reform and the Role of the Plan*) the World Bank says that only 500 products were under price and distribution controls in China, against more than 20,000 in the USSR. In *China 2020*, based on work by B. Naughton (*Growing out of the Plan: Chinese Economic Reform, 1978–93*, New York: Cambridge University Press, 1995), the Bank has upped the figures to 600 and 60,000 respectively (p. 13). The 800-plus figure is taken from Tidrick, 'Planning and supply', in Tidrick and Jiyuan, *China's Industrial Reform*.

20. For instance, in the early 1980s there was a thriving market in China for 'bonsai' – Japanese dwarf trees grown in a vase. These bonsai trees cost upward of $200, but were selling briskly at a time when the semi-skilled worker earned $25 a month and the plant director $50.

21. World Bank, *China 2020*, p. 32, box 3.4, and elsewhere.

22. Ibid., p. 11.
23. As explained to the author by the vice-chairman of the Guangzhou branch of the All China Federation of Trades Unions, from the top to the bottom the message sent out was the same.

9. IS CHINA'S TRANSFORMATION SUSTAINABLE?

1. 'The death of gradualism', *The Economist*, China survey, 8 March 1977, p. 17.
2. Andrew Tanzer, 'Small is beautiful', *Forbes* magazine, 23 September 1996, p. 90.
3. Anita Chan and Robert A. Senser, 'China's troubled workers', *Foreign Affairs*, March–April 1997, p. 104.
4. World Bank, *China 2020* (Washington DC, 1996), pp. 2, 19.
5. Nicholas R. Lardy, 'China and the Asian contagion', *Foreign Affairs*, July/August 1998.
6. 'The death of gradualism', *The Economist*, p. 17.
7. Reuters/Bloomberg News, 'China's debt crisis ripples beyond Guangdong', *International Herald Tribune* (*IHT*), 20 January 1999.
8. Neil C. Hughes, 'Smashing the iron rice bowl', *Foreign Affairs*, July/August 1998, p. 70.
9. Beijing, August 1985. The conference was organised by the World Bank and the Institute of Economics of the Chinese Academy of Social Sciences, to discuss 'Enterprise guidance in socialist and mixed economies' and received ten seconds on the national news, although not the portion in which Dong made his proposal. Barely two months later the government announced the setting up of a capital market for the shares of public enterprises.
10. Lardy, 'China and the Asian contagion', p. 79.
11. World Bank, *China 2020*, pp. 3–36.
12. Ibid., p. 34, figure 3.7.
13. For a brief description see ibid., pp. 32–3, boxes 3.4, 3.5.
14. For a more detailed analysis of the stabilisation programme see World Bank, *China: Macro-economic Stability in a Decentralised Economy*, Country Study 1995, pp. 18–23.
15. World Bank, *China: Between Plan and Market*, Country Study 1990, p. 5 and chart 1.2.
16. Ibid., p. 9. Not until September 1988 was a price-linked interest rate introduced for savings of three years or longer. But apart from the fact that this covered only a part of bank deposits, inflation rates in China have tended to be substantially underestimated. This has made it necessary to depend mainly on credit ceilings to contain inflation.
17. Newspaper reports. A daily digest of important economic news was maintained by the Indian embassy in Beijing. I am grateful to the embassy

and Ambassador C.S. Dasgupta for giving me access to it. Unfortunately, since my purpose then was to write for the newspapers, the idea for this book not having germinated, I was less than punctilious about noting the sources.

18. World Bank, *China 2020*, p. 28. The proportion of SOEs losing money climbed from 26 per cent in 1992 to 50 per cent in 1996. Their combined operating loss in 1996 was 1 per cent of GDP. This did not include interest, or replacement of capital assets, let alone depreciation.

19. 'Condemned to live China's greatest contradiction (socialist market economy)', *The Economist*, 14 December 1996, p. 61.

20. Lardy, 'China and the Asian contagion', p. 81.

21. This is the most commonly cited estimate of foreign analysts. Chinese estimates are lower. At the National Peoples' Congress in March 1999, Sheng Huaren, chairman of the State Economic and Trade Commission said that 2,300 out of 7,680 large and medium sized companies were making losses. But the Chinese definition of loss is the inability to cover operating costs. If depreciation, interest and loan amortisation costs are taken into account the proportion would probably exceed 50 per cent. Some estimates run as high as 70 per cent.

22. Bloomberg News quoted in *IHT*, 5 January 1999, 'China has $240 billion bad loans at its biggest banks'. Lardy also quotes the figure of 25 per cent, citing high officials including Dai Xianglong, the governor of the Reserve Bank (Lardy, 'China and the Asian contagion', p. 83), but this figure is getting increasingly politicised. In March 1999, Dai Xianglong claimed that only 10 per cent of the loans were non-performing. However, the head of the China Construction Bank admitted that 25 per cent of his bank's loans were non-performing (Bloomberg News in *IHT*, 27–8 March 1999, 'China reconsiders company to manage bad debt').

23. By official estimates the GDP was Y7.9748 trillion in 1998 (*Xinhua*, 30 December 1998).

24. *The Economist*, 'Condemned to live China's greatest contradiction', p. 61.

25. World Bank, *China 2020*, p. 12.

26. Hughes, 'Smashing the iron rice bowl', p. 72.

27. World Bank, *China 2020*.

28. World Bank, *The Chinese Economy: Fighting Inflation, Deepening Reforms*, Country Study 1996. Contains a passing reference to the reimposition of informal controls on prices of some products.

29. There is an implicit criticism of the government in the World Bank's comments upon this, but as has been pointed out in the previous section this is an integral part of what Deng Xiaoping called the socialist market economy with Chinese characteristics. It is very doubtful whether any sudden withdrawal of these privileges would have been acceptable or indeed feasible.

30. In 1993, on the way back by train from Tianjin to Beijing, in the 'soft berth'

(i.e. first) class, my guide fell into conversation with a conservatively dressed man who had apparatchik written all over him. He later told me that the man belonged to the railway security police and was going home from the southern town where he was posted to the steel city of Wuhan for a short leave. Some weeks earlier he had learned that the railway workshops in his town were in desperate need of a special kind of steel. Since he had friends at the Wuhan steel plant, he was able to obtain the steel through his connections. He made a profit on the deal of Y8,000 ($1,400) – for him, a little over two years' of his basic salary in 1993. Such deals are being struck in the thousands every day all over China. They are made possible by the rudimentary nature of the market and the consequent lack of information about buyers and sellers. This situation is partly natural, and partly being prolonged by provincial authorities who do not want orders to go out to plants outside their provinces.

31. In 1996, the state prosecuted 65, 424 persons on charges of corruption, embezzlement and bribery. These included a number of senior officials belonging to the party and the government. World Bank, *China 2020*, p. 37.

32. Hughes, 'Smashing the iron rice bowl', p. 75. The number is based on his estimation that there are 118,000 SOEs, and therefore probably refers only to industrial enterprises.

33. World Bank, *Reform and the Role of the Plan*, Country Study 1992, table 8.3, p. 248.

34. Told to a Harvard University Center for International Affairs visiting team in May 1995 by scholars of the Institute of Economics of the Chinese Academy of Social Sciences.

35. S. Cook, *Surplus Labour and Productivity in Chinese Agriculture* (Sussex: Institute of Development Studies, 1996).

36. This estimate is for 1995 (given in World Bank, *China 2020*). The most recent estimate available to the author, for mid-1998, is 11 million (*IHT*, 9/10 August).

37. Typical of the solutions being proposed was one by Nicholas Lardy of the Brookings Institution, Washington DC. Lardy suggested that the central government should issue bonds to the value of the banks' bad debts, and pay interest on them to the banks. The banks' funds would thus become unblocked and their non-performing assets would start to perform. This would improve their balance sheets and enable them to pay interest to their depositors. The SOEs would be freed from the burden of non-performing debt. They would therefore be able to invest more without an increase in the money supply. Quoted in *The Economist*, 'The death of gradualism', China survey.

38. Chan and Senser ('China's troubled workers') quote Beijing's *Economic Daily* which first reported this in May 1989. Epidemics of job security panic broke out among workers in 1992, 1993 and 1994, particularly in the Northeast 'rust belt' where the majority of the heavy industries in the state

sector are located. Writing at the end of 1996, Chan and Senser claim that 'Today a state of near panic grips a large section of China's work force.' Migrant workers typically earned only 70 to 80 per cent of what residents of the booming towns could expect, and could extract almost none of the social security benefits that their counterparts enjoyed.

39. Chan and Senser, 'China's troubled workers'.
40. See chapter 8, pp. 115–17.
41. Zhao Minghua and Theo Nichols in *China Journal* July 1996. Quoted by Chan and Senser, 'China's troubled workers'.
42. Chan and Senser, 'China's troubled workers'.
43. See World Bank, *China 2020*, p. 8. The Gini coefficient has risen from 0.28 in the 1980s to 0.40 in the 1990s. It must have been even lower in the 1970s. Although income is still more equally distributed in China than in even some East Asian countries, what is disturbing is the rate of increase in income inequality.
44. Chan and Senser. This was still the norm in 1985, when a plant director earned about Y300 a month ($110), a skilled workman or shop superintendent around Y150 and the unskilled or semi-skilled worker Y76, although fringe payments and benefits had begun to appear, and the 10,000-yuan family had appeared in the rural communes after the freeing of agriculture.
45. Ibid.
46. The Chinese seldom miss an opportunity to talk about the number of Rolls Royce and Mercedes cars now being sold in Shanghai.
47. World Bank, *China 2020*, p. 8. In South Korea when the urban–rural income ratio climbed to 3 in the late 1970s, the government became sufficiently concerned to launch the Semaul Undong (New Village) programme. Its main aim was to bring the ratio down to 2:1.
48. From discussions with fellows from the Harvard Center for International Studies. The author was present.
49. Discussions with the author in June 1993.

10. CHINA'S UNDECLARED RECESSION

1. Laid-off workers in China continue to receive a minimal salary. They also continued to live in state-provided lodgings and dormitories.
2. Neil C. Hughes, 'Smashing the iron rice bowl', *Foreign Affairs*, July/August 1998, pp. 69–70.
3. Nicholas R. Lardy, 'China and the Asian contagion', *Foreign Affairs*, July/August 1998, p. 86.
4. Hughes, 'Smashing the iron rice bowl', p. 76.
5. 'No letup in economic overhaul, China pledges', *IHT*, 6–7 March 1999.
6. Seth Faison, 'China's exports tumble, raising fears of decline', *IHT*, 14 April 1999 (*New York Times* service).

7. *IHT*, 12 January 1999.
8. John Pomfret, 'China says its economy expanded by 7.8 per cent but some question data', *IHT*, 1 January 1999 (*Washington Post* service).
9. Elizabeth Rosenthal (*NYT*) in *IHT*, 16–17 January 1999.
10. *IHT*, 'No letup in economic overhaul'.
11. Seth Faison in *IHT*, 1 January 1999.
12. *IHT*, 'General Motors' China venture at the cross roads', 18 December 1998.
13. *Xinhua* report datelined Beijing, 8 February. Reproduced in *News From China*, 17 February 1999, p. 35.
14. Seth Faison, 'China's cutback surprises Boeing and Airbus', *IHT*, 10 February 1999.
15. Ibid.
16. 'Chinese truck, motorcycle production up', *Xinhua*, 26 October 1998.
17. Li Jianlin, 'Economy good despite severe crisis and flood', *China Daily*, 30 December 1998. Jianlin, citing economists of the Chinese Academy of Social Sciences writes: 'It is widely recognised that the root cause for the low efficiency of China's economy lies in overly duplicated industrial structures and overflowing similar products, which have brought a pervasive glut relative to Houseold consumption demands in the domestic market.'
18. Ibid.
19. 'China sees stable economic growth', *Xinhua*, 15 June 1999.
20. Reuters, 'High savings rate cuts into Chinese economy', *IHT*, 6–7 March 1999.
21. 'News analysis: Interest rate cut to benefit economic growth', *Xinhua*, 10 June 1999.
22. Ibid.
23. Kou Zhenglin, 'Stimulating individual consumption, maintaining steady development', *Beijing Review*, 4–10 February 1998. Interview with Hou Ruoshi, reproduced in *News From China*, 17 February 1999, pp. 22–5.
24. Lardy, 'China and the Asian contagion', p. 82.
25. Joshua Cooper Ramo, 'The Shanghai bubble', *Foreign Policy*, Summer 1998, p. 69.
26. Lardy, 'China and the Asian contagion', p. 82. Also *Xinhua*, 3 December 1999, 'Residential housing glut in Beijing'. In Beijing a study of 96 real estate companies by the Beijing Municipal Statistics Bureau showed that at the end of August 1998 they had 801,000 sq.m. of unsold/rented housing space. In all, Beijing had over 2.3 million sq.m. of unsold housing.
27. Cooper, 'The Shanghai bubble', p. 71.
28. Lardy, 'China and the Asian contagion', p. 81.
29. Pomfret, 'China says its economy expanded'.
30. *IHT*, 18 December 1999.
31. Ibid.

32. Philip Segal, 'Profitless companies pull out of China', *IHT*, 27 April 1999.

33. This was the explanation favoured by the Chinese government, most Chinese economists, and foreign analysts who had not entertained any serious doubts about China's dazzling performance in the years of the Great Inflation. They ascribed the economic slowdown in 1997 and 1998 to the collapse of demand from East and South East Asia, and the recession in Japan, which caused a sharp decline in demand for China's exports and a stagnation in the level of foreign direct investment. For example the IMF's deputy director for research, Flemming Larsen, said at a press conference in Beijing on 20 May 1999 that China had 'pulled through the Asian economic crisis very successfully', and that its long term economic prospects were 'quite optimistic'. (*News From China*, published by the Chinese Embassy in New Delhi, 2 June 1999, p. 17.)

34. The high savings rate in China, as in Russia, was partly attributable to people having incomes but no goods to buy, or at least not enough of a variety of goods to make people want to spend more. So there was a large sum of disposable cash for spending on new consumer goods when these became available. Since at the advent of reforms the state was still doing most of the saving for the people – such as building homes, providing schools and medical facilities – the propensity to spend the 'private' saving on consumer goods, particularly consumer durables, was especially high.

35. Lin Yi Fu, 'Energising the market in rural areas', *China Daily*, 27 January 2000.

36. In 1996, some 25,000 washing machines were sold in India against almost a million in China.

37. Cooper, 'The Shanghai bubble'.

38. This was reflected by the warning the Shenzen government issued to companies that 'borrowed in dollars to invest in Yuan', that they could no longer expect bailouts. (Reuters/Bloomberg News, 'China promises to cut bailouts', *IHT*, 13–14 March 1999.)

39. *China Daily*, 20 November 1997.

40. *China Daily*, 10 January 2000.

41. Quoted in the *Business Standard*, New Delhi, from the *Business Weekly* of the *China Daily* (end April), p. 5.

42. Pomfret, 'China says its economy expanded'.

43. Philip Segal, 'Foreign banks turn wary of China', *IHT*, 11 January 1999.

44. Philip Segal, 'China's capitalist road gets bumpier', *IHT*, 13 May 1999.

45. Ibid.

46. 'China asks patience on $4 billion in bad loans', *IHT*, 11 January 1999.

47. 'China provinces to cut bailouts', *IHT*, 13–14 February 1999.

48. This was over and above the direct borrowing of Chinese companies controlled by provincial governments.

49. Segal, 'China's capitalist road gets bumpier'.
50. 'China province to curb bailouts', *IHT*, 13–14 February 1999.
51. 'Development Bank urges Moody's to exhibit objectivity', *Xinhua*, 8 December 1998.
52. Lardy, 'China and the Asian contagion', p. 85.
53. *IHT*, 20 January 1999. Reuters/Bloomberg News.
54. 'China lifts dollar saving rate to stem outflow', *IHT*, 10 March 1999.
55. 'A delay as China rethinks company to manage bad debt', *IHT*, 27–28 March 1999. Bloomberg News.
56. Faison, 'China's cutback surprises Boeing and Airbus'.
57. Benjamin Kang Lim and Ben Savadore, 'Beijing sets new high in deficit spending', *IHT*, 4 March 1999.
58. *IHT*, 19 April 1999. Bloomberg News/ Reuters.
59. Segal, 'China's capitalist road gets bumpier'.
60. Ma Yu, an official of the foreign trade ministry, gave the foreign investment estimate. *IHT*, 10 March 1999, 'China lifts dollar saving rate'.
61. Highlights of trade-related news released by *Xinhua* between 24 January and 30 January 2000.
62. John Pomfret, 'Beijing's law and order problem', *Washington Post*. Reproduced in *IHT*, 19 January 1999.
63. Described to a group of scholars from Harvard University's Center for International affairs by the deputy mayor of Shenzen in June 1995.
64. Eric Eckholm (*New York Times*), 'Migrants find they are not welcome at Beijing's party', *IHT*, 19 April 1999.
65. Pomfret, 'Beijing's law and order problem'.
66. Michael Laris (*Washington Post*), 'Chinese police foil bomb attempt', *IHT*, 30–31 January 1999.
67. Pomfret, 'Beijing's law and order problem'.
68. John Pomfret, 'China detains top police aide in corruption enquiry', *IHT*, 11 January 1999.
69. Elizabeth Rosenthal (*NYT*) in *IHT*, 16–17 January 1999.
70. *IHT*, 'No letup in economic overhaul'.
71. Rosenthal in *IHT*, 16–17 January 1999.
72. Eric Eckholm (*NYT*), 'China expanding a secret army for riot control', *IHT*, 29 March 1999.

11. REFORM IN THE SHADOW OF RECESSION

1. IMF, *World Economic Outlook, 1997*, annex 1, 'China: Growth and economic reforms'.
2. Neil C. Hughes, 'Smashing the iron rice bowl', *Foreign Affairs*, July/August 1998, p. 72.
3. Ibid.

4. Ibid.

5. John Pomfret, 'Beijing back pedals on some reforms', *International Herald Tribune (IHT)*, 28 October 1998.

6. *China News* and *Report No. 16*, 15 August 1998, 'Initial results in expanding domestic demand'.

7. *Xinhua*, 20 April 1999, '7 percent target attainable – SDPC spokesman'.

8. Bloomberg News/AFP in *IHT*, 12 February 1999.

9. *Xinhua*, 9 June 1999, 'China reporting rapid industrial growth'.

10. *Xinhua*, 15 June 1999, 'China sees stable economic environment'.

11. *Xinhua*, 14 June 1999, 'China reports May export increase'. May was the first month in 1999 when exports rose in relation to the previous year.

12. Bloomberg News in *IHT*, 15–16 May 1999, 'China's reserves data spark growth concern'.

13. *Xinhua*, 16 June 1999, 'Imports surge in first five months'.

14. Report in *Peoples' Daily*. Published in *News From China*, a weekly news digest published by the Chinese embassy, New Delhi, 26 January 2000, p. 7.

15. From $139 billion at the end of 1998 to $154 billion in 1999. These and the above figures, however, need to be treated with caution. According to an article written by Li Rongxia in the *Beijing Review* of 11 January 2001, exports in 1999 were only $139.2 billion, while imports were $117.5 billion.

16. Bloomberg News/Reuters in *IHT*, 9 April 1999.

17. Bao Daozu, ''99 growth target achievable', *China Daily*, 21 April 1999.

18. Figures given by Du Yuzhou, director general of the State Administration of Textiles, in a press conference. *Xinhua*, 29 April 1999.

19. *IHT*, 6–7 March 1999, 'No letup in economic overhaul, China pledges'.

20. *Xinhua*, 24 November 1998.

21. *Xinhua*, 8 December 1999.

22. Philip Segal, 'Foreign managers get new powers in China', *IHT*, 21 May 1999.

23. *IHT*, 10 March 1999, 'China lifts dollar saving rate to stem outflow'.

24. Michael Laris (*Washington Post* service), 'Businesses bank on China's vows', *IHT*, 11 March 1999.

25. Bloomberg News, 'A delay as China rethinks company to manage bad debt', *IHT*, 27–28 March 1999.

26. Bloomberg News, 'China has $240 billion of bad loans at its biggest banks', *IHT*, 5 January 1999.

27. *IHT*, 6–7 March 1999, 'No letup in economic overhaul, China pledges'.

28. See note 18 (*Xinhua*, 29 April 1999).

29. John Pomfret, 'Why Beijing spring cooled; dissidents overstepped', *IHT*, 4 January 1999.

30. Bloomberg News, 'China has $240 billion in bad loans at its banks', *IHT*, 5 January 1999.

31. *IHT*, 27 January 1999, 'Beijing asks that an electoral first also be a last'.
32. Eric Eckholm, 'China expanding secretive army for riot control', *IHT*, 29 March 1999.
33. John Pomfret, 'China aides reveal wave of corruption', *IHT*, 11 March 1999.
34. Ibid.
35. John Pomfret, 'China detains top aide in corruption enquiry', *IHT*, 8 January 1999.
36. John Pomfret, 'Beijing's law and order problem', *IHT*, 19 January 1999.
37. Elizabeth Rosenthal (*NYT*) in *IHT*, 16–17 January 1999.
38. Michael Laris, 'Chinese police foil bomb attempt', *IHT*, 30–31 January 1999.
39. Yang Qixian, 'Economy mixed for 2000', *China Daily*, 10 January 2000. This was prevented from happening by bounding exports to the USA and bottoming-out of the fall in consumer prices and demand in 2000.
40. 'Zhu maps out economic work for 2000', reproduced from the *China Daily* in *News From China*, 19 January 2000, p. 5.
41. *Beijing Review*, 10 January 2000, 'GDP growth reaches 7.1 percent'.
42. 'China's imports record historic high since 1994', reproduced from the *China Daily* in *News From China*, 19 January 2000.
43. Ibid.
44. In January 2001, US industrial production fell for a fourth straight month. Bloomberg News, 'US inflation data drive dollar down', *IHT*, 17–18 February 2001, p. 13.

12. THE PARADOX OF INDIA'S SLOW TRANSITION

1. Irfan Habib, 'Potentialities of capitalistic development in the economy of Mughal India', in Irfan Habib, *Essays in Indian History* (New Delhi: Tulika, 1995).
2. Amiya Kumar Bagchi, 'Transition from Indian to British systems of money and banking, 1800–1850', *Modern Asian Studies*, 19 (3), 1985, pp. 501–19.
3. Centre for Monitoring the Indian Economy, Bombay, *Basic Statistics – All India*, August 1991, table 8.23. In 1980 there were 13. 23 million enterprises employing fewer than six workers. By 1998 the figure has probably exceeded 20 million.
4. Ashutosh Varshney, *Democracy, Development and the Countryside: Urban Rural Struggles in India* (Cambridge University Press, 1995), chapter 3. See also Daniel Thorner, *The Shaping of Modern India* (New Delhi: Allied Publishers, 1980), chapter 11, 'The emergence of capitalist agriculture in India'.
5. Jagdish N. Bhagwati and Padma Desai, *India: Planning for Industrialisation* (Oxford University Press, 1970), chapter 4, 'Industrialisation and trade policies since 1951'. See also Francine Frankel, *India's Political Economy: The Gradual Revolution* (Princeton University Press, 1978; Oxford Univer-

sity Press, India, 1980), chapters 3 and 4.

6. The best analysis of India's recurrent foreign exchange crises is to be found in Vijay Joshi, and I.M.D. Little, *India: Macroeconomics and Political Economy 1964–1991* (Delhi: Oxford University Press, 1994), chapters 4–7.

7. Ibid., pp.73–4.

8. Ibid., p. 142.

9. Ibid.

10. *Economic Survey 1998–99* (Government of India: Ministry of Finance), p. s-1, table 1.

11. CRR and VSS (authors' full names not given), 'What are Indians importing after the QR era?', *The Hindu*, 22 February 2001. In 1996 close to 3,000 products at the eight-digit level of classification of imports were under one or other form of Quantitative Restriction.

12. Even with the help of subsidies and devaluation, exports grew by 114 per cent between 1981 and 1991 (*Economic Survey 1998–99*, p. s-37) against 113 per cent growth of industry. This was not sufficient to prevent the external payments gap from widening. Some idea of the growth rate needed to sustain an 8.2 per cent annual increase in industrial output can be had from the experience of 1992–93 to 1995–96. In these years an average industrial growth rate of 9.1 per cent was accompanied by a 20 per cent growth of exports. The balance of payments deficit still widened from 0.4 per cent of GDP in 1993–94 to 1.6 per cent in 1995–96 (Centre for Monitoring the Indian Economy, monthly reviews).

13. Prem Shankar Jha, *In the Eye of the Cyclone* (New Delhi: Viking Books, 1993), chapter 6.

13. THE SUCCESS OF GRADUAL REFORM – 1992–96

1. World Bank, *India: Country Economic Memorandum*, 30 May 1995, table A2.1.

2. The dilemma is not peculiar to India. It arises from the fact that the very same reforms that reassure the foreign constituency tend to erode support for the government at home. Since nearly all countries that have experienced an economic crisis have first done so in their external payments, all of them have faced the same dilemma. Stable authoritarian regimes and some democracies have been able to ignore these pressures for a little while and create an apolitical space in which technocrats and economists can take decisions. But the strategy has not always worked, as the reversal in 1993 of the economic reforms enacted in Venezuela, between 1989 and 1991, showed. But the pressure not to alienate the domestic constituency is much greater in democracies than in authoritarian regimes. What has therefore distinguished the Indian economic reforms is the government's determination to give priority to the concerns of its domestic constituency.

3. This anomaly was itself a product of piecemeal, incomplete reform. In 1978, following the recommendations of the Alexander Committee, a committee on trade liberalisation headed by a former secretary of the department of commerce, the government had sharply reduced the number of commodities whose import was banned or restricted. In succeeding years the list was pruned down further, but no effort was made to create a climate conducive to exports.

4. This was the finding of a committee headed by Mr D.V. Kapur, member for industry of the Planning Commission.

5. This figure, taken from the *Economic Survey 1997–98* (p. 21) is markedly different from the estimate published by the government in its *Economic Survey 1999–2000*, of 4.3 per cent of GDP. The difference is explained by two changes made in the basis of calculation. In 1998, the government shifted the base year for calculation of GDP from 1980–81 to 1993–94. The resulting GDP series was about 11 per cent higher than the old, and reflected the fuller inclusion of a host of new industries and services. This change lowered the ratio of fiscal deficit to GDP by a corresponding amount. In 1999 the government shifted borrowings made under the Small Savings scheme and transferred to the state governments, out of the central government's gross borrowing. This further reduced the government's fiscal deficit by about 0.6 per cent, but increased the states' deficit by the same amount.

6. *Economic Survey 1995–96*, p. 31. Government of India.

7. World Bank, *India: 1998 Macro Economic Update*, 30 June 1998, annex tables, table 10.

8. *Economic Survey 1995–96*, p. 31.

9. Centre for Monitoring the Indian Economy, *Monthly Review of the Indian Economy*, February 1997, p. 140.

10. World Bank, *India: Country Economic Memorandum*, 8 August 1996, pp. 77–8. In theory farmers should have been ambivalent about reforms, for while they increased the prices of inputs, by permitting exports and lifting the system of procurement, they would also have raised the price of outputs. But these were arguments that applied only to rich farmers who had a surplus to sell in the market. These make up barely 4 per cent of the farmers and cultivate a third of the land. The remainder would have suffered from the price increase of inputs but had little surplus to sell.

11. For a complete list of capital and primary market reforms see *Economic Survey 1995–96*, p. 61.

12. From January 1994, the government of West Bengal began to take out four-page supplements annually in the London *Financial Times*, extolling the virtues of West Bengal as an investment destination. By March 1996, West Bengal had become the third largest destination for foreign direct investment in India.

13. A good example was Philips, which increased its shareholding in a moribund Indian branch that had done very little business for two decades, and immediately launched a wide range of music systems, videos and televisions on the market.

14. All the statistics in this paragraph are based on 1980–88 = 100. In 1998, the base year was shifted to 1992–93. This has increased all the figures given here.

15. Centre for Monitoring the Indian Economy, monthly reviews – March, April and May 1994.

16. Manufacturing output rose by 12.8 per cent in the period April to August, over the previous year.

17. *National Income Statistics*, September 1998, p. 2. Centre for Monitoring the Indian Economy.

18. *Economic Survey 1996–97*, p. 98, table 6.11.

19. Shankar Acharya (chief economic adviser to the government of India) at a seminar at the Harvard Institute for International Development, November 1996.

20. Acharya at Harvard.

21. *Economic Survey 1998–99*, p. 147, table 10.9.

22. Ibid., p. 145, table 10.5.

23. Acharya at Harvard.

24. 1992–93 = 100. On the earlier base of 1980–81, it was 5.5 per cent. This was cited by Acharya at Harvard.

14. THE CONGRESS DEFEAT AND SETBACK FOR REFORM

1. I was one of those who had predicted this in June 1994, in an op-ed piece in *The Economic Times*. My reasoning was based on the fourfold increase in capital raised by the private corporate sector between 1991–92 and 1993–94. This had sooner or later, I reasoned, to be converted into investment. At the prevailing debt-to-equity and capital-output ratios, and assuming a small shrinkage in the share of the small scale and unorganised sector in industrial output, this, I had calculated, would yield a 15 per cent rate of growth of industrial output. My prediction turned out to be correct. In January to March 1996 industrial growth touched 16.2 per cent.

2. See Chapter 2: 'A society in torment'.

3. The Congress Working Committee set up two sub-committees to examine the causes of the defeat. One concluded that the reforms were not popular, the other that the Congress had lost the support of the minorities and backward castes. The interesting feature about their terms of reference was that they were not asked to identify the causes of the debacle, but simply to ascertain whether these were indeed the causes. The dice were therefore loaded in advance against any finding that went counter to the intuitive conclusions that

powerful leaders were already pushing within the party. Both the charges were aimed at weakening the prime minister and Congress president, Mr P.V. Narasimha Rao, and less directly the finance Minister, Dr Manmohan Singh.

4. Told to the author by Dr Manmohan Singh in July 1995.

5. Bruce Graham, 'Hindu Nationalism and Indian Politics: The Origins and Development of the Jana Sangh (Cambridge University Press, 1990), p. 158. 'The Jana Sangh's rhetoric was directed neither to the closed world of the village nor to the open world of India's modern cities but to the middle world between the two extremes, that of the rural towns, the provincial professions, small industry and country trading and banking.'

6. Kapur had earlier been the chief of planning in the Indian power generation giant, Bharat Heavy Electricals. He had set up the National Thermal Power Corporation, which was later lauded by the World Bank as one of the most efficient companies of its kind in the world, and had ended his career in the government as a secretary in the ministry of industry, where he pushed relentlessly for an easing of autarchic controls on domestic and foreign investment.

7. In very few Indian companies did the promoters hold more than 12 to 14 per cent of the shares. Often their holding was even lower. In most large companies government-owned financial institutions held 40 per cent or more of the shares. So long as these remained absolutely neutral or did not disinvest, the promoters were usually the largest single private shareholder. But the neutrality of the financial institutions came under suspicion during the first opening of the Indian market to foreign (non-resident Indian) shareholders by Indira and Rajiv Gandhi in 1984 and 1985. Takeover bids by non-resident Indians with dubious backgrounds became common in the late 1980s, and after 1993 it became possible for individuals abroad to buy a controlling share in an Indian company via a portfolio fund. When the government also prevented Indian promoters from increasing their shareholding by issuing themselves blocks of shares at highly concessional prices, as it had done in the case of around 160 foreign companies, the fear of the Indian entrepreneurial class turned to alarm.

8. India's Energy Sector (Bombay: Centre for Monitoring the Indian Economy (CMIE), July 1995), p. 14. By 1999–2000 the per unit subsidy had risen to Rs. 1.65 per unit, rural sector consumptoion to 31 per cent of the total and the subsidy to the rural sector to Rs. 310 billion ($4 billion). See Economic Survey 1999–2000.

9. For details see the next chapter.

10. This was the average rate used for the calculations of the cost of thermal power plants in the Eighth Plan estimates. Coal-based power projects cleared by the Central Electricity Authority in 1993 cost Rs. 32.5 million ($1.03 million) per megawatt. See India's Energy Sector (CMIE).

11. Reports in the press in the week before the project was cancelled on 3 August, showed that the chief minister, Manohar Joshi, was making a strong bid inside the government to prevent it. Joshi had found out, within days of assuming office, just how precarious the power position in Maharashtra actually was. The state had 10,772MW of installed capacity and planned to add 7,922MW by 2002. These plans were way behind schedule. Apart from Enron there were only three other private projects that had gone beyond the discussion stage. These would add 1,892MW to Enron's 2,015MW. Thus Maharashtra needed to tie up another 4,000MW worth of projects. Like the central government three years earlier, Mr Joshi's thoughts had immediately turned to the USA. He had been in the act of finalising a delegation to the USA to solicit investment in power projects, when the publication of the details of the agreement between Maharashtra and the company forced him to announce a 'review' of the project. Mr Joshi's reluctance to cancel the project deepened during his US trip where one chief executive after another told him, in unambiguous terms, to forget foreign investment if his government cancelled a solemn contract without due cause. On his return, therefore, Joshi expressed his dissatisfaction with the report prepared by a cabinet sub-committee under the BJP hard-line deputy chief minister, Gopinath Munde, which had unambiguously recommended the cancellation of the project. In a bid to prevent the cancellation Joshi had set up his own committee of senior government and Maharashtra State Electricity Board officials, to advise him. This committee had unambiguously told him that cancellation would be most unwise as it would affect three other projects whose negotiations were in the final stages. *The Hindu* (Delhi edn), 11 August 1995, p. 4; and *Times of India*, 23 August 1995.

12. *Times of India*, 1 April 1995.

13. Reported in the *New York Times* and *International Herald Tribune*, and virtually all Indian newspapers in early May 1995.

14. The tone of a letter written by Ravindra Mahajan, convenor of the Swadeshi Jagran Manch, to the Dabhol Power Company on 14 July, makes this amply clear. It read:

> Your Ms. Linda Powers is reported to have stated that 'our company has spent an enormous amount of its own money, approximately $20 million on this education and project development process alone, not including any project costs'. We request you to provide us the complete details of your interactions with the said Indian bureaucrats and bankers along with the expenditure in each case. Inter alia we require the following:
>
> • all items construing 'educating Indians'
>
> • 'type and content' of the education process

- the chronological order and the names of the persons and the places including hotels and locations abroad where 'education' was imparted

- whether this 'education' was solicited by those Indians or whether Enron had to 'pursuade' [sic] them or whether it was offered and willingly accepted by them ...

And so on. In a last flourish of rhetoric the letter ended, 'We eagerly look forward to these details, inter alia, to evaluate what the nation has "learnt" [sic].'

15. Testimony given by Ms Linda Powers before the Committee on Appropriations, Sub-committee on Foreign Operations, of the US House of Representatives, 31 January 1995. This evidence was given three months before the Dabhol power plant ran into trouble.

16. Reported in the *New York Times* and *International Herald Tribune*, and virtually all Indian newspapers in early May 1995.

17. *Times of India*, 29 August 1995.

18. Ibid.

19. Major breakdowns occurred on 17 August 1989, 24 November 1990, 25 October 1991, 2 February 1992. In 1995 there were breakdowns on 19 April, in July, and on 16 November; so three occurred even as the Enron project was being cancelled. (Newspaper reports).

20. Told to the author by Dr Manmohan Singh.

21. *Financial Times' India Business Intelligence*, 29 November 1995.

22. Although the detailed project report had forecast that Enron would earn at least a 25 per cent return on the first phase of the project, in her testimony before the US House of Representatives, Enron's Linda Powers had admitted that various delays and cost escalation had reduced this estimate to around 20 per cent.

23. *Economic Survey 1999–2000* (Government of India), p. 169.

24. CMIE monthly review, March–April 1999, p. 10.

25. *Economic Survey 1995–96*, pp. 42–3, 76–7.

26. CMIE monthly review, February 1999, GDP new series, 1993–94 = 100.

27. CMIE, *Capital Markets*, published October 1998, p. 127. This is by a share price index constructed by the CMIE. This index has a much broader base, and is more stable than the BSE-SENSEX (sensitive index), which is the most often quoted share price index in the country.

28. CMIE monthly review, January 1996, p. 44.

29. CMIE monthly survey, February 1997, p. 199.

30. Output grew by 4.1 per cent in May, declined by 1.8 per cent in June, rose again by 7.9 per cent in July, but then fell by 8.4 per cent in August, and a whopping 19.3 per cent in September (CMIE monthly reviews of September, October and November 1997).

31. Data are all from the CMIE monthly reviews of September, October and November 1997.
32. Ibid., November 1997.
33. 1993–94 = 100.
34. Figures for growth in the tertiary sector were inflated by the inclusion of salary increases and arrears paid to central government employees. But if this was excluded, growth in the services sector had also slowed down. See below.
35. See ministry of finance economic surveys for 1996–97, and subsequent years until 1999–2000.

15. REFORM GRINDS TO A HALT

1. In other words, they made changes in column 3 of the model given in Chapter 1 of this book (see Table 1.1), when what India desperately needed was to complete the sequence of reforms given in column 1 of that model.
2. Centre for Monitoring the Indian Economy (CMIE), *Basic Statistics – All India*, August 1991, table 4.23.
3. CMIE, various monthly reports and periodic reports on energy.
4. Ibid.
5. *Economic Survey 1999–2000*. Government of India.
6. Calculated from data given in the *Economic Survey 1999–2000* and *2000–2001*, and CMIE report on energy, March 2000.
7. Even this was not sufficient. In 2000 the states owed the central public sector a total of Rs. 200 billion in unpaid bills, and the central government was considering raising the annual deductions from their Plan and other allocations to 30 per cent.
8. Mahesh Vijapurkar, 'Enron deal: Mid-course options before MSEB' and 'A question of ability to pay', *The Hindu* Business/Science Review, 21 December 2000. By March 2001, the state governments' refusal to raise the yield from electricity tariffs by reducing subsidies and curbing theft of power had created a situation in which not a single private investor was prepared to put any money into power generation. In 13 private power projects with a generating capacity of 6,275MW, promoters had not invested a single dollar or rupee despite having achieved financial closure and received all government clearances. The Indian financial institutions were forced to cancel loans to ten of them (Economist Intelligence Unit, *Business Indian Intelligence*).
9. Deepak Arya and Surajeet Dasgupta, 'Hughes cover encashed', *Business Standard*, 11 May 1999. These were a company called Usha Telecom, which had a licence for Bihar, and Hughes-Ispat, an Indo-American collaboration, which had a licence for the state of Karnataka in the south.
10. Compiled by the author from publicly available information in December 1997.
11. Foreign direct investment (FDI) in India since economic reforms

Year	92–93	93–94	94–95	95–96	96–97	97–98	98–99	99–00
FDI	315	586	1314	2133	2696	3198	2062 (1678)*	1279*
Total	559	4153	5138	4892	6153	5385	2401 (1282)*	3325*

* The figure for total FDI differs from the one given there because the value of shares sold in dollars has been deducted to maintain comparability of the Economic Survey of India data with that of the CMIE.

Source: Government of India, *Economic Survey 1999–2000*, table 6.7, p. 100.

12. As of the end of 1998 there were no less than eleven other models of foreign cars being made or assembled in India.

13. The description and interpretation of what went wrong is based entirely on my talks over an extended period of time with the Indian and Japanese directors of Suzuki Japan and Maruti Udyog, India. It was published in *The Hindu*, Madras.

14. Indian law requires any major decision, such as the closing down, selling off, change of ownership or purpose of an enterprise, to obtain 76 per cent of the votes of the shareholders.

16. THE SECOND CRISIS AND FALSE DAWN

1. Old series. By the new series (1993–94 = 100) industrial growth touched 12.8 per cent in 1995–96.

2. 5.6 per cent by the new series.

3. The Central Statistical Office's preliminary estimate of industrial growth for January 2001 was 2.8 per cent.

4. These and the following figures for the economy, where not sourced separately, have been taken from the CMIE's (Centre for the Monitoring the Indian Economy) monthly review of the Indian economy, various months in 1999 and 2000, and the *Economic Survey 1999–2000* and *2000–2001*. An irritating feature of all Indian statistics is the frequency with which they are revised, albeit though the revisions are marginal. So they may not necessarily coincide with the estimates given in 2000 either by the CMIE or the economic survey. CMIE's data sources are all official releases of the ministries of finance and commerce, the Reserve Bank of India and other government agencies.

5. See Chapter 13.

6. *Economic Survey 1998–99*, p. 35. Government of India.

7. Ibid.

8. Total employment in the public sector grew from 10.4 million in 1971 to 19.5 million in 1996. The central government contributed only 670,000 to the increase. The state and 'quasi-government' sectors were responsible for the

rest. State government employment, in departments and district offices, rose from 3.9 to 7.4 million (source: *Economic Survey*, various years).

9. In March 2000 the total 'loans' of this kind added up to more than Rs. 200 billion. In 1999 the central government had negotiated an arrangement with the state governments to cut 15 per cent of their plan allocations towards payment of these bills. This was proving insufficient as it barely covered the interest on these overdues.

10. Calculated by the author from tables supplied by CMIE in its publication *Public Finance February 1999*.

11. Calculated from GDP estimates given in the *Economic Survey*, and the CMIE's report *Public Finance, India's Central and State Governments*, June 1996, table 3, p. 3.

12. The combined fiscal deficit of the Centre and states, which fell from 10.2 per cent in the crisis year of 1990–91 to 7.5 per cent in 1992–93, rose steeply after that to touch 11.7 per cent in 1998–99 (by the old GDP series based on 1981–82 weights). Even this rise does not reflect the full deterioration in state finances. Increasingly strapped for cash, they have been using the public sector as a banker of last resort, buying power, water, coal and other essentials from them and not paying them for it. As of now these debts have risen to over Rs. 200 billion, or 1.2 per cent of GDP. Assuming that three-quarters of the deterioration has taken place since 1990–91, the true fiscal deficit of the Centre and the states is now a full 2.4 per cent higher than it was during the crisis of 1990–91.

The fiscal deficit has increased despite the 30 per cent cut in developmental expenditure described in the text. Finally, there has also been a decline in the share of defence spending from 3.5 per cent to 2.2 per cent. The overall deterioration in the finances of the Indian state thus amounts to a minimum of 9.5 per cent of GDP, or Rs. 1.7 trillion! Compiled from the CMIE *Public Finance*, June 1996 and February 1999. The data on forced lending by the public sector enterprises to the state governments was provided to the author by government officials in the course of research for an article published in *The Hindu*, Madras, on 18 February 2000 entitled 'Budget reflections 1: India's fiscal crisis'.

13. *Economic Survey 1998–99*, p. 24. The figure given in the *Economic Survey 1999–2000* of 8.3 per cent in 1990–91 is suspiciously different.

14. Told to the author by the prime minister I.K. Gujral's principal secretary, N.N. Vohra in September 1997.

15. *Economic Survey 1998–99*, p. 23.

16. Newspaper reports – all papers.

17. Anil Padmanabhan, 'Current account deficit estimated at 1 percent', *Business Standard*, 3 May 1999, p. 1.

18. CMIE monthly review of the Indian economy, December 1998.

19. Change in major components of balance of payments, 1998–99 ($ million)

Year/ month	1997–98 (actual)	1998 (April to July)	1998 (August to October)	1998–99 (estimate)
Aid	3162	NA	–1197	–1500
Foreign institutional investors	1583	–1.281)	–2286	–2400
FDI	3226	–276	–740	–1000
Global depository receipts	291	–100	–96	–100
Non-resident Indian deposits	20402	NA	–850[a]	–1200
Trade balance	–6807[b]	–1479	–3332[c]	–4500
TOTAL	–1707	–3126	–8481	–10700

[a] April to 30 September 1998.

[b] DGCI&S estimates. The RBI estimates of trade deficit are about $8 billion higher.

[c] April to November 1998.

Source: compiled from data and tables prepared by CMIE, in monthly review of the Indian economy, July and December 1998.

20. Calculated from the survey data by the author. See Tables 16.2 and 16.3.

21. *Economic Survey 1999–2000*, chapter 1.

22. Ibid.

23. Yashwant Sinha, Budget Speech, Part A, para 84. 28 February 2001.

24. According to CMIE, the estimated GDP in 2000–01 will be Rs. 20 trillion. Assuming this grows in nominal terms by 13 per cent per annum it will rise to Rs. 735 billion. If GDP grows by 14 per cent per annum it will be Rs. 850 billion.

25. *Economic Survey 2000–2001*, p. 138, box. 7.3.

26. This had become necessary not, as the Left kept insisting, to save money at the expense of the urban and rural poor, but to adjust the public distribution system to a sustained improvement in living standards. 1991–92 was the last year in which the offtake of subsidised foodgrains from the ration shops more or less matched the allocations made to them. Since then it has hovered between 50 and 65 per cent. In the last two years offtake fell to 24.5 million tonnes while food procurement rose to 58 million tonnes. As a result the government found itself saddled with 45.7 million tonnes of foodgrains, against a required average buffer stock of around 19 million tonnes. (CMIE monthly review for January 2001, p. 17.)

27. It could fall a great deal more if the government front-loads the reduction in subsidy. In actual fact there is a good deal of implicit front-loading. Most of the impact of the interest rate reduction will be felt in the next year;

foodgrains purchases by central government will decline most sharply in the next two harvest seasons as it tried to draw down its stocks, and the impact of petroleum price deregulation will be felt in 2002–03.

28. This shift had begun in 1980 as farmers realised that they could not rely on government support forever. Between 1980–81 and 1999–2000 the area under foodgrains declined from 126.7 million to 23.1 million hectares. The area under major cash crops rose from 30.5 to 40.1 million hectares. (*Economic Survey 2000–2001*, table 1.13, p. s-17.)

29. Ibid., p. 146.

30. S.D. Naik, 'SSI continues to be ignored', *The Hindu* Business Line, 6 March 2001.

31. Ibid.

32. *Statistical Report on General Elections 1998 to the Twelfth Lok Sabha* (Election Commission of India), vol. 1, ver. i.

17. CONCLUSION: STATE AND MARKET IN ECONOMIC REFORM

1. Manuel Castells, *End of Millennium* (Oxford: Blackwell, 1988), vol. 3, p. 7.

2. Twelfth Golden Jubilee Paper at the National Council for Applied Economic Research, presented by Montek Singh Ahluwalia, member of the Planning Commission, Government of India. New Delhi, April 2000.

3. Ibid. The conclusion has been derived from data given in the body of the lecture and tables 8 and 9.

Index

Compiled by Sue Carlton